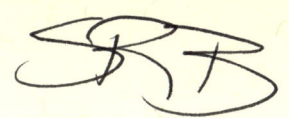

COMPUTER APPLICATIONS
IN ELECTRICAL ENGINEERING SERIES
Franklin F. Kuo, *Editor*

| | |
|---|---|
| Bowers and Sedore | *SCEPTRE: A Computer Program for Circuit and Systems Analysis* |
| Cadzow and Martens | *Discrete-Time and Computer Control Systems* |
| Davis | *Computer Data Displays* |
| Friedman and Menon | *Fault Detection in Digital Circuits* |
| Jensen and Lieberman | *IBM Circuit Analysis Program: Techniques and Applications* |
| Kuo and Magnuson | *Computer Oriented Circuit Design* |
| Lin | *An Introduction to Error-Correcting Codes* |
| Sifferlen and Vartanian | *Digital Electronics with Engineering Applications* |
| Stoutemyer | *PL/1 Programming for Engineering and Science* |

# FAULT DETECTION IN DIGITAL CIRCUITS

PRENTICE-HALL INTERNATIONAL, INC., *London*
PRENTICE-HALL OF AUSTRALIA PTY. LTD., *Sydney*
PRENTICE-HALL OF CANADA, LTD., *Toronto*
PRENTICE-HALL OF INDIA PRIVATE LIMITED, *New Delhi*
PRENTICE-HALL OF JAPAN, INC., *Tokyo*

# FAULT DETECTION IN DIGITAL CIRCUITS

Arthur D. Friedman
Premachandran R. Menon

*Bell Telephone Laboratories*

*Prentice-Hall, Inc., Englewood Cliffs, New Jersey*

© 1971 by
Bell Telephone Laboratories, Incorporated
Murray Hill, N.J. 07974

All rights reserved. No part of this
book may be reproduced in any form
or by any means without permission
in writing from the publisher.

Current printing (last digit):
10 9 8 7 6 5 4 3 2

SBN: 13-308197-4
Library of Congress Catalog Card Number: 71-149975

Printed in the United States of America

# PREFACE

In recent years, much effort has gone into the development of efficient algorithms for the generation of tests to detect and locate faults in digital circuits. As the circuits get larger, it becomes increasingly impractical to generate such tests except by computers. Furthermore, the efficiency of the set of tests affects the time required for the maintenance of the circuit and consequently the time available for useful computation.

This book presents the most useful algorithms that have been developed for test generation. In addition, recent work on some procedures which are not practical for deriving tests for presently used circuits, but may become useful for future technologies, is presented. Beginning with an explanation of the types of faults considered, procedures for deriving tests for combinational and sequential circuits and iterative arrays are discussed. The concluding chapter contains some suggested techniques for the design of circuits that are easily tested and also a discussion on the improvement of the reliability of a system by means of redundancy and self-checking.

The book may be used as a textbook for a graduate level course in Electrical Engineering or Computer Science. It will also be useful to the practicing engineer and the research student who is interested in fault diagnosis. The book is essentially self-contained, pressupposing only the normal background of a beginning graduate student, although some knowledge of switching theory is likely to be useful. Problems at the end of the chapters include exercises as well as some unsolved problems, which are identified by asterisks.

We are thankful to our colleagues who read the manuscript and made several useful comments, especially D. B. Armstrong, A. Friedes, F. M. Goetz and M. D. McIlroy. We would also like to thank Mrs. Dorothy Luciani and Miss Geraldine A. Marky for an excellent job of typing the manuscript. Finally, we would like to express our appreciation of the facilities made available to us for this work by Bell Telephone Laboratories.

ARTHUR D. FRIEDMAN
PREMACHANDRAN R. MENON

*Murray Hill, New Jersey*

# CONTENTS

**CHAPTER 1—INTRODUCTION**      1

    LOGIC CIRCUITS     2
        Combinational Circuits    3
        Sequential Circuits    4
        Iterative Arrays    7
    LOGICAL FAULTS     7
    REFERENCES     9

**CHAPTER 2—COMBINATIONAL CIRCUITS**      11

    DERIVATION OF TESTS     12
        Truth Table Method    12
        Method of Boolean Differences    14
        Path Sensitizing    16
        The D-Algorithm    19
        Poage's Method    34
        The Equivalent Normal Form    41
    MINIMIZATION OF TEST SETS     46
        Fault Table Methods    46
        Near Minimal Test Sets Using the
        Equivalent Normal Form    49
        Diagnosing Tree    52
    REDUNDANCY     53
    SUMMARY     56
    REFERENCES     56
    PROBLEMS     57

## CHAPTER 3—SEQUENTIAL CIRCUITS  62

    CIRCUIT TESTING APPROACH  62
        Successor Tree  65
        Path-Sensitization and the D-Algorithm  68
        Sequential Analyzer  70
    MACHINE IDENTIFICATION  70
        Hennie's Procedure  73
        Hsieh's Procedure  85
        Ad Hoc Methods  90
        Checking Sequences Under
        Restricted Fault Assumptions  93
        Asynchronous Sequential Circuits  97
    SUMMARY  100
    REFERENCES  101
    PROBLEMS  102

## CHAPTER 4—ITERATIVE LOGIC ARRAYS  106

    ONE-DIMENSIONAL ARRAYS  108
        Testability  108
        Derivation of Tests  114
        Bounds on the Number of Tests  119
        Location of Faults  120
    TWO-DIMENSIONAL ARRAYS  125
        Application of Cell Inputs  126
        Propagation of Faults  133
        Bounds on the Number of Tests  141
        Limitations of the Test-Derivation Procedures  142
    ARRAYS OF SEQUENTIAL MACHINES  144
    TREE STRUCTURES  145
    SUMMARY  147
    REFERENCES  147
    PROBLEMS  148

## CHAPTER 5—SIMULATION TECHNIQUES  151

    THE SEQUENTIAL ANALYZER  153
    ARMSTRONG'S METHOD  158
    SUMMARY  164

CONTENTS                                                                    xi

      REFERENCES    165
      PROBLEMS      166


**CHAPTER 6—DESIGN TECHNIQUES**                                          **168**

      DESIGN TO SIMPLIFY TESTING    169
          Combinational Circuits with Small Test Sets    169
          Fault Locatable Combinational Circuits    171
          Sequential Circuits with Distinguishing Sequences    178
          Double-Rank and Multiple-Rank Circuits    182
          Circuits with Completion Signals    187
          System Organization    189
      REDUNDANCY TECHNIQUES    191
          Theoretical Estimates of Reliability    192
      FAULT MASKING TECHNIQUES    193
          Voting Schemes    193
          Quadded Logic    195
          Radial Logic    201
          Use of Error-Correcting Codes    202
      SELF-CHECKING SYSTEMS    204
          Electronic Switching System (ESS)    205
          Self-Testing and Repair (STAR) Computer    207
          A Theoretical Model of Self-Checking    208
      SUMMARY    209
      REFERENCES    210
      PROBLEMS    212


**INDEX**                                                                **215**

# FAULT DETECTION
IN
DIGITAL CIRCUITS

CHAPTER 1

# INTRODUCTION

One of the prime requirements of a computing system is the ability to operate correctly over a sufficiently long period of time. This requirement is particularly stringent in computers that operate in a real-time or time-sharing environment. In order to satisfy this requirement, the system has to be tested periodically to determine if it is functioning properly. If any malfunction is detected, the faulty unit must be identified and repaired or replaced. The set of tests used should be complete in that it is capable of detecting any fault that is likely to occur. The set should be as small as possible, in order to minimize the time required for this maintenance function. If a fault is found, additional tests may then be necessary to identify the faulty unit.

The major portion of this book is devoted to the problem of deriving efficient tests for different classes of switching circuits. In addition to a comprehensive survey of the procedures applicable to the types of switching circuits encountered in present day digital computers, some results which are currently of theoretical interest are presented. It is hoped that these results may stimulate further research in these areas and that some of them may become applicable to future technologies.

The number of tests required and the ease with which they can be derived are both dependent on the circuit design. Some techniques for designing circuits which are relatively easy to test are presented. Redundant circuits where the effects of faults are intentionally masked are also considered. Such circuits find application in systems which are required to operate correctly even in the presence of faults for a relatively short period of time. Finally, systems which utilize redundancy as well as testing and repair, in order to ensure reliable operation over long periods of time, are considered.

## LOGIC CIRCUITS

We will be concerned primarily with the testing of digital circuits contained in computers rather than testing at the system level. Since we will be concerned only with the effects of faults on the logical behavior of these circuits, we will be interested in the logical description of these circuits but not their physical implementations.

We shall consider logic circuits made up of AND, OR, NOT, NAND, NOR and exclusive-OR elements (gates). Fig. 1.1 shows the symbols that will be used throughout the book to represent these elements. The circuits may also contain memory elements like set-reset (SR) flip-flops and delays. Fig. 1.2

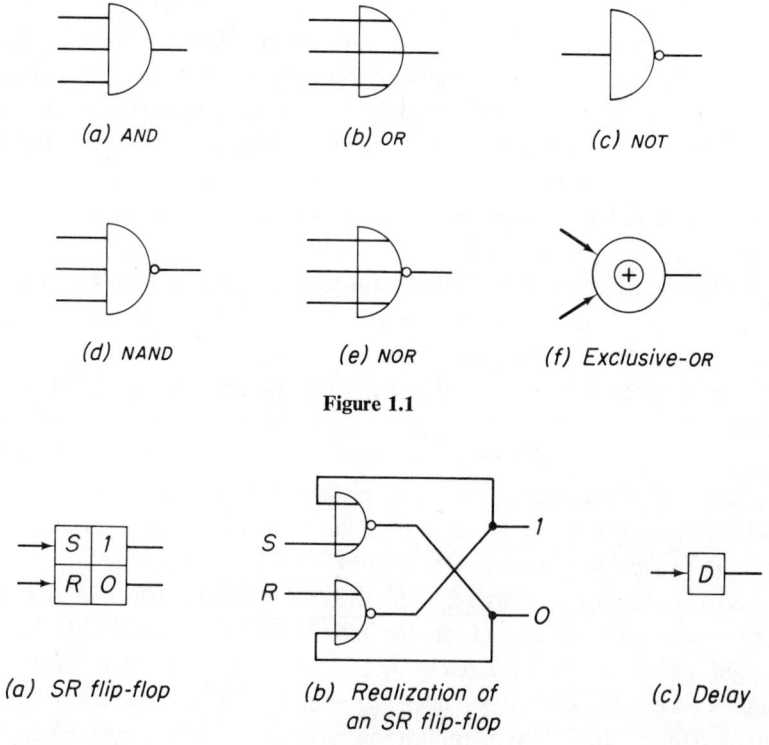

**Figure 1.1**

**Figure 1.2**

# LOGIC CIRCUITS

shows the representation of these elements and also a realization of an SR flip-flop using NOR gates.

## Combinational Circuits

The circuits normally used in a digital computer are usually divided into two types: combinational circuits and sequential circuits. Combinational circuits are used to realize combinational functions and are characterized by the absence of feedback (i.e., closed loops). A combinational function $y_i$ of a set of variables $\{x_1, x_2, \ldots, x_n\}$ is dependent only on the present values of the inputs; i.e., $y_i = f_i(x_1, x_2, \ldots, x_n)$. A combinational function may be represented by a truth table which specifies the value of the function for each combination of input values. Another method of representation is by means of a Karnaugh map. An example of a combinational function, its different representations and a realization are shown in Fig. 1.3. Note that it is the exclusive-OR function.

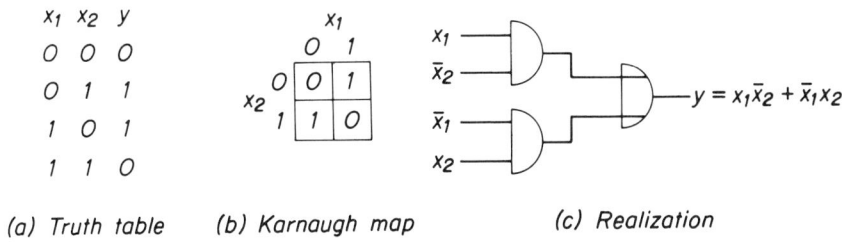

(a) Truth table    (b) Karnaugh map    (c) Realization

**Figure 1.3**

The type of realization shown where the outputs of AND's are inputs to an OR is called a *two-level sum-of-products* (SP) realization. The function can also be written in the form $y = (x_1 + x_2)(\bar{x}_1 + \bar{x}_2)$ and realized by connecting the outputs of two OR gates to an AND gate. This is a *two-level product-of-sums* realization. If a function is expressed in the sum-of-products form, each product term in the expression is called an *implicant* of the function. The function assumes the value of 1 whenever any of its implicants has the value of 1. A *prime implicant* of a function is an implicant such that any proper subset of its variables does not form an implicant of the function. A minimal two-level SP realization of a function is obtained by finding the set of prime implicants with the smallest number of input variable appearances such that for every input combination for which the function is required to have the value of 1, some prime implicant contained in the set is 1. This problem is usually referred to as the *prime implicant covering problem*. There exist several techniques for solving this problem (McCluskey, 1956).

*Sequential Circuits*

A *sequential function* depends not only on the present values of the inputs but on the past values of the inputs as well. The mathematical model which realizes such a function is usually referred to as a *sequential machine* or a *finite-state machine* and the logic circuit realizing the behavior is called a *sequential circuit*. The past values of inputs are represented by the *internal states* of the sequential machine.

Two different models of sequential machines have been presented by Mealy (1955) and Moore (1956) and bear their names. In a Mealy machine, the output at any time is dependent on the input and internal state at that time, whereas in the Moore machine, the output is a function of only the internal state. Let $x(t)$, $s(t)$ and $z(t)$ be the input, state and output at time $t$. Then the next state is given by:

$$s(t+1) = N(x(t), s(t))$$

for both models;

$$z(t) = Z(x(t), s(t))$$

for the Mealy machine; and

$$z(t) = Z'(s(t))$$

for the Moore machine. $N$ and $Z$ (or $Z'$) are referred to as the next-state and output functions, respectively. Any sequential machine may be represented by either model and conversion from one model to the other is always possible.

Sequential machines are usually represented by *state diagrams* or *state tables* (*flow tables*). A state diagram for a Mealy machine is a directed graph whose nodes correspond to states of the machine and whose edges correspond to state transitions. Each edge is labeled with the input and output associated with the transition. The state diagram of a Moore machine is similar, except that outputs are associated with the nodes of the graph instead of the edges. In the flow table representation of a machine, the rows of the table correspond to states and the columns to inputs. The entries in the table

# LOGIC CIRCUITS

are the next state and output associated with each combination of inputs and internal state.* Fig. 1.4 shows the state diagram and the flow table of a machine with inputs $\{x_1, x_2, x_3\}$, states $\{s_1, s_2, s_3\}$ and outputs $\{z_1, z_2\}$.

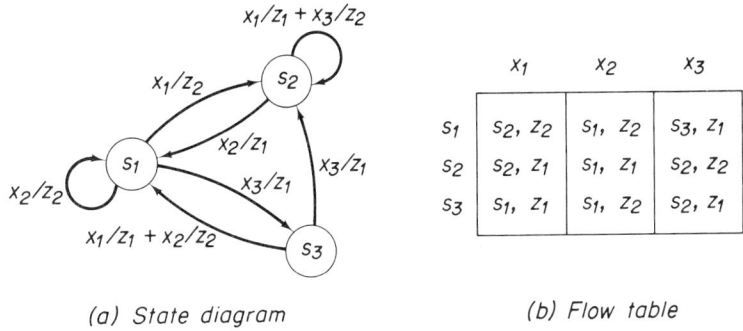

(a) State diagram

(b) Flow table

**Figure 1.4**

In a sequential machine $M$, two states $s_i$ and $s_j$ are *equivalent*, if for every input sequence, the output sequences generated by $M$ in initial states $s_i$ and $s_j$ are identical. A machine is said to be *reduced* if no two states in it are equivalent. A sequential machine is said to be *strongly connected* if for every pair of states $(s_i, s_j)$, there exists an input sequence which takes the machine from $s_i$ to $s_j$. The machine of Fig. 1.4 is reduced and strongly connected.

A sequential circuit realizing a machine is provided with memory elements to store the internal state. The general model of a sequential circuit proposed by Huffman (1954) is shown in Fig. 1.5. The state of the machine is

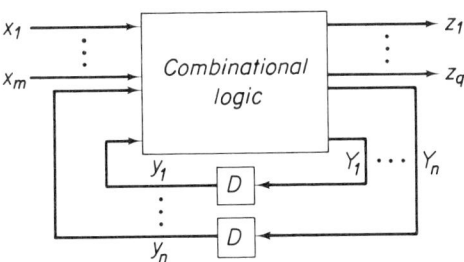

**Figure 1.5**

*Since we are interested in deriving tests for existing circuits, we shall restrict ourselves to flow tables in which all entries are specified. Even if the original flow table of the sequential function is incompletely specified, every realization of the function has a completely specified flow table.

represented by the state variables $y_1, \ldots, y_n$, the next-state values of which are denoted by $Y_1, \ldots, Y_n$. The delays constitute the memory elements. In actual practice, a set of flip-flops and clock signals may be used instead of the delays shown in the model. If the output of the machine can be determined from the knowledge of a finite number of past inputs (such a machine is said to realize a *definite event*), it can be realized without feedback. However, we shall use the general model of Fig. 1.5 in discussing sequential circuits.

Sequential circuits are classified as *synchronous* or *asynchronous* depending on whether the circuit is operating under the control of clock pulses or not. Synchronous circuits are commonly characterized by pulsed inputs (although this is not necessary) and asynchronous circuits by level inputs and outputs. For a synchronous circuit, the inputs are assumed to occur at discrete intervals of time, and each input pulse causes at most one internal state transition. The output pulses are also in synchronism with the clock pulses.

In asynchronous circuits (Unger, 1969) state transitions are initiated by changes in the inputs. The inputs are allowed to change only when the circuit has reached a stable state. This mode of operation is called the *fundamental mode*. Unlike the synchronous case, the flow table of an asynchronous machine will contain stable and unstable next-state entries. If for a state $s_i$ and input $x_j$, the next state is also $s_i$, then $s_i$ is said to be stable in that column and is usually circled. A flow table is said to be a *normal mode* flow table if every transition in it leads directly to a stable state and no output is required to change more than once during any transition.

In synchronous circuits, the next state and outputs are determined from signal values that are present when a clock pulse appears. Hence transient conditions during the change of inputs or state variables do not affect the operation. Since asynchronous circuits are not controlled by clock pulses, it is necessary to ensure that the operation is not affected by transients or by the order in which signals change during a transition. If two or more state (or input) variables change during a transition (referred to as a *race*) it is necessary to analyze the circuit to determine the stable state reached for every order in which the variables may change. If the final state depends on the order of changes, the race is called a *critical race*. For proper operation, all races in the circuit should be noncritical. The state assignment should be such that only one state variable changes at a time or all variables that change do so without critical races. The combinational circuit should also be designed so that it produces no transients.

*Iterative Arrays*

Another type of logic circuit to be considered is the iterative array. Although such arrays have not found widespread use in digital computers, they have been included because of the insight they give to the problem of testing logic circuits with regular structure. Furthermore, it has been shown (Minnick, 1967; Arnold et al, 1970) that any combinational or sequential function can be realized using such arrays, with some modification in the interconnection pattern in cells along certain boundaries.

Most of our discussion of iterative arrays will be restricted to one-dimensional and two-dimensional arrays of combinational cells. All cells in the array are identical and the outputs of each cell serve as inputs to its neighbors. One-dimensional arrays of sequential machines and tree structures of combinational cells will also be briefly discussed.

## LOGICAL FAULTS

The type of faults that we shall be concerned with are *logical faults;* faults which produce some change in the logical behavior of the circuit. Thus, component failures which affect voltages, currents, shapes of pulses or delays in the circuit, but do not alter the logical functions realized by the circuit will not be considered. Also excluded are failures of power supply and clock signals. We shall assume that such failures are tested for and corrected so that they do not affect the logical behavior of the circuits.

The malfunctioning of a circuit may be due to a permanent fault or an intermittent one. Although intermittent faults do occur in practice, the theory is lacking in procedures for testing for them. Since the fault may disappear when a test is applied, there are no reliable means of detecting their occurrence. In this book, we shall be concerned only with permanent (solid) faults, which do not occur, disappear, or change their nature during testing.

The derivation of tests is greatly simplified if we assume that the circuit cannot have more than one fault at any time. This assumption (which is used in most of the methods of deriving tests) is justifiable only if testing is frequent enough so that the probability of the occurrence of more than one fault during the interval between tests is negligibly small. The probability of the occurrence of a single physical fault which produces several simultaneous logical faults should also be negligibly small. Even then, the single-fault assumption may not be valid for the initial check-out of a circuit. Except where otherwise stated, the single-fault assumption will be implied throughout the book.

The class of faults to be considered in testing a logic circuit depends on the type of circuit. However, most of the faults in currently used circuits (Millman and Taub, 1964) like diode-resistor logic circuits (DR), diode-transistor logic circuits (DTL), transistor-resistor logic circuits (TRL) and transistor-transistor logic circuits (TTL), can be represented by an input or the output of some gate being *stuck-at-one* (s-a-1) or *stuck-at-zero* (s-a-0). That is, an input or output of some gate may assume a fixed logical value, independent of the inputs applied to the circuit. This covers most of the faults in circuits with discrete components as well as integrated circuits.

In deriving tests for detecting s-a-0 and s-a-1 faults, it is important to remember that the faulty wires do not actually assume the corresponding signal values, but the logic circuit behaves as though the particular gate input or output assumes that fixed value. For example, in Fig. 1.6(a) if the wire $\alpha$ becomes stuck at the signal value corresponding to logical 1, the wire $\beta$ which is directly connected to it will also become 1. However, if the input lead $\alpha$ to the AND gate becomes open-circuited, the output $\gamma$ becomes independent of the value of $B$, but the output $\delta$ of the second AND gate is still $BC$. This fault can be conveniently represented by $\alpha$ s-a-1, which has no effect on $\beta$ or $\delta$. Similarly, in Fig. 1.6(b), $\alpha$ s-a-0 may be used to represent an open-circuit in the lead $\alpha$ to the OR gate.

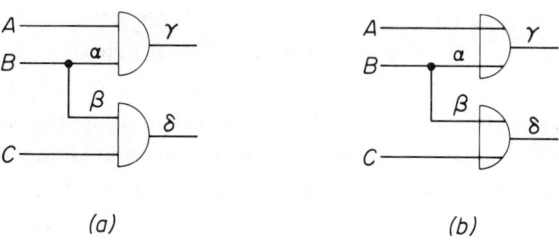

(a)                    (b)

**Figure 1.6**

A more complex fault which can be analyzed in a manner similar to the procedures for s-a-1 and s-a-0 faults is a short-circuited input diode in diode-resistor logic or diode-transistor logic (e.g. Millman and Taub, 1964). The output of the faulty gate is unaffected but the input connected to the faulty diode and all fan-out leads from that input are forced to a value dependent on the output. For example, let us assume that positive logic (where logical 1 represented by a higher voltage than logical 0) is used in Fig. 1.6(a).

If the diode connected to $\alpha$ is shorted and $A = 0$, then $\gamma = 0$ and $\alpha$ and $\beta$ are forced to 0 independent of the value of $B$. Similarly, in Fig. 1.6(b), short-circuiting the diode connected to $\alpha$ causes both $\alpha$ and $\beta$ to be forced to 1 if $A = 1$, assuming negative logic (where 0 is represented by the higher voltage). A shorted diode in a DTL NAND (NOR) gate is analyzed by treating it as an AND (OR) gate followed by an inverter.

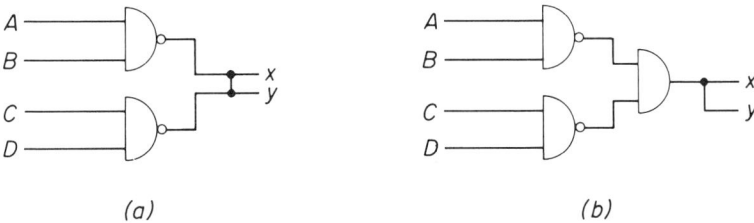

Figure 1.7

As an example of single faults that cannot be represented by s-a-0 or s-a-1, consider the circuits of Fig. 1.7. Let us assume DTL NAND gates and positive logic. If the outputs of two independent NAND gates are connected together by the fault, as shown in Fig. 1.7(a), both outputs become equal to the AND of the NAND-gate outputs as shown in Fig. 1.7(b). Similarly, short-circuiting the outputs of NOR gates realized by negative logic causes the outputs to be the OR of the individual NOR-gate outputs. Some of the methods presented in this book may also be used for deriving tests for these and other similar faults.

## REFERENCES

Arnold, T. F., Tan, C. J. and Newborn, M. M., "Iteratively Realized Sequential Circuits", *IEEE Trans. Computers* C-19, 54–66, 1970.

Huffman, D. A., "The Synthesis of Sequential Switching Circuits", *J. Franklin Inst.* 257, 161–190; 273–303, 1954.

McCluskey, E. J., Jr., "Minimization of Boolean Functions", *Bell System Tech. J.* 35, 1417–1444, 1956.

Mealy, G. H., "A Method for Synthesizing Sequential Circuits", *Bell System Tech. J.* 34, 1045–1080, 1955.

Millman, J. and Taub, H., *Pulse, Digital and Switching Waveforms*, McGraw-Hill, Inc., New York, 1965.

Minnick, R. C., "A Survey of Microcellular Research", *J. ACM* 14, 203–241, 1967.

Moore, E. F., "Gedanken-Experiments on Sequential Machines", *Automata Studies*, Princeton University Press, Princeton, New Jersey, 1956.

Unger, S. H., *Asynchronous Sequential Switching Circuits*, Wiley-Interscience, New York, 1969.

CHAPTER 2

# COMBINATIONAL CIRCUITS

A physical fault in a combinational circuit usually results in a change in one or more of the combinational functions realized by the circuit. As a consequence, some outputs of the faulty circuit will be different from their normal values for some input combinations applied to the circuit. Any such input combination which produces an incorrect output when a particular fault is present is a *test* for *detecting* that fault because the presence of the fault can be detected by applying this input combination and observing the outputs. In general, a particular input combination may be a test for detecting several faults in a circuit and there may be several tests for detecting a given fault.

In some circuits, the presence of certain physical faults does not alter any of the functions realized by the circuit. This implies that such faults cannot be detected by applying inputs to the circuit and observing the outputs. It will be shown later in this chapter, that the undetectability of certain faults in a circuit is caused by redundancy, in the sense that certain components or connections may be eliminated without altering the function realized by the circuit. For the present, we shall restrict our attention to irredundant circuits.

Clearly, any irredundant circuit with $n$ inputs can be completely tested by applying all $2^n$ input combinations to it. As $n$ becomes large, this procedure becomes undesirable due to the large number of input combinations to be applied in order to detect all faults. A smaller set of tests is often sufficient for detecting all faults that are likely to occur. Thus, one of the important problems associated with the testing of large combinational circuits is that of obtaining an *efficient* set of fault detection tests.

In addition to detecting faults in a circuit, it may be desirable to locate the fault to a specific gate or a replaceable module. We shall refer to this as the diagnosis problem. As in the case of fault detection, an efficient set of diagnostic tests is also desirable.

## DERIVATION OF TESTS

In this section, we discuss several methods of deriving tests for a given fault in a combinational circuit. The circuit is assumed to be irredundant and only a single fault can be present at any time. Initially, we shall consider only faults where any wire in the circuit is stuck-at-zero (s-a-0) or stuck-at-one (s-a-1). A few additional types of faults will be considered later.

### Truth-Table Method

The most obvious method of deriving tests for a particular fault is by comparing the truth tables of the normal and faulty circuits. Let the inputs to a combinational circuit be $x_1, x_2, \ldots, x_n$ and let its outputs be $z_1, z_2, \ldots, z_m$, where $z_i = f_i(x_1, x_2, \ldots, x_n)$, $i = 1, 2, \ldots, m$. For any set of faults, F, and any fault $\alpha \in F$, let $z_i^\alpha = f_i^\alpha(x_1, x_2, \ldots, x_n)$ be the value of the $i^{\text{th}}$ output when the fault $\alpha$ is present. Then an input vector $\mathbf{x}^j = (x_1^j, x_2^j, \ldots, x_n^j)$ is a test for detecting the fault $\alpha$ if and only if

$$f_i(\mathbf{x}^j) \oplus f_i^\alpha(\mathbf{x}^j) = 1 \quad \text{for some } i, \quad 1 \leq i \leq m,$$

where $\oplus$ represents the exclusive-OR operator. The above equation implies that the fault $\alpha$ is detected by applying the input $\mathbf{x}^j$ and observing the output $z_i$. All the tests which detect any given fault can be obtained in a straightforward manner by comparing the truth tables of the normal and faulty circuits as shown in the following example.

**Example 2.1:** Consider the circuit shown in Fig. 2.1 and let the wire $\alpha$ be s-a-1. The truth tables of the output functions of the normal and faulty circuits are shown in Table 2.1.

# DERIVATION OF TESTS

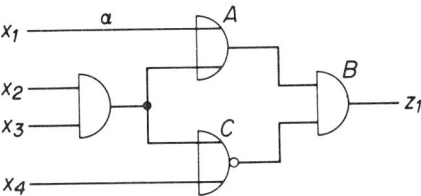

**Figure 2.1**

| $x_1$ | $x_2$ | $x_3$ | $x_4$ | $z_1$ | $z_1^\alpha$ | $z_1 \oplus z_1^\alpha$ |
|---|---|---|---|---|---|---|
| 0 | 0 | 0 | 0 | 0 | 1 | 1 |
| 0 | 0 | 0 | 1 | 0 | 0 | 0 |
| 0 | 0 | 1 | 0 | 0 | 1 | 1 |
| 0 | 0 | 1 | 1 | 0 | 0 | 0 |
| 0 | 1 | 0 | 0 | 0 | 1 | 1 |
| 0 | 1 | 0 | 1 | 0 | 0 | 0 |
| 0 | 1 | 1 | 0 | 0 | 0 | 0 |
| 0 | 1 | 1 | 1 | 0 | 0 | 0 |
| 1 | 0 | 0 | 0 | 1 | 1 | 0 |
| 1 | 0 | 0 | 1 | 0 | 0 | 0 |
| 1 | 0 | 1 | 0 | 1 | 1 | 0 |
| 1 | 0 | 1 | 1 | 0 | 0 | 0 |
| 1 | 1 | 0 | 0 | 1 | 1 | 0 |
| 1 | 1 | 0 | 1 | 0 | 0 | 0 |
| 1 | 1 | 1 | 0 | 0 | 0 | 0 |
| 1 | 1 | 1 | 1 | 0 | 0 | 0 |

**Table 2.1**

From Table 2.1, it is seen that the following three tests detect the fault $\alpha$ s-a-1:

$$(x_1, x_2, x_3, x_4) = (0, 0, 0, 0); (0, 0, 1, 0); (0, 1, 0, 0).$$

It is often convenient to represent tests by the corresponding minterms*. The set of tests in Example 2.1 can be written as $\bar{x}_1\bar{x}_2\bar{x}_3\bar{x}_4$, $\bar{x}_1\bar{x}_2 x_3\bar{x}_4$ and $\bar{x}_1 x_2\bar{x}_3\bar{x}_4$. From the first two tests we see that $x_1 = x_2 = x_4 = 0$ is a test independent of the value of $x_3$. Similarly, $x_1 = x_3 = x_4 = 0$ is a test indepen-

---

*A *minterm* is a product of all the variables of a function, where each variable may appear in the complemented or uncomplemented form.

dent of the value of $x_2$. The tests can be represented by the Boolean expression $\bar{x}_1\bar{x}_2\bar{x}_4 + \bar{x}_1\bar{x}_3\bar{x}_4$. Tests for detecting other faults in the circuit can be determined in a similar manner.

It is obvious from the example that the method would be impractical even for circuits of moderate size, because a truth table will have to be constructed for every possible fault. We shall now discuss some methods of deriving tests without constructing these truth tables.

*Method of Boolean Differences*

The test which detects a given fault is an input combination which produces an incorrect output if the fault is present. It follows that the necessary and sufficient conditions for a test to detect a given fault are: (1) the signal value at the site of the fault should be opposite to that caused by the fault. (2) Any change of signal value at the site of the fault should cause a change of at least one output of the circuit. It can be verified that these two conditions are satisfied by the tests derived in Example 2.1.

Tests satisfying these conditions can be derived directly from the Boolean equations representing the functions realized by the circuit (Sellers et al., 1968). We shall discuss the method for single-output combinational circuits. Tests for multi-output circuits can be derived by treating each output separately.

We define the *Boolean difference* of a function $F(x_1, x_2, \ldots, x_n)$ with respect to one of its inputs $x_i$ (denoted by $dF(\mathbf{x})/dx_i$) as follows:

$$\frac{dF(\mathbf{x})}{dx_i} = F(x_1, x_2, \ldots, 0, \ldots, x_n) \oplus F(x_1, x_2, \ldots, 1, \ldots, x_n).$$

Note that the Boolean difference is not a derivative although such a notation is used. If $dF(\mathbf{x})/dx_i \equiv 0$, this implies that $F$ is independent of $x_i$. Similarly, if $dF(\mathbf{x})/dx_i \equiv 1$, any change in $x_i$ will affect the output independent of the values of all $x_j, j \neq i$. In general, $dF(\mathbf{x})/dx_i$ will be a function of some (or all) the $x_j$'s, $j \neq i$. The value of the function will depend on the value of $x_i$ if and only if the remaining variables assume values such that $dF(\mathbf{x})/dx_i = 1$. In order to test for a fault on $x_i$, we set $x_i$ opposite to its faulty value and assign values to the remaining inputs such that $dF(\mathbf{x})/dx_i = 1$. The set of tests for a fault on $x_i$ can be represented by the following expressions:

$$x_i \frac{dF(\mathbf{x})}{dx_i} \text{ for } x_i \text{ s-a-0,}$$

# DERIVATION OF TESTS

and

$$\bar{x}_i \frac{dF(\mathbf{x})}{dx_i} \quad \text{for } x_i \text{ s-a-1.}$$

The following operations enable us to find the Boolean difference of complex circuits in terms of the Boolean difference of simpler circuits:

$$\frac{d\bar{F}(\mathbf{x})}{dx_i} = \frac{dF(\mathbf{x})}{dx_i},$$

$$\frac{dF(\mathbf{x})}{dx_i} = \frac{dF(\mathbf{x})}{d\bar{x}_i},$$

$$\frac{d}{dx_i}\left(\frac{dF(\mathbf{x})}{dx_j}\right) = \frac{d}{dx_j}\left(\frac{dF(\mathbf{x})}{dx_i}\right),$$

$$\frac{d[F(\mathbf{x})G(\mathbf{x})]}{dx_i} = F(\mathbf{x})\frac{dG(\mathbf{x})}{dx_i} \oplus G(\mathbf{x})\frac{dF(\mathbf{x})}{dx_i} \oplus \frac{dF(\mathbf{x})}{dx_i}\frac{dG(\mathbf{x})}{dx_i},$$

$$\frac{d[F(\mathbf{x}) + G(\mathbf{x})]}{dx_i} = \bar{F}(\mathbf{x})\frac{dG(\mathbf{x})}{dx_i} \oplus \bar{G}(\mathbf{x})\frac{dF(\mathbf{x})}{dx_i} \oplus \frac{dF(\mathbf{x})}{dx_i}\frac{dG(\mathbf{x})}{dx_i},$$

and

$$\frac{d[F(\mathbf{x}) \oplus G(\mathbf{x})]}{dx_i} = \frac{dF(\mathbf{x})}{dx_i} \oplus \frac{dG(\mathbf{x})}{dx_i}.$$

Tests for an internal wire $h$ in the circuit can be found by expressing $F$ as a function of $h$, $F(x_1, x_2, \ldots, x_n, h)$, and $h$ as a function of the inputs, $h(x_1, x_2, \ldots, x_n)$. Then $h(x_1, x_2, \ldots, x_n) \cdot dF/dh$ gives tests for $h$ s-a-0 and $\bar{h}(x_1, x_2, \ldots, x_n) \cdot dF/dh$ gives tests for $h$ s-a-1.

**Example 2.2**

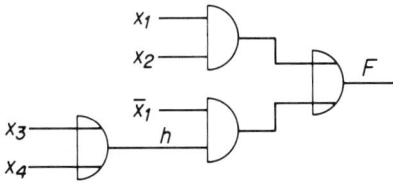

Figure 2.2

$$F = x_1 x_2 + \bar{x}_1(x_3 + x_4) = x_1 x_2 + \bar{x}_1 h$$
$$= G(x_1, x_2) + H(x_1, h)$$

$$\frac{dF}{dh} = \bar{G}\frac{dH}{dh} \oplus \bar{H}\frac{dG}{dh} \oplus \frac{dG}{dh} \cdot \frac{dH}{dh}$$
$$= (\bar{x}_1 + \bar{x}_2)\bar{x}_1 \oplus 0 \oplus 0 = \bar{x}_1.$$

Tests for $h$ s-a-0 are given by

$$h \cdot \frac{dF}{dh} = (x_3 + x_4)\bar{x}_1 = \bar{x}_1 x_3 + \bar{x}_1 x_4$$

and $h$ s-a-1 by

$$\bar{h} \cdot \frac{dF}{dh} = \overline{(x_3 + x_4)} \cdot \bar{x}_1 = \bar{x}_1 \bar{x}_3 \bar{x}_4.$$

*Path Sensitizing*

Instead of using the Boolean difference method to determine the conditions under which a change in the signal value on a wire in the circuit will affect the value of the output, the conditions for propagating a change to an output along any path can be determined from a knowledge of the logic circuit. This is done by assigning input values to each gate along the chosen path such that its output depends only on one particular input. The conditions required for a change in one of the inputs to a gate to cause a change in its output depend on the type of gate involved. For AND and NAND gates all inputs except the changing one should be 1. For OR and NOR gates these inputs should be set to 0.

Returning to Example 2.1, $x_1 = 0$ in all the tests. In order for the output of the OR gate to be sensitive to any change on wire $\alpha$, the other input to gate $A$ should be 0, leading to the condition $x_2 x_3 = 0$. For $z_1$ to be sensitive to any change in $\alpha$, the other input to gate $B$ should be 1, and the output of the NOR gate $C$ should be 1. This, in turn, requires that $x_4 = 0$. The three tests derived in the example satisfy these conditions.

The general procedure for deriving tests using path sensitizing is as follows: The faulty wire is assigned a value opposite to the fault condition. That is, a value of 1 is assigned to a wire with a s-a-0 fault and vice versa for a s-a-1 fault. A path is chosen from the fault to one of the output terminals. The inputs to the gates along this path are assigned values so as to propagate any change on the faulty wire along the chosen path to the output terminal.

# DERIVATION OF TESTS

The path is now said to be *sensitized*. One or more tests for detecting the particular fault are obtained by determining network inputs which will produce the desired values on the gate inputs along the sensitized path. This is done by tracing back from gates along the sensitized path towards the network inputs and assigning values to a sufficient number of inputs to obtain the desired signal values in the circuit. This procedure may not yield a unique set of inputs for sensitizing a particular path. An arbitrary choice is made wherever different possibilities exist. If a contradiction is encountered, the process is repeated with a different choice, if such a choice exists. Otherwise, it may be necessary to select a different path for sensitizing. If a consistent input combination is obtained, some inputs in it may be unspecified. This means that the test is independent of those inputs and they may be assigned any values desired for the purpose of minimizing the test set. The following example demonstrates the procedure.

**Example 2.3**

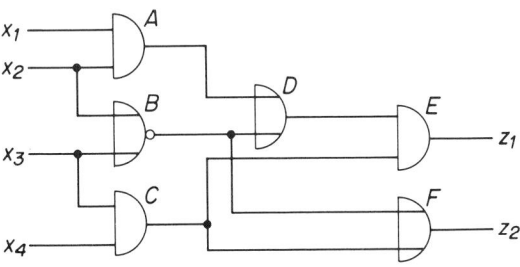

Figure 2.3

In Fig. 2.3, let the output of the NOR gate $B$ be s-a-0. Referring to the outputs of gates by the names of the gates, we require $B = 1$ in order to detect the s-a-0 fault. Let us arbitrarily choose to sensitize the path $BDE$ to the output $z_1$. In order to sensitize this path we need $A = 0$ and $C = 1$. But $B = 1$ implies $x_2 = x_3 = 0$. This also makes $A = 0$. In order to make $C = 1$, we require $x_3 = x_4 = 1$ leading to a contradiction in the assignment of $x_3$. Since no arbitrary choices were made during the assignment of input values, and $BDE$ is the only path from $B$ to $z_1$, it follows that a s-a-0 fault at $B$ cannot be detected at the output $z_1$. However, the fault can be detected at $z_2$ since $x_2 = x_3 = 0$ sensitizes the path $BF$ and also makes $B = 1$. Inputs $x_1$ and $x_4$ are unspecified for this test.

The path sensitizing technique, as we have discussed it so far, attempts to sensitize only one path in the circuit at a time. The following example shows the inadequacy of this procedure.

**Example 2.4:** In the circuit of Fig. 2.4, let us try to derive a test for detecting the fault, $\alpha$ s-a-0 by sensitizing the path $ABJ$.

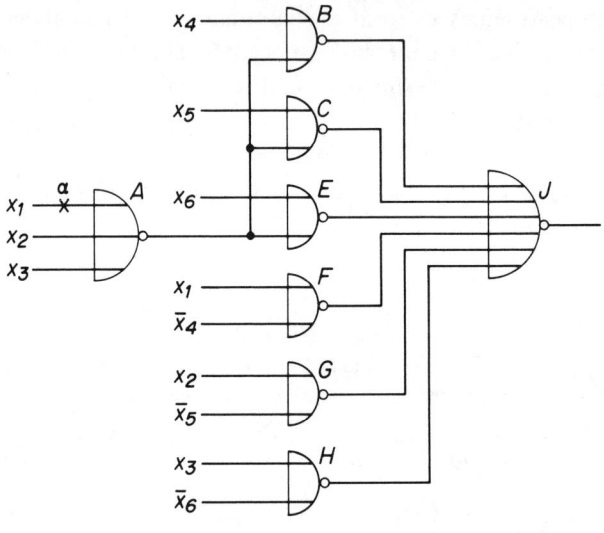

Figure 2.4

We set $x_1 = 1$, $x_2 = x_3 = 0$ so as to apply a signal opposite to the faulty value to $\alpha$ and propagate the effect of the fault through gate $A$. Setting $x_4 = 0$ propagates it through gate $B$. In order to propagate it through gate $J$, we require $C = E = F = G = H = 0$. Setting $x_5 = x_6 = 1$ to make $C = E = 0$, we find that $G = H = 1$ and we are unable to propagate through $J$. Similarly, we can show that it is impossible to sensitize the single paths ACJ or AEJ. However, we note that $x_4 = x_5 = x_6 = 0$ sensitizes the three paths simultaneously and also makes $F = G = H = 0$. Thus, three inputs to $J$ change from 1 to 0 as a result of the fault $\alpha$ s-a-0, while the remaining three inputs are fixed at 0. The fault will cause the output of $J$ to change from 0 to 1 and $x_1 \bar{x}_2 \bar{x}_3 \bar{x}_4 \bar{x}_5 \bar{x}_6$ is a test for $\alpha$ s-a-0. Similarly, if we set $x_1 = x_2 = x_3 = 0$ to detect $\alpha$ s-a-1, the output of $A$ will change from 1 to 0 as a result of the fault. Here again, the three paths $ABJ$,

# DERIVATION OF TESTS

$ACJ$ and $AEJ$ have to be sensitized simultaneously by setting $x_4 = x_5 = x_6 = 0$ in order to detect the fault.

The above example shows the necessity of sensitizing more than one path, in deriving tests for certain faults. In order to sensitize more than one path, we need some method of identifying signals whose values depend on the fault. This is the principal idea behind the D-algorithm (Roth, 1966).

*The D-Algorithm*

We shall first present an informal version of the D-algorithm, which may be considered to be path sensitization with the fault-dependent signals uniquely identified. Let us use the symbol D to represent a signal that is 1 in the normal circuit and 0 in the faulty circuit. The symbol $\bar{D}$ will be used to represent the signal that is normally 0, but becomes 1 when the fault is present. Note that the definitions of D and $\bar{D}$ could be interchanged, but should be consistent throughout the circuit. Thus, all D's in a circuit imply the same value whether 0 or 1 and all $\bar{D}$'s will have the opposite value. With this meaning associated with D the following logical operations are easily verified:

| + | 0 | 1 | D | $\bar{D}$ |
|---|---|---|---|---|
| 0 | 0 | 1 | D | $\bar{D}$ |
| 1 | 1 | 1 | 1 | 1 |
| D | D | 1 | D | 1 |
| $\bar{D}$ | $\bar{D}$ | 1 | 1 | $\bar{D}$ |

(a) OR

| · | 0 | 1 | D | $\bar{D}$ |
|---|---|---|---|---|
| 0 | 0 | 0 | 0 | 0 |
| 1 | 0 | 1 | D | $\bar{D}$ |
| D | 0 | D | D | 0 |
| $\bar{D}$ | 0 | $\bar{D}$ | 0 | $\bar{D}$ |

(b) AND

Table 2.2

**Example 2.5:** The circuit of Example 2.4 is repeated in Fig. 2.5. In order to derive a test for $\alpha$ s-a-0, we assign a D to the line $\alpha$ and try to propagate the D to the output. Setting $x_1 = 1$ applies a 1 to the wire $\alpha$. $x_2 = x_3 = 0$ causes the output to gate $A$ to be $\bar{D}$. We arbitrarily choose to sensitize the path $ABJ$, by setting $x_4 = 0$ and also note that gates C and E both have a $\bar{D}$ on one input. Attempting to make all inputs to gate $J$ except $B$ equal to 0 results in contradiction.

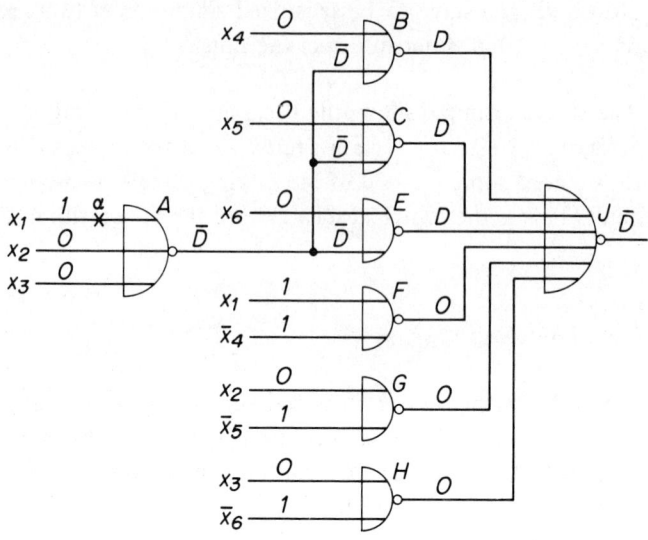

**Figure 2.5**

However, if we set $x_5 = x_6 = 0$, we have $B = C = E = D$ and $F = G = H = 0$. Now $J = \bar{D}$ and $\alpha$ s-a-0 is detected. The signal values in the circuit for this test are shown in Fig. 2.5.

In the formal D-algorithm, a function of $n$ variables $f(x_1, x_2, \ldots, x_n)$ is represented as a function of $(n + 1)$ variables $g(x_1, x_2, \ldots, x_{n+1})$, such that $g(a_1, a_2, \ldots, a_{n+1}) = 1$ if and only if $a_{n+1} = f(a_1, a_2, \ldots, a_n)$. A set of prime implicants covering the function $g$ represents the truth table of the function $f$ in a concise manner. The set of cubes defined by these prime implicants is called the *singular cover* of the function $f$. As an example, a two-input NOR gate and its singular cover are shown in Fig. 2.6, where x denotes

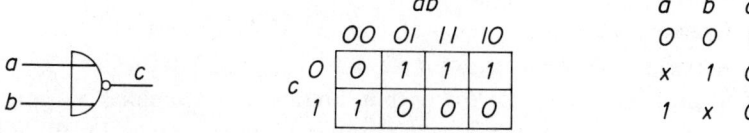

**Figure 2.6**

# DERIVATION OF TESTS

"don't care" values. The singular cover of the NOR gate states that its output will be 1 if both inputs are 0, and 0 if one of the inputs is 1.

In deriving tests for combinational circuits, it is useful to identify two special types of inputs to a logic block. The first type are those inputs which cause the output of the block (assuming single-output blocks) to be different from its normal value, if a given fault is present in the block. These inputs are represented by the *primitive D-cubes of the fault*. The second type of inputs, represented by the *propagation D-cubes* of a block (Chang et al., 1970), are those that cause the output of the block to depend only on one or more of its specified inputs (and hence to propagate a fault on these inputs to the output).

For simple blocks, such as a NOR gate, and simple faults like an input s-a-1, both types of D-cubes can be written down by inspection. For example, if the input lead $a$ of the NOR gate of Fig. 2.6 is s-a-1, $a = 0$, $b = 0$ will cause the output $c = 0$ if the fault is present and $c = 1$ otherwise. This is represented by the following primitive D-cube of the fault:

| $a$ | $b$ | $c$ |
|---|---|---|
| 0 | 0 | D |

where D represents the condition under which the normal output is 1 and the faulty output is 0. Note that this choice is arbitrary and the opposite choice could have been made.

On the other hand, if we are interested in propagating the effect of a fault (external to the particular gate) through the NOR gate of Fig. 2.6, the following D-cubes of the block are of interest, assuming that only one input to the gate may be faulty:

| $a$ | $b$ | $c$ |
|---|---|---|
| D | 0 | $\bar{D}$ |
| 0 | D | $\bar{D}$ |

Here, the interpretation of the symbol D is slightly different. D may be 0 or 1, but all D's in a D-cube always have the same value. $\bar{D}$ always has the value complementary to D. The two propagation D-cubes of the NOR gate merely state that if one of its inputs is zero, the output is the complement of the other input. If multiple-input changes are to be propagated through the NOR gate, $DD\bar{D}$ should be added to the list of propagation D-cubes.

Although the D-cubes of small blocks and simple faults can be written down by inspection, algorithms may be useful for larger blocks and more complicated types of faults. These algorithms involve the intersections of cubes contained in singular covers. The intersection of two cubes is obtained by intersecting each coordinate of the two cubes according to the following rules: $a \cap x = a$; $a \cap a = a$; $a \cap b = b \cap a$; $0 \cap 1 = \phi$; where $a, b = 0, 1$ or x and $\phi$ is the null intersection. If any coordinate of the intersection is null, the intersection is empty and is denoted by $\Phi$.

The primitive D-cubes of any fault in a logic block can be obtained from the singular covers of the normal and faulty blocks. Let $\alpha_0$ and $\alpha_1$ be sets of cubes in the singular cover of the good circuit, whose output coordinates are 0 and 1 respectively. Let $\beta_0$ and $\beta_1$ be the corresponding sets in the singular cover of the faulty circuit. The primitive D-cubes of the fault are obtained as follows: (1) Ignoring the output coordinate, members of $\alpha_1$ are intersected with members of $\beta_0$. The nonempty intersections correspond to those inputs under which the output of the good circuit will be 1 and that of the faulty circuit 0. The output coordinates of these cubes are assigned D. (2) Members of $\alpha_0$ are intersected with members of $\beta_1$, ignoring the output coordinate. The output coordinates in the intersection are assigned the value $\bar{D}$. The nonempty intersections correspond to those inputs which produce a 0 output from the good circuit and a 1 output from the faulty circuit.

**Example 2.6**

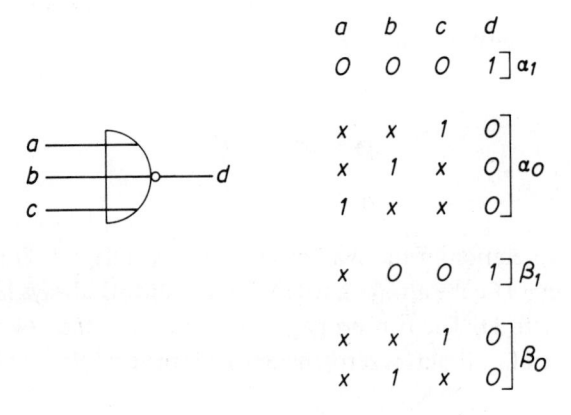

Figure 2.7

# DERIVATION OF TESTS

The singular cover for the NOR gate shown in Fig. 2.7 consists of the sets marked $\alpha_1$ and $\alpha_0$. If input $a$ is s-a-0, the faulty circuit has the singular cover consisting of $\beta_1$ and $\beta_0$. Ignoring the output coordinate, $\alpha_1 \cap \beta_0 = \Phi$. Intersecting $\alpha_0$ and $\beta_1$, ignoring the coordinate $d$, and assigning $\bar{D}$ to the output coordinate as specified in the above algorithm, we obtain the primitive D-cube of the fault as: $100\bar{D}$. This means that if the inputs are 100 the output of the normal gate will be 0 but if input $a$ is s-a-0, the output will be 1. This result could have been obtained by inspection (as in most other simple cases) as explained in the preceding section.

The algorithm is applicable to a wider class of faults than wires stuck at 0 or 1. For instance, if a fault in an exclusive-OR causes it to operate as an OR gate, the singular covers for the two cases are shown below:

$$\left.\begin{array}{ccc}0 & 1 & 1\\ 1 & 0 & 1\end{array}\right\}\alpha_1 \qquad \left.\begin{array}{ccc}x & 1 & 1\\ 1 & x & 1\end{array}\right\}\beta_1$$

$$\left.\begin{array}{ccc}1 & 1 & 0\\ 0 & 0 & 0\end{array}\right\}\alpha_0 \qquad \left.\begin{array}{ccc}0 & 0 & 0\end{array}\right\}\beta_0$$

Intersecting $\alpha_0$ and $\beta_1$, we obtain the primitive D-cube of this fault: $11\bar{D}$. With both inputs equal to 1, the normal circuit will produce an output of 0, whereas the faulty circuit will produce an output of 1.

Primitive D-cubes of faults in blocks with multiple outputs can also be treated in an analogous manner. We divide the singular covers of the good and faulty circuits into blocks according to their outputs, the good and faulty circuits being denoted by $\alpha$ and $\beta$ respectively with subscripts corresponding to the outputs. Primitive D-cubes of the fault are obtained by intersecting members of sets $\alpha$ and $\beta$ with different subscripts, ignoring the output coordinates as before. If an intersection is not empty, the output coordinates are assigned as follows: If both members have the same output, that value is assigned to the corresponding coordinate of the intersection. If the member of $\alpha$ has an output of 1 and the member of $\beta$ has the same output equal to 0, the corresponding coordinate in the intersection is assigned D. If the reverse is true, $\bar{D}$ is assigned to the coordinate.

## Example 2.7

(a) Normal circuit   (b) Faulty circuit

|  | a | b | c | d |
|---|---|---|---|---|
| $\alpha_{00}$ | 0 | 0 | 0 | 0 |
| $\alpha_{01}$ | 0 | 1 | 0 | 1 |
| $\alpha_{10}$ | 1 | 0 | 1 | 0 |
| $\alpha_{11}$ | 1 | 1 | 1 | 1 |

|  | a | b | c | d |
|---|---|---|---|---|
| $\beta_{00}$ | 0 | x | 0 | 0 |
|  | x | 0 | 0 | 0 |
| $\beta_{11}$ | 1 | 1 | 1 | 1 |

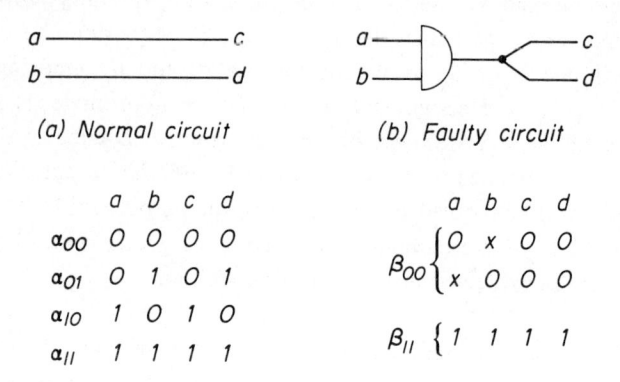

**Figure 2.8**

Figure 2.8 shows what may happen as a result of a short-circuit between two independent wires in the circuit. In the normal circuit, $c = a$ and $d = b$. The fault causes the circuit to realize $c = d = a \cdot b$. From the singular covers of the normal and faulty circuits given in Fig. 2.8, we see that the only nonempty intersections are those of $\alpha_{01}$ with $\beta_{00}$ and $\alpha_{10}$ with $\beta_{00}$. These yield the following primitive D-cubes of the fault: 010D and 10D0. Other faults in multi-output combinational logic blocks can be treated in an analogous manner.

The propagation D-cubes of a single-output block for a change in the $i^{th}$ input variable are obtained in the following manner:

1. Obtain the singular cover of the block and group the cubes in the singular cover into sets $\alpha_0$ and $\alpha_1$, according to their output coordinates.
2. For each cube in $\alpha_0$ (or $\alpha_1$), complement the $i^{th}$ input, if it is not x, and the output to form the set of cubes $\beta_1$ (or $\beta_0$).
3. Intersect the cubes in $\beta_0$ with $\alpha_0$ (or $\beta_1$ with $\alpha_1$). These cubes represent the points for which a change in the $i^{th}$ input will cause a change in the output.
4. For each cube in the intersection, assign D to the $i^{th}$ input and D or $\bar{D}$ to the output coordinate, depending on whether the value of the output in the original $\alpha$ cube was the same as or opposite to the $i^{th}$ input.

# DERIVATION OF TESTS

**Example 2.8:** Consider a three-input AND gate whose inputs are labeled $a$, $b$ and $c$ and whose output is labeled $d$. The singular cover of the gate is given below:

$$\begin{array}{cccc} a & b & c & d \\ 0 & x & x & 0 \\ x & 0 & x & 0 \\ x & x & 0 & 0 \\ 1 & 1 & 1 & 1 \end{array} \begin{array}{l} \\ \alpha_0 \\ \\ \alpha_1 \end{array}$$

For a change in input $a$, the $\beta$-cubes are:

$$\begin{array}{cccc} 1 & x & x & 1 \\ 0 & 1 & 1 & 0 \end{array} \begin{array}{l} \beta_1 \\ \beta_0 \end{array}$$

$\alpha_0 \cap \beta_0 = 0110$ yields the propagation D-cube D11D. Note that the same D-cube is obtained from $\alpha_1 \cap \beta_1 = 1111$.

More than one propagation D-cube may be associated with a block for the same input variable. For example, consider an exclusive-OR whose inputs are labeled $a$ and $b$ and whose output is labeled $c$. The singular cover consists of four cubes:

$$\begin{array}{ccc} a & b & c \\ 0 & 0 & 0 \\ 1 & 1 & 0 \\ 0 & 1 & 1 \\ 1 & 0 & 1 \end{array} \begin{array}{l} \alpha_0 \\ \\ \alpha_1 \end{array}$$

Complementing the first input and the output of the cubes in $\alpha_0$ we obtain:

$$\begin{array}{ccc} 1 & 0 & 1 \\ 0 & 1 & 1 \end{array} \beta_1$$

and the propagation D-cubes D0D and D1$\bar{\text{D}}$ are obtained from the intersection $\alpha_1 \cap \beta_1$.

D-cubes for multiple input changes can be constructed in an analogous manner. The algorithm for deriving propagation D-cubes can also be modified to make it applicable to blocks with more than one binary output. If the block has $k$ outputs, step (2) of the algorithm is modified so as to construct $2^k - 1$ sets of $\beta$ cubes for each $\alpha$ set, each set of $\beta$ cubes corresponding to one possible output combination resulting from an input change. Although the D-algorithm can be used with multi-output blocks of logic, there seems to be no advantage in doing so. We shall therefore restrict ourselves to single-output blocks.

The algorithm for deriving tests involves intersections of the primitive D-cube of the fault with propagation D-cubes. While intersecting two D-cubes, $a = (a_1, \ldots, a_n)$ and $b = (b_1, \ldots, b_n)$, it is important to remember that all D's in a propagation D-cube may be 0 or 1 and that $\bar{\text{D}}$'s will always have the opposite value. Thus, if we complement all D's and $\bar{\text{D}}$'s in a propagation D-cube, the set of vertices they represent do not change. The intersection of a D-cube $a$ and a propagation D-cube $b$ is undefined unless:

**1** in all positions in which $b$ has a D($\bar{\text{D}}$), $a$ has a D($\bar{\text{D}}$),

or in all positions in which $b$ has a D($\bar{\text{D}}$) $a$ has a $\bar{\text{D}}$(D)

and **2** in any position in which $a$ has a D or $\bar{\text{D}}$, $b$ does not have a 0 or 1.

If these two conditions are satisfied, then $a \cap b$ agrees with $a$ in all coordinates in which $a$ has a D or $\bar{\text{D}}$. The remaining coordinates of the intersection are defined as in the intersection of cubes contained in singular covers. If any coordinate intersection $a_i \cap b_i = \phi$, then $a \cap b = \Phi$.

As examples, consider $a = 11\text{xD0}\bar{\text{D}}$ and $b = \text{x10}\bar{\text{D}}\text{xD}$. Then $a \cap b = 110\text{D0}\bar{\text{D}}$. If $c = \text{x1x}\bar{\text{D}}\text{0}\bar{\text{D}}$, $a \cap c = \Phi$.

The procedure for deriving a test for a given fault consists of two parts: (1) A primitive D-cube of the fault is chosen and intersected successively with propagation D-cubes of the blocks of the circuit in order to form a connected chain of D-coordinates to an output. This procedure is called the *D-drive*. (2) The D-cube obtained in (1) is intersected with the singular covers of blocks of the circuit until a sufficient number of inputs have been specified. This is called the *consistency* operation. These two operations correspond to the sensitizing of a path from the fault to an output and the tracing back from the gates in the path towards the inputs in order to specify a sufficient number of inputs to produce the desired internal signals.

The first step in deriving tests is to obtain the singular covers and the

# DERIVATION OF TESTS

propagation D-cubes of the blocks of the circuit. Only single-input propagation D-cubes are computed initially. Multiple-input D-cubes in which more than one input coordinate is D or $\bar{D}$ are computed as necessary. These will be necessary when more than one path in a circuit containing reconvergent fan-out* has to be sensitized in order to detect a fault. Before attempting the D-drive, the blocks of the circuit are ordered so that every block appears after the blocks to whose outputs it is connected. This can always be done in circuits without feedback.

Any D-cube which represents a partially formed test during the D-drive is called a *test cube* and is represented by *tc* and a superscript denoting the step at which it is obtained. Associated with each test cube is an *activity vector*, consisting of the circuit wires to which D or $\bar{D}$ has been propagated at this stage in the test generation. Thus, the activity vector gives the successors through which the D-chain already constructed may be extended.

One of the primitive D-cubes of the fault under consideration is chosen as the initial test cube $tc^0$. It is intersected with the propagation D-cube of one of the members of the activity vector of $tc^0$ so that $tc^0$ and the D-cube with which it is intersected have a D or $\bar{D}$ in at least one common coordinate. The intersection is the new test cube which is then labeled $tc^1$. The activity vector of $tc^1$ is determined and the procedure is repeated until at least one output coordinate of the circuit is contained in the activity vector of the last test cube computed. At each step, coordinates that can be determined from the values of coordinates that have already been specified are also entered in the test cube.

The D-drive using single-input propagation D-cubes may terminate prematurely before reaching an output terminal if the circuit contains reconvergent fan-out. This will happen when all intersections of the test cube with the propagation D-cubes of all blocks of its activity vector are empty. Two types of empty intersections may be encountered. In the first, both the test cube and the D-cube have opposite values 0 or 1 specified for some coordinate. This happens when conditions necessary for propagation in the earlier part of the D-chain prevent further propagation. In this case the particular D-chain has to be abandoned and a new D-chain using a different member of the activity vector at the step of the last arbitrary selection is attempted. In the second type, the intersection is empty because the propagation D-cube has a 0 or 1 in a coordinate assigned D or $\bar{D}$ in the test cube.

---

*If there are two or more paths from any fan-out point in a circuit to the inputs of some gate, the fan-out is said to be reconvergent.

This implies that another path in the circuit has been accidentally sensitized. The D-drive can be continued only if a suitable multiple-input D-cube can be derived for the particular block. This corresponds to the case where a particular path can be sensitized only along with other paths, but not by itself. Multiple-input D-cubes with D's or $\bar{D}$'s in the desired coordinate positions can be derived in a manner analogous to that for the single input D-cubes. If the intersections with the appropriate multiple D-cubes are also empty, we have to back-track to the last step where a choice of path was made and try a different path.

On the successful completion of a D-drive, the consistency operation is begun. Here the unspecified coordinates in the test cube are assigned values consistent with the singular cover. The consistency operation is carried out by intersecting the test cube successively with cubes in the singular cover until a sufficient number of circuit inputs for generating the signal values specified in the test cube have been assigned. Since the D's and $\bar{D}$'s in the test cubes will be mutually consistent by our construction, it is sufficient to ensure that 0's and 1's which are not inputs are consistent with the circuit inputs. For every coordinate in the test cube that represents the output of a block and is assigned 0 or 1, the test cube is intersected with cubes in the singular cover of that block. The test cube is replaced by the intersection if the latter is not empty. As in the case of the D-drive, an inconsistent result indicated by empty intersections will necessitate back-tracking. It may be necessary to return to the D-drive phase and obtain a new D-chain before the consistency operation can be completed successfully.

It is interesting to examine how the response to a test T of a normal circuit and the same circuit with the fault $F$ in it can be represented in terms of D-cubes. Treating the inputs, outputs and internal connections as coordinates, the signal values in the normal circuit can be represented by a cube contained in the singular cover of the circuit. (If all inputs are specified, the signal values will correspond to a single vertex.) Similarly, the signal values in the faulty circuit can be represented by another cube. From these two cubes, we construct a D-cube $c(T, F)$ as follows: If a coordinate has the same value (including x) in both cubes, the corresponding coordinate is assigned the same value in the D-cube. If a coordinate is 1 in the cube of the normal circuit and 0 in the cube of the faulty circuit, the corresponding coordinate in the D-cube is set to D. The opposite condition is assigned $\bar{D}$. Note that the D-cube $c(T, F)$ as defined above is analogous to a primitive D-cube of the fault, if the entire combinational circuit is treated as a single block. For any given fault $F$, the D-algorithm attempts to construct a D-cube $c(T, F)$ from the

# DERIVATION OF TESTS

primitive D-cubes of the fault and the propagation D-cubes of some of the blocks of the circuit, so that the coordinate associated with some circuit output has a D or $\bar{D}$. The input coordinates of $c(T, F)$ specify the test T.

**Example 2.9:** We shall demonstrate the application of the formal D-algorithm by deriving a test for detecting the fault $\alpha$ s-a-0 in the circuit of Fig. 2.9.

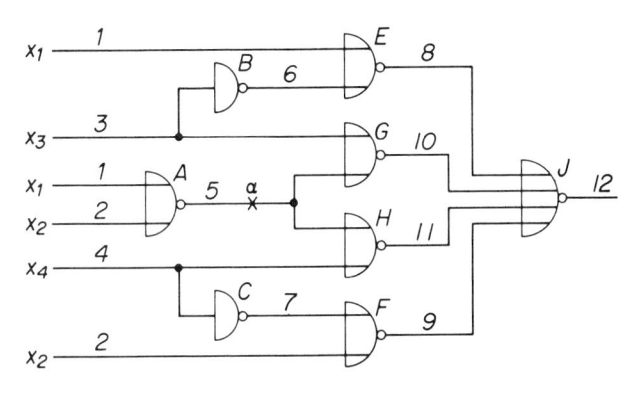

**Figure 2.9**

The singular cover of the circuit and the propagation D-cubes of the blocks are shown in Table 2.3(a) and (b) respectively. The entries that are left blank are unspecified and are treated as x's while performing intersections. The first D-drive for $\alpha$ s-a-0 is shown in the top part of Table 2.3(c). The primitive D-cube of the fault, $tc^0$, has a D in coordinate 5. Propagation D-cubes $i_d$ and $k_d$ both have D in this coordinate and $i_d$ is chosen arbitrarily for the D-drive. $tc^{1*}$ is obtained by specifying all signal values which can be determined from $tc^1$. The D-cube $n_d$ has a D in column 10 corresponding to the activity vector of $tc^{1*}$ and the D-drive terminates with the test cube $tc^2$ which has a D in the output coordinate 12.

In the consistency operation shown in the lower half of the table, the test cube is intersected with the singular cover of each block whose output coordinate is already specified. It terminates unsuccessfully due to the null intersection $tc^6$. Choosing $k_d$ instead of $i_d$ in the D-drive also leads to unsuccessful termination as shown in Table 2.3(d). Since both choices for the D-drive ended in inconsistency, we attempt the D-drive along both paths simultaneously. This is shown in Table 2.3(e). Since the activity vector of $tc^{1*}$ has two coordinates (10 and

|   |   | 1 | 2 | 3 | 4 | 5 | 6 | 7 | 8 | 9 | 10 | 11 | 12 |
|---|---|---|---|---|---|---|---|---|---|---|----|----|----|
| A | a | 0 | 0 |   |   | 1 |   |   |   |   |   |   |   |
|   | b | 1 | x |   |   | 0 |   |   |   |   |   |   |   |
|   | c | x | 1 |   |   | 0 |   |   |   |   |   |   |   |
| B | d |   |   | 0 |   |   | 1 |   |   |   |   |   |   |
|   | e |   |   | 1 |   |   | 0 |   |   |   |   |   |   |
| C | f |   |   |   | 0 |   |   | 1 |   |   |   |   |   |
|   | g |   |   |   | 1 |   |   | 0 |   |   |   |   |   |
| E | h | 0 |   |   |   |   | 0 |   | 1 |   |   |   |   |
|   | i | 1 |   |   |   |   | x |   | 0 |   |   |   |   |
|   | j | x |   |   |   |   | 1 |   | 0 |   |   |   |   |
| F | k |   | 0 |   |   |   |   | 0 |   | 1 |   |   |   |
|   | l |   | 1 |   |   |   |   | x |   | 0 |   |   |   |
|   | m |   | x |   |   |   |   | 1 |   | 0 |   |   |   |
| G | o |   |   | 0 |   | 0 |   |   |   |   | 1 |   |   |
|   | p |   |   | 1 |   | x |   |   |   |   | 0 |   |   |
|   | q |   |   | x |   | 1 |   |   |   |   | 0 |   |   |
| H | r |   |   |   | 0 | 0 |   |   |   |   |   | 1 |   |
|   | s |   |   |   | 1 | x |   |   |   |   |   | 0 |   |
|   | t |   |   |   | x | 1 |   |   |   |   |   | 0 |   |
| J | u |   |   |   |   |   |   |   | 0 | 0 | 0 | 0 | 1 |
|   | v |   |   |   |   |   |   |   | 1 | x | x | x | 0 |
|   | w |   |   |   |   |   |   |   | x | 1 | x | x | 0 |
|   | x |   |   |   |   |   |   |   | x | x | 1 | x | 0 |
|   | y |   |   |   |   |   |   |   | x | x | x | 1 | 0 |

Table 2.3 (a)
Singular Cover

|   |   | 1 | 2 | 3 | 4 | 5 | 6 | 7 | 8 | 9 | 10 | 11 | 12 |
|---|---|---|---|---|---|---|---|---|---|---|----|----|----|
| A | $a_d$ | 0 | D |   |   | $\bar{D}$ |   |   |   |   |   |   |   |
|   | $b_d$ | D | 0 |   |   | $\bar{D}$ |   |   |   |   |   |   |   |
| B | $c_d$ |   |   | D |   |   | $\bar{D}$ |   |   |   |   |   |   |
| C | $d_d$ |   |   |   | D |   |   | $\bar{D}$ |   |   |   |   |   |
| E | $e_d$ | 0 |   |   |   |   | D |   | $\bar{D}$ |   |   |   |   |
|   | $f_d$ | D |   |   |   |   | 0 |   | $\bar{D}$ |   |   |   |   |
| F | $g_d$ |   | 0 |   |   |   |   | D |   | $\bar{D}$ |   |   |   |
|   | $h_d$ |   | D |   |   |   |   | 0 |   | $\bar{D}$ |   |   |   |
| G | $i_d$ |   |   | 0 |   | D |   |   |   |   | $\bar{D}$ |   |   |
|   | $j_d$ |   |   | D |   | 0 |   |   |   |   | $\bar{D}$ |   |   |
| H | $k_d$ |   |   |   | 0 | D |   |   |   |   |   | $\bar{D}$ |   |
|   | $l_d$ |   |   |   | D | 0 |   |   |   |   |   | $\bar{D}$ |   |
| J | $m_d$ |   |   |   |   |   |   |   | 0 | 0 | 0 | D | $\bar{D}$ |
|   | $n_d$ |   |   |   |   |   |   |   | 0 | 0 | D | 0 | $\bar{D}$ |
|   | $o_d$ |   |   |   |   |   |   |   | 0 | D | 0 | 0 | $\bar{D}$ |
|   | $p_d$ |   |   |   |   |   |   |   | D | 0 | 0 | 0 | $\bar{D}$ |
|   | $q_d{}^*$ |   |   |   |   |   |   |   | 0 | 0 | D | D | $\bar{D}$ |

*Double D-cube.

Table 2.3 (b)
Propagation D-cubes

|  | 1 | 2 | 3 | 4 | 5 | 6 | 7 | 8 | 9 | 10 | 11 | 12 | Activity vector |
|---|---|---|---|---|---|---|---|---|---|---|---|---|---|
| *D-drive* | | | | | | | | | | | | | |
| $tc^0$ | 0 | 0 | | | D | | | | | | | | 5 |
| $tc^1 = tc^0 \cap i_d$ | 0 | 0 | 0 | | D | | | | | $\bar{D}$ | | | 10 |
| $tc^{1*}$ | 0 | 0 | 0 | | D | 1 | | 0 | | $\bar{D}$ | | | 10 |
| $tc^2 = tc^{1*} \cap n_d$ | 0 | 0 | 0 | | D | 1 | | 0 | 0 | $\bar{D}$ | 0 | D | 12 |
| *Consistency* | | | | | | | | | | | | | |
| $tc^3 = tc^2 \cap j$ | 0 | 0 | 0 | | D | 1 | | 0 | 0 | $\bar{D}$ | 0 | D | |
| $tc^4 = tc^3 \cap m$ | 0 | 0 | 0 | | D | 1 | 1 | 0 | 0 | $\bar{D}$ | 0 | D | |
| $tc^5 = tc^4 \cap s$ | 0 | 0 | 0 | 1 | D | 1 | 1 | 0 | 0 | $\bar{D}$ | 0 | D | |
| $tc^6 = tc^5 \cap f$ | 0 | 0 | 0 | $\varphi$ | D | 1 | 1 | 0 | 0 | $\bar{D}$ | 0 | D | |

Table 2.3 (c)

**D-drive Along *AGJ* and Consistency Operation**

|  | 1 | 2 | 3 | 4 | 5 | 6 | 7 | 8 | 9 | 10 | 11 | 12 | Activity vector |
|---|---|---|---|---|---|---|---|---|---|---|---|---|---|
| *D-drive* | | | | | | | | | | | | | |
| $tc^0$ | 0 | 0 | | | D | | | | | | | | 5 |
| $tc^1 = tc^0 \cap k_d$ | 0 | 0 | | 0 | D | | | | | | $\bar{D}$ | | 11 |
| $tc^{1*}$ | 0 | 0 | | 0 | D | | 1 | | 0 | | $\bar{D}$ | | 11 |
| $tc^2 = tc^{1*} \cap m_d$ | 0 | 0 | | 0 | D | | 1 | 0 | 0 | 0 | $\bar{D}$ | D | 12 |
| *Consistency* | | | | | | | | | | | | | |
| $tc^3 = tc^2 \cap j$ | 0 | 0 | | 0 | D | 1 | 1 | 0 | 0 | 0 | $\bar{D}$ | D | |
| $tc^4 = tc^3 \cap m$ | 0 | 0 | | 0 | D | 1 | 1 | 0 | 0 | 0 | $\bar{D}$ | D | |
| $tc^5 = tc^4 \cap p$ | 0 | 0 | 1 | 0 | D | 1 | 1 | 0 | 0 | 0 | $\bar{D}$ | D | |
| $tc^6 = tc^5 \cap d$ | 0 | 0 | $\varphi$ | 0 | D | 1 | 1 | 0 | 0 | 0 | $\bar{D}$ | D | |

Table 2.3 (d)

**D-drive Along *AHJ* and Consistency Operation**

|  | 1 | 2 | 3 | 4 | 5 | 6 | 7 | 8 | 9 | 10 | 11 | 12 | Activity vector |
|---|---|---|---|---|---|---|---|---|---|---|---|---|---|
| $tc^0$ | 0 | 0 | | | D | | | | | | | | 5 |
| $tc^1 = tc^0 \cap i_d \cap k_d$ | 0 | 0 | 0 | 0 | D | | | | | $\bar{D}$ | $\bar{D}$ | | 10, 11 |
| $tc^{1*}$ | 0 | 0 | 0 | 0 | D | 1 | 1 | 0 | 0 | $\bar{D}$ | $\bar{D}$ | | 10, 11 |
| $tc^2 = tc^{1*} \cap q_d$ | 0 | 0 | 0 | 0 | D | 1 | 1 | 0 | 0 | $\bar{D}$ | $\bar{D}$ | D | 12 |

Table 2.3 (e)

**Simultaneous D-drive Along *AGJ* and *AHJ***

11), we need a double D-cube for the block $J$, with D's in these coordinates. Intersecting $tc^2$ with the cubes $j, m, s, f, p$ and $d$ of the singular cover, we obtain the final test cube, $tc = tc^2$. Thus $\bar{x}_1 \bar{x}_2 \bar{x}_3 \bar{x}_4$ is a test for detecting $\alpha$ s-a-0.

In Example 2.9, we assigned the same label to all lines which fan out from any point. This labeling is sufficient if we are interested in deriving tests only for faults on the outputs of blocks. If we wish to derive tests for faults on the inputs of blocks as well, the fan-out lines should be labeled individually. Fan-out points may then be treated as single-input, multi-output blocks whose singular covers and propagation D-cubes are used in the formal D-algorithm.

It can be shown that the D-algorithm will yield a test for a fault if a test exists (Roth, 1966). The algorithm as described above, involving the intersection of D-cubes and singular covers can be used for test generation using a digital computer. For relatively small circuits, the informal method presented earlier, which is a path-sensitizing technique, preserving the identity of signals sensitive to the fault, seems to be more convenient, especially for manual computations.

The D-algorithm can be extended in a rather straightforward manner to make it applicable to multiple stuck type faults. We shall consider only an informal version of the algorithm.

The first step in the informal D-algorithm for multiple faults is to label wires which are s-a-0 with D and those which are s-a-1 with $\bar{D}$. As in the single-fault cases, we attempt to propagate a D or $\bar{D}$ to the circuit output. In doing so, the effect of a fault may propagate to some other faulty wire. If $x \rightarrow y$ indicates that a signal $x$ reaches a faulty wire whose state is represented by $y$, where $x = 0, 1$, D or $\bar{D}$ and $y =$ D or $\bar{D}$, the following additional rules may be defined: $D \rightarrow D = D$; $\bar{D} \rightarrow \bar{D} = \bar{D}$; $D \rightarrow \bar{D} = 1$; $\bar{D} \rightarrow D = 0$; $1 \rightarrow D = D$; $1 \rightarrow \bar{D} = 1$; $0 \rightarrow D = 0$; $0 \rightarrow \bar{D} = \bar{D}$. These rules, in effect, represent the consistency operation in the presence of multiple faults. The validity of the above equations will be clear if we use our interpretation of D and $\bar{D}$. $D \rightarrow D$ means that a signal that is normally 1 but changes to 0 in the presence of some fault propagates to a wire which is s-a-0. The signal on the wire will be 1 if neither fault is present but will be 0 if both faults are present. Similarly $D \rightarrow \bar{D}$ implies that a signal that changes from 1 to 0 propagates to a wire which is s-a-1. The signal on the wire will be 1 both in the normal and faulty circuits. The remaining equations can be verified in the same manner.

# DERIVATION OF TESTS

**Example 2.10**

*(a)*

*(b)*

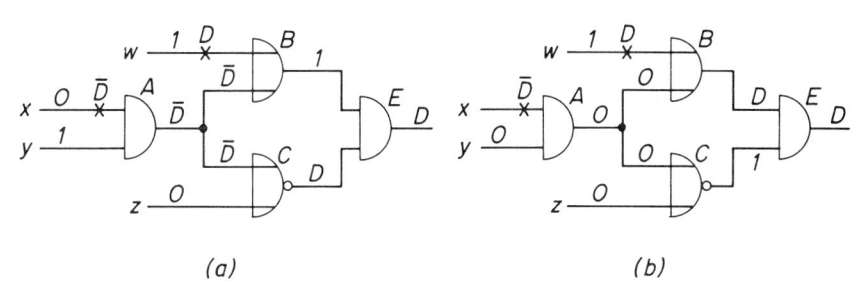

**Figure 2.10**

Figure 2.10 shows a circuit with $w$ s-a-0 and $x$ s-a-1. The signals shown on the wires are obtained by representing the two faults by D and $\bar{\text{D}}$ respectively and propagating a D to the output. First let us try to propagate the fault $x$ s-a-1 to the output in the presence of $w$ s-a-0. To propagate the fault to the output of gate $A$ we set $x = 0$, $y = 1$. At this stage we have a choice as to paths. Choosing path $ACE$ we must set $z = 0$ resulting in D as output from gate $C$. If $w = 0$ the output of $B$ is $\bar{\text{D}}$, the output of $E$ is $\text{D} \cdot \bar{\text{D}} = 0$ and the fault is not detected. However, if $w = 1$ the inputs to gate $B$ are D and $\bar{\text{D}}$, the output is 1 and the output of gate $E$ is D. This test, $w\bar{x}y\bar{z}$, is shown in Fig. 2.10(a).

It is also possible to propagate the fault $w$ s-a-0, by the input combination $w\bar{y}\bar{z}$. This case is shown in Fig. 2.10(b). Note that the output of the first AND gate will be 0 whether or not $x$ is s-a-1, because $y = 0$. The tests derived by this procedure are guaranteed to detect the simultaneous presence of all the multiple faults considered. Individual faults may or may not be detected by these tests. For example, $w\bar{x}y\bar{z}$ will detect $w$ s-a-0, $x$ s-a-1 or both whereas $w\bar{y}\bar{z}$ will detect $w$ s-a-0 or the double fault, but not $x$ s-a-1.

**Example 2.11:** Consider the same circuit repeated in Fig. 2.11 with $x$ s-a-0 and $\alpha$ s-a-1. In Fig. 2.11(a) we attempt to propagate the D on $x$ to the output of gate $E$ along the path $ACE$. If $w = 0$, the output of $B$ is D. Gate $E$ produces a $\bar{\text{D}}$ output with $\alpha$ s-a-1 because $\text{D} \to \bar{\text{D}} = 1$. If $w = 1$, the output of $B$ is 1 and $1 \to \bar{\text{D}} = 1$ causing the output of $E$ to be $\bar{\text{D}}$, as shown in Fig. 2.11(b). Both the tests $\bar{w}xy\bar{z}$ and $wxy\bar{z}$ detect the simultaneous presence of $x$ s-a-0 and $\alpha$ s-a-1. The test $wxy\bar{z}$ will detect the single-fault $x$ s-a-0, but not the single-fault $\alpha$ s-a-1, and $\bar{w}x\bar{y}z$

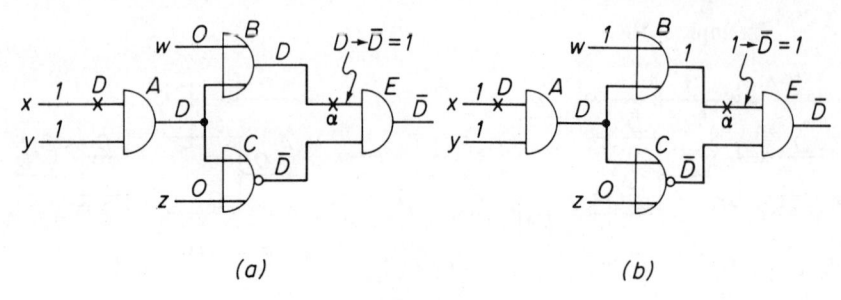

**Figure 2.11**

will not detect either single fault. The multiple-fault and the single-fault $\alpha$ s-a-1 can also be detected by $\bar{w}\bar{y}z$, which is derived by setting $y = 0$ so as not to propagate the fault on $x$ and then propagating the fault on $\alpha$.

*Poage's Method*

The methods discussed so far are useful for deriving individual tests for faults in a circuit. If the complete set of tests for detecting all faults in a circuit is desired, these methods will have to be used repeatedly. Poage (1963) has proposed a method which may be useful for deriving the complete set of tests.

The method derives functional descriptions of each output of the circuit, which also represent the structure of the circuit. Each functional expression represents not only the relationship of the output variables to the signals on the input and internal lines, but also the effect of faults on the output. The disadvantage of the method is that it is practical only for relatively small circuits. Though the procedure is applicable to both gate circuits and relay-contact circuits, we shall restrict our attention to the former type.

In order to include the effect of faults in the function realized by a circuit, three binary variables are used to specify the state of each wire $e_i$ in the circuit. These element variables are defined as follows:

$e_{in}$: $e_{in} = 1$ if and only if $e_i$ is normal

$e_{i1}$: $e_{i1} = 1$ if and only if $e_i$ is s-a-1

$e_{i0}$: $e_{i0} = 1$ if and only if $e_i$ is s-a-0

For each wire $a$, the totality of conditions under which it can have a signal 1

# DERIVATION OF TESTS

is represented by the proposition $P_a$. Similarly, $P'_a$ represents the conditions under which the signal on the wire can be 0. If $w$ is the input proposition for the wire $a$, then

$$P_a = wa_n + a_1$$

(i.e., $a$ will have a signal value of 1 if $w = 1$ and $a$ is normal or if $a$ is s-a-1). Similarly, $P'_a = \bar{w}a_n + a_0$. For any single-output function, the output propositions representing the conditions under which the output assumes the values of 1 and 0 can be expressed in terms of the input propositions of the circuit and the variables associated with each wire. From the output propositions, tests can be derived for all faults in the circuit as shown in the following example.

**Example 2.12**

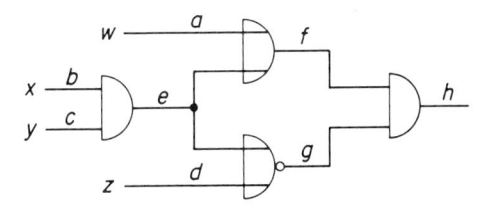

Figure 2.12

The circuit of Fig. 2.12 is the same as that in Fig. 2.1, with the wires suitably labeled. The output propositions $P_h$ and $P'_h$ are obtained from the element (wire) propositions as shown below:

$$P_a = wa_n + a_1$$
$$P'_a = \bar{w}a_n + a_0$$
$$P_b = xb_n + b_1$$
$$P'_b = \bar{x}b_n + b_0$$
$$P_c = yc_n + c_1$$
$$P'_c = \bar{y}c_n + c_0$$
$$P_d = zd_n + d_1$$
$$P'_d = \bar{z}d_n + d_0$$

$$P_e = (P_b \cdot P_c)e_n + e_1$$
$$= (xb_n + b_1)(yc_n + c_1)e_n + e_1$$

$$P'_e = (P'_b + P'_c)e_n + e_0$$
$$= (\bar{x}b_n + b_0 + \bar{y}c_n + c_0)e_n + e_0$$

$$P_f = (P_a + P_e)f_n + f_1$$
$$= \{wa_n + a_1 + (xb_n + b_1)(yc_n + c_1)e_n + e_1\}f_n + f_1$$

$$P'_f = (P'_a \cdot P'_e)f_n + f_0$$
$$= (\bar{w}a_n + a_0)\{(\bar{x}b_n + b_0 + \bar{y}c_n + c_0)e_n + e_0\}f_n + f_0$$

$$P_g = (P'_d \cdot P'_e)g_n + g_1$$
$$= (\bar{z}d_n + d_0)\{(\bar{x}b_n + b_0 + \bar{y}c_n + c_0)e_n + e_0\}g_n + g_1$$

$$P'_g = (P_d + P_e)g_n + g_0$$
$$= \{zd_n + d_1 + (xb_n + b_1)(yc_n + c_1)e_n + e_1\}g_n + g_0$$

$$P_h = (P_f \cdot P_g)h_n + h_1$$
$$= [\{wa_n + a_1 + (xb_n + b_1)(yc_n + c_1)e_n + e_1\}f_n + f_1]$$
$$\cdot [(\bar{z}d_n + d_0)\{(\bar{x}b_n + b_0 + \bar{y}c_n + c_0)e_n + e_0\}g_n + g_1]h_n + h_1$$

$$P'_h = (P'_f + P'_g)h_n + h_0$$
$$= [(\bar{w}a_n + a_0)\{(\bar{x}b_n + b_0 + \bar{y}c_n + c_0)e_n + e_0\}f_n + f_0$$
$$+ \{zd_n + d_1 + (xb_n + b_1)(yc_n + c_1)e_n + e_1\}g_n + g_0]h_n + h_0.$$

The effect of any fault on the output can be determined by assigning appropriate values to the element variables. For example, if $a$ is s-a-1, we set $a_n = a_0 = 0$, $a_1 = 1$, all other variables with subscript $n$ at 1 and the remaining variables at 0. Denoting the output propositions of the normal circuit by $P_h(n)$ and $P'_h(n)$ and those of the faulty circuit by $P_h(a_1)$ and $P'_h(a_1)$, we have:

$$P_h(n) = (w + xy)\bar{z}(\bar{x} + \bar{y})$$

$$P'_h(n) = \bar{w}(\bar{x} + \bar{y}) + z + xy$$

$$P_h(a_1) = \bar{z}(\bar{x} + \bar{y})$$

$$P'_h(a_1) = z + xy.$$

# DERIVATION OF TESTS

The set of tests for detecting a s-a-1 fault on wire $a$ is given by:

$$\begin{aligned}
T(a_1) &= P_h(n) \cdot P'_h(a_1) + P'_h(n) \cdot P_h(a_1) \\
&= (w + xy)\bar{z}(\bar{x} + \bar{y})(z + xy) \\
&\quad + \{\bar{w}(\bar{x} + \bar{y}) + z + xy\}\bar{z}(\bar{x} + \bar{y}) \\
&= \bar{w}\bar{x}\bar{z} + \bar{w}\bar{y}\bar{z}
\end{aligned}$$

$T(a_1)$ represents the three tests 0000, 0010 and 0100 which were derived for the same fault in Example 2.1. Though the derivation of the output propositions is rather cumbersome, once they have been derived the tests for all faults can be derived by simply assigning appropriate values to the element variables. Tests for multiple faults can also be derived using the same procedure. For instance, if $a$ is s-a-0 and $b$ is s-a-1, then

$$P_h(a_0, b_1) = y \cdot \bar{z} \cdot \bar{y} = 0$$

$$P'_h(a_0, b_1) = \bar{y} + z + y = 1$$

$$\begin{aligned}
T(a_0, b_1) &= P_h(n) = (w + xy)\bar{z}(\bar{x} + \bar{y}) \\
&= w\bar{x}\bar{z} + w\bar{y}\bar{z}.
\end{aligned}$$

In the circuit of Fig. 2.12, the wire $e$ fans out to the OR gate whose output is $f$ and the NOR gate whose output is $g$. Since the fan-out wires themselves have not been labeled, faults on these wires cannot be represented in the output propositions in the present form. Tests for faults in the individual branches can be derived by labeling each branch and assuming that each branch contains an element whose normal output is equal to its input. Labeling the fan-out branches as $j$ and $k$ we have:

$$P_j = P_e \cdot j_n + j_1; \quad P'_j = P'_e \cdot j_n + j_0$$

$$P_k = P_e \cdot k_n + k_1; \quad P'_k = P'_e \cdot k_n + k_0$$

The OR gate $f$ will have wires $a$ and $j$ as inputs and the NOR gate $g$ will have $d$ and $k$ as inputs. The output propositions $P_h$ and $P'_h$ can then be derived in the usual manner.

A more convenient representation for the propositions for any wire in a circuit is in terms of literal propositions. A *literal proposition* is an expression containing a single input literal and having a nested structure as in the example shown below:

$$((((xa_n + a_0)c_n + c_1)d_n + d_0)g_n + g_0).$$

Because of the regularity of the nested structure of literal propositions, a compressed notation may be used for representing them. The compressed notation for the example shown above is:

$$x(a_0 c_1 d_0 g_0).$$

It can be shown (Poage, 1963) that the propositions for any wire in a circuit can be written in terms of literal propositions. Using the compressed notation, the output propositions for the circuit of Fig. 2.12 can be written as follows:

$$P_a = w(a_1)$$

$$P'_a = \bar{w}(a_0)$$

$$P_b = x(b_1)$$

$$P'_b = \bar{x}(b_0)$$

$$P_c = y(c_1)$$

$$P'_c = \bar{y}(c_0)$$

$$P_d = z(d_1)$$

$$P'_d = \bar{z}(d_0).$$

$$P_e = (P_b \cdot P_c)e_n + e_1 = (P_b e_n + e_1)(P_c e_n + e_1)$$
$$= x(b_1 e_1) \cdot y(c_1 e_1)$$

$$P'_e = (P'_b + P'_c)e_n + e_0 = (P'_b e_n + e_0) + (P'_c e_n + e_0)$$
$$= \bar{x}(b_0 e_0) + \bar{y}(c_0 e_0)$$

Similarly

$$P_f = w(a_1 f_1) + x(b_1 e_1 f_1) \cdot y(c_1 e_1 f_1)$$

# DERIVATION OF TESTS

$$P'_f = \bar{w}(a_0 f_0) \cdot (\bar{x}(b_0 e_0 f_0) + \bar{y}(c_0 e_0 f_0))$$

$$P_g = \bar{z}(d_0 g_1) \cdot (\bar{x}(b_0 e_0 g_1) + \bar{y}(c_0 e_0 g_1))$$

$$P'_g = z(d_1 g_0) + x(b_1 e_1 g_0) \cdot y(c_1 e_1 g_0)$$

$$P_h = (w(a_1 f_1 h_1) + x(b_1 e_1 f_1 h_1) \cdot y(c_1 e_1 f_1 h_1))$$
$$\cdot \bar{z}(d_0 g_1 h_1) \cdot (\bar{x}(b_0 e_0 g_1 h_1) + \bar{y}(c_0 e_0 g_1 h_1))$$

$$P'_h = \bar{w}(a_0 f_0 h_0) \cdot (\bar{x}(b_0 e_0 f_0 h_0) + \bar{y}(c_0 e_0 f_0 h_0))$$
$$+ z(d_1 g_0 h_0) + x(b_1 e_1 g_0 h_0) \cdot y(c_1 e_1 g_0 h_0)$$

The output propositions can be expressed in the sum-of-products form as given below:

$$P_h = w(a_1 f_1 h_1) \bar{x}(b_0 e_0 g_1 h_1) \bar{z}(d_0 g_1 h_1)$$
$$+ w(a_1 f_1 h_1) \bar{y}(c_0 e_0 g_1 h_1) \bar{z}(d_0 g_1 h_1)$$
$$+ x(b_1 e_1 f_1 h_1) y(c_1 e_1 f_1 h_1) \bar{z}(d_0 g_1 h_1) \bar{x}(b_0 e_0 g_1 h_1)$$
$$+ x(b_1 e_1 f_1 h_1) y(c_1 e_1 f_1 h_1) \bar{z}(d_0 g_1 h_1) \bar{y}(c_0 e_0 g_1 h_1)$$

$$P'_h = \bar{w}(a_0 f_0 h_0) \bar{x}(b_0 e_0 f_0 h_0) + \bar{w}(a_0 f_0 h_0) \bar{y}(c_0 e_0 f_0 h_0)$$
$$+ z(d_1 g_0 h_0) + x(b_1 e_1 g_0 h_0) \cdot y(c_1 e_1 g_0 h_0)$$

Note that $P_h$ contains a term which has literal propositions with $x$ and $\bar{x}$. This term cannot be omitted because the literal propositions are not complements of each other as can be verified by expanding them.

$$x(b_1 e_1 f_1 h_1) = ((((xb_n + b_1)e_n + e_1)f_n + f_1)h_n + h_1)$$

$$\bar{x}(b_0 e_0 g_0 h_1) = ((((\bar{x}b_n + b_0)e_n + e_0)g_n + g_0)h_n + h_1)$$

Both of these expressions will have the value 1 when $h_1 = 1$ and are therefore not complements of each other.

A literal proposition can be evaluated directly from its compressed notation. By examining the expanded form of the proposition, we see that the proposition will have the same value as the literal if the elements contained in it are normal. If one or more elements in the proposition are faulty, the value of the proposition will be 1 if the variable corresponding to the faulty wire appearing last in the proposition is 1, and 0 otherwise. For example, consider the following literal proposition:

$$x(b_1 e_1 g_1 h_0) = (((xb_n + b_1)e_n + e_1)g_n + g_1)h_n + h_0$$

If the wires $b$, $e$, $g$ and $h$ are fault-free, the literal proposition will be 1 if and only if $x$ is 1. It will also have the value of 1 if $b$, $e$ or $g$ is s-a-1 or if $h$ is s-a-0, or if any combination of these faults occurs. If $b$ is s-a-0 and $g$ is s-a-1, the proposition will have the value of 1. On the other hand, if $b$ is s-a-1 and $g$ is s-a-0, the proposition will be 0.

The compressed notation may be used for deriving all tests which detect a given fault or a set of faults occurring simultaneously, using the method discussed earlier in this section. This procedure can be repeated to obtain tests for all possible single and multiple faults. It is also possible to determine the complete set of faults detected by a given input combination in the following manner: For any input combination, the normal output is determined by assigning appropriate values to the literals in the output propositions. The faults detected by the particular input combination are obtained by assigning all permissible mutually consistent values to the element propositions so as to cause the output to have a value opposite to the normal output.

As an example, consider the circuit of Fig. 2.12 with $w = 1$, $x = y = z = 0$. The output of the normal circuit will be 1. The faults detected by this input combination are those which will cause the output to be 0. For these faults,

$$\begin{aligned}P'_h = &\ \bar{w}(a_0 f_0 h_0)\bar{x}(b_0 e_0 f_0 h_0) + \bar{w}(a_0 f_0 h_0)\bar{y}(c_0 e_0 f_0 h_0) \\ &+ z(d_1 g_0 h_0) + x(b_1 e_1 g_0 h_0)y(c_1 e_1 g_0 h_0) = 1\end{aligned}$$

If only single faults are to be considered, the following will be detected by this test: $a_0, d_1, e_1, f_0, g_0, h_0$; i.e., $a, f, g$ or $h$ s-a-0 or $d$ or $e$ s-a-1. The first two terms of $P'_h$ become 1 when $a_0, f_0$ or $h_0$ is equal to 1. Similarly, $d_1, g_0$ or $h_0$ equals 1 causes the third term to be 1. $e_1, g_0$ or $h_0$ have to become equal to 1 to set the last term to 1. A similar procedure may be used for determining the multiple faults that will be detected by the test. For example, the first term of $P'_h$ will be 1 if and only if $\bar{w}(a_0 f_0 h_0)$ and $\bar{x}(b_0 e_0 f_0 h_0)$ are 1. $\bar{w}(a_0 f_0 h_0)$ will be 1 if $a_0 = 1, f_0 = 1$ or $h_0 = 1$. Since $\bar{x} = 1$, $\bar{x}(b_0 e_0 f_0 h_0)$ will be 1 if $b, e, f$ or $h$ is s-a-0 or they are all normal. If two faults are present simultaneously, the following pairs of faults will cause the first term to be 1: $(\alpha, a_0), (\beta, f_0), (\gamma, h_0)$, where $\alpha \neq b_1, e_1, f_1, h_1$; $\beta \neq f_1, h_1$; $\gamma \neq h_1$. In obtain-

# DERIVATION OF TESTS

ing this list of pairs of faults, we have made use of the fact that if more than one element in a literal proposition is faulty, the value of the literal proposition is determined by the fault appearing last in it: e.g., $\bar{w}(a_0 f_0 h_0) = 1$ if $a_1 = 1, f_0 = 1$. Also, an element proposition not appearing in a literal proposition does not affect the value of the latter. For example, faults on wires $c$, $d$ or $g$ do not affect the value of the first term of $P_h'$. The complete set of faults detected by any test can be determined in this manner. Poage's method can be used to find a minimal set of fault-detection tests. We shall consider these techniques later in this chapter.

*The Equivalent Normal Form*

Armstrong (1966) has proposed a method for deriving a *nearly* minimal set of fault-detection tests, making use of the *equivalent normal form* (enf) of the circuit. He has conjectured, but not proved, that this method will yield tests for detecting all single faults in an irredundant circuit. The enf of a circuit is similar to its output proposition as defined by Poage in that it represents the dependence of the output on the inputs and the states of internal wires. However, some information regarding the type of fault that may be present on each wire is omitted.

The enf of a circuit is obtained by expressing the output of each gate as a function of its inputs and preserving the identity of each gate by a suitable subscript. Thus, if the inputs to an AND gate are labeled $a$ and $b$ and the output is labeled $c$, we represent this by $c = (a \cdot b)_c$. Applying this procedure to all gates in the circuit, we obtain an expression (usually in a factored form) of the output in terms of the input variables. This factored expression is then expanded into the sum-of-products form in the usual manner except that when a pair of parentheses is removed, the subscript associated with it is concatenated to the subscripts of the variables within the pair of parentheses. Each subscripted input variable in the enf is referred to as a *literal*. If an input variable appears in the enf with different subscripts, they are considered to be distinct literals. Thus, a literal in the enf is similar to a literal proposition in Poage's output proposition and represents a path from the input to the output.

**Example 2.13:** We shall illustrate the procedure for deriving the enf for the circuit of Fig. 2.12 which is repeated on the following page:

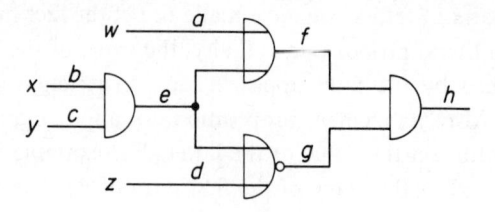

## Figure 2.13

Since input wires have been labeled with a symbol distinct from the input variables, we may treat each of them as a logic element whose output has the same value as its input. This also allows us to compare the enf to the output propositions obtained earlier.

$$\begin{aligned}
h &= (f \cdot g)_h = ((a + e)_f \cdot (\bar{d} \cdot \bar{e})_g)_h \\
&= (((w)_a + (bc)_e)_f \cdot ((\bar{z})_d \cdot (\bar{b} + \bar{c})_e)_g)_h \\
&= (((w)_a + ((x)_b \cdot (y)_c)_e)_f \cdot ((\bar{z})_d \cdot ((\bar{x})_b + (\bar{y})_c)_e)_g)_h \\
&= ((w_a + (x_b \cdot y_c)_e)_f \cdot (\bar{z}_d \cdot (\bar{x}_b + \bar{y}_c)_e)_g)_h \\
&= ((w_a + x_{be} \cdot y_{ce})_f \cdot (\bar{z}_d(\bar{x}_{be} + \bar{y}_{ce}))_g)_h \\
&= ((w_{af} + x_{bef} y_{cef})(\bar{z}_{dg} \bar{x}_{beg} + \bar{z}_{dg} \bar{y}_{ceg}))_h \\
&= w_{afh} \bar{x}_{begh} \bar{z}_{dgh} + w_{afh} \bar{y}_{cegh} \bar{z}_{dgh} \\
&\quad + x_{befh} \bar{x}_{begh} y_{cefh} \bar{z}_{dgh} + x_{befh} y_{cefh} \bar{y}_{cegh} \bar{z}_{dgh}
\end{aligned}$$

Comparing the enf with the compressed form of the output proposition $P_h$ obtained earlier, we see that the enf is obtained by omitting the subscripts of the element variables and using the variables within parentheses as the subscripts for the corresponding literals. The complemented enf is obtained by complementing the enf and converting it to the sum-of-products form. The correspondence between the complemented enf and the output proposition $P'_h$ can also be readily established. However, the manner in which the enf is used for deriving tests differs from Poage's method.

An appearance of a literal in the enf is usually tested for s-a-1 by assigning the value of 0 to it, 1's to all other literals in the term and suitable values to additional variables so as to cause all other terms in the enf to be 0. An appearance of a literal is tested for s-a-0 by assigning the value of 1 to all literals in the term containing it and making all other terms equal to 0. Alternatively, an appearance of the same literal in the complemented enf may be tested for s-a-1. In Example 2.13, the literal $w_{afh}$ in the first term can be tested for s-a-1 by the input combinations $\bar{w}\bar{x}\bar{z}$ and for s-a-0 by $w\bar{x}\bar{y}\bar{z}$. We shall show

# DERIVATION OF TESTS 43

later that in certain circuits with reconvergent fan-out it may be necessary to test for several literals simultaneously.

Armstrong (1966) has shown that any test for a literal appearance in the enf also sensitizes the path in the original circuit represented by the subscripts of the literal. Thus a test for a literal will test the wires represented by its subscripts for s-a-1 or s-a-0. A set of tests for detecting all s-a-1 and s-a-0 faults in the circuit can be obtained if it were possible to (1) select a set of literals such that their subscripts cover all wires in the circuit and (2) derive a set of tests which test at least one appearance of each such literal in the enf (or the complemented enf) for s-a-1 and s-a-0. Alternatively, each literal in both the enf and its complement may be tested for s-a-1 (or s-a-0). The set of tests so obtained may contain more than one test for each fault, because the same wire may be in more than one path sensitized by the sets of tests. Also note that testing every literal in the enf for both s-a-1 and s-a-0 (if this is possible) is sufficient for testing the entire circuit but not necessary. This leads us to the following conjecture by Armstrong (1966): Testing every testable literal in the enf of a circuit for both s-a-0 and s-a-1 is sufficient for detecting all s-a-0 and s-a-1 faults in an irredundant circuit.

If the above conjecture is true, certain terms in the enf may be omitted, since they cannot be used for testing any literal. If an input variable and its complement appear in the same term of an enf, but with different subscripts, that term may be omitted. Such terms in the enf correspond to two (or more) reconvergent fan-out paths, where the number of inversions along one path is even and along another is odd. Unless a fault is present in one of the fan-out branches, this term will always have the value of 0 and therefore will have no effect on the derivation of tests for literals in other terms. If terms containing complementary variables are discarded, the reduced enf so obtained may not contain literals corresponding to some connections in the circuit. It has *not* been shown that the faults on these connections will be detected by tests derived for other literals in the reduced enf, but no counterexample has been found.

The enf for the circuit of Fig. 2.13 can be reduced to:

$$h = w_{afh}\bar{x}_{begh}\bar{z}_{dgh} + w_{afh}\bar{y}_{cegh}\bar{z}_{dgh}$$

The complemented enf for the circuit is

$$\bar{h} = \bar{w}_{afh} + x_{begh}y_{cegh} + z_{dgh}$$

**Example 2.14:** As an example where the reduced enf does not contain a set of literals whose subscripts cover all connections in the circuit,

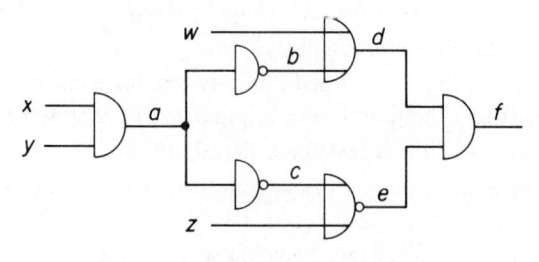

**Figure 2.14**

consider the circuit of Fig. 2.14. Note that this circuit is redundant and a s-a-0 fault on wire $b$ cannot be detected. The enf for the circuit is

$$f = w_{df}x_{acef}y_{acef}\bar{z}_{ef} + \bar{x}_{abdf}x_{acef}y_{acef}\bar{z}_{ef}$$
$$+ x_{acef}\bar{y}_{abdf}y_{acef}\bar{z}_{ef}$$

The last two terms may be discarded because each contains a variable and its complement. This leads to the reduced enf

$$f = w_{df}x_{acef}y_{acef}\bar{z}_{ef}$$

and the complemented enf

$$\bar{f} = \bar{w}_{df} + \bar{x}_{acef} + \bar{y}_{acef} + z_{ef}$$

neither of which contains a literal with subscript $b$. The tests $\bar{w}xy\bar{z}$, $w\bar{x}y\bar{z}$ and $wxy\bar{z}$ will detect $a, c, d, e$ or $f$ s-a-0 or s-a-1. $b$ s-a-0 is undetectable, but $b$ s-a-1 can be detected by $\bar{w}xy\bar{z}$ which is contained in the test set derived by using the reduced enf and its complement. Notice that the fault $b$ s-a-1 is equivalent to the fault $w$ s-a-1 in that both faults have the same set of tests and $w$ s-a-1 is detectable by $\bar{w}xy\bar{z}$.

When a term contains two or more literals pertaining to the same input variable, it may be necessary to test all these literals in the term simultaneously by setting them all to 0 and setting the remaining literals in the term to 1. All other terms are made to assume the value of 0, as before. It may also be necessary to test for two or more literals corresponding to the same input variable but contained in different terms, simultaneously. These cases occur when the circuit has reconvergent fan-out and two or more paths have to be sensitized simultaneously, as in the following example.

## Example 2.15

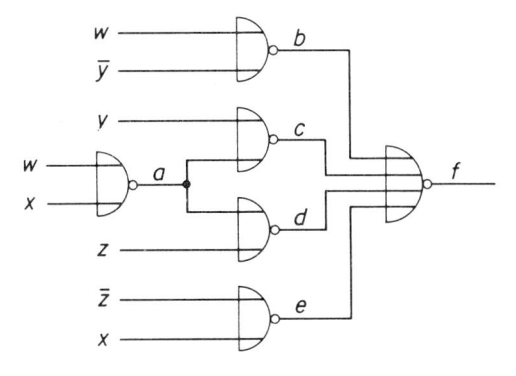

**Figure 2.15**

The reduced enf for the circuit of Fig. 2.15 is:

$$\bar{w}_{acf}\bar{w}_{adf}\bar{x}_{acf}\bar{x}_{adf}\bar{y}_{bf}\bar{z}_{ef} + w_{bf}x_{ef}y_{cf}z_{df}$$

The literals $\bar{w}_{acf}$ and $\bar{w}_{adf}$ in the first term cannot be tested for s-a-1 individually. However, they can be tested simultaneously by the input $w\bar{x}\bar{y}\bar{z}$. The same comment applies to the literals $\bar{x}_{acf}$ and $\bar{x}_{adf}$. The complemented enf for this circuit is:

$$\bar{w}_{bf}y_{bf} + w_{acf}\bar{y}_{cf} + x_{acf}\bar{y}_{cf} + w_{adf}\bar{z}_{df} + x_{adf}\bar{z}_{df} + \bar{x}_{ef}z_{ef}$$

Let us test the literals in the second term for s-a-0 by setting $w = 1$ and $y = 0$. In order to make the third and fourth terms equal to 0, we need $x = 0$ and $z = 1$. This causes both literals in the last term to be 1. Thus we are able to test for literals in these terms, simultaneously for s-a-0, but not individually. However, both these terms will change from 1 to 0 simultaneously if and only if the fault is on lead $f$, and the test will detect a fault only on that lead. The input combination $wx\bar{y}z$ will test literals in the second and third terms for s-a-0 and will therefore detect faults on $a$, $c$ or $f$.

Though the enf method is simpler than Poage's method of deriving tests, the latter has the advantage that tests can be derived for multiple faults. Both methods are practical only for relatively small circuits. For larger circuits, the path sensitizing technique or the D-algorithm or a combination of these methods seems to be preferable. Another method of deriving tests for large circuits involves simulation of the circuit on a digital computer. We shall discuss this in Chapter 5.

## MINIMIZATION OF TEST SETS

The methods discussed in the preceding section are useful for deriving a set of tests for detecting any fault in an irredundant combinational circuit. The set of tests so obtained may be much larger than necessary for detecting all faults. Thus, one of the practical problems is that of obtaining a minimal or near minimal set of fault-detection tests. Another problem of interest is that of locating the fault in a circuit to a gate or a module. This is the diagnosis problem. A minimal or near minimal set of diagnostic tests is also desirable.

Tests may be applied to a circuit using a *fixed* (*combinational*) *schedule* or an *adaptive* (*sequential*) *schedule* of testing. In fixed schedules, the order in which tests are applied is irrelevant. Fixed schedules are particularly suited for fault detection in circuits where all faults are equally likely to occur. In adaptive schedules, the next test to be applied is determined by the outcome of earlier tests. Adaptive schedules may require fewer tests than fixed schedules for locating faults and also may be useful for detecting faults when the faults are not equally probable.

*Fault-Table Methods*

A fault table can be used for obtaining minimal sets of tests for detection and diagnosis, when a fixed schedule of testing is used. The fault table for minimizing the set of fault-detection tests has a row for each test and a column for each fault. In the table, an entry $c_{ij}$ is 1 if the test $T_i$ detects the fault $f_j$, and 0 otherwise. For the diagnosis problem, the columns of the fault table correspond to pairs of faults that have to be distinguished. If a circuit is made up of modules, each of which contains many gates, it may not be necessary to distinguish between the different faults that may occur in the same module, because the entire faulty module will be replaced in the event of a fault. An entry $c_{ij}$ is 1 if test $T_i$ produces different outputs for the pair of faults represented by column $j$. If a minimal set of tests for detection and diagnosis is desired, a combined table which has a column corresponding to every fault to be detected and for every pair of faults to be distinguished is used. Minimal sets of tests for fault detection and/or diagnosis are obtained by finding the smallest set of rows such that every column of the appropriate fault table has a 1 in at least one of the rows in the set.

The problem of finding a minimal set of tests is similar to the prime-implicant covering problem (McCluskey, 1956) and methods of solution of the latter are also applicable to the former. As the first step in the minimization, it may be possible to delete certain rows and columns of the fault table. A row (column) $x$ of a fault table is said to *cover* (*dominate*) a row (column) $y$ if $x$ has 1's in all columns (rows) that $y$ has 1's. Any row of a fault table that is covered by another row can be deleted from the table, because all the faults detected (or pairs of faults distinguished) by the test corresponding to the row which is deleted will be detected (or distinguished) by the test corresponding to the row that covers it. Any column that covers another column may also be deleted. This is justifiable because any test which detects the fault (or distinguishes between the pair of faults) represented by the remaining column also detects (or distinguishes between) the fault (or faults) represented by the deleted column. The deletion of columns and rows may be carried out in any order until no further deletions are possible.

Several methods have been proposed (McCluskey, 1956; Pyne and McCluskey, 1962; Gimpel, 1965) for obtaining minimal covers for the prime-implicant problem, all of which are applicable to the minimization of the fault detection and diagnosis test sets. We shall present one such method which is useful for solving small problems by hand computation.

Let a binary variable $x_i$ be associated with every test $T_i$ and let $x_i$ have the value of 1 if the test $T_i$ is to be included in the test set. Let the number of faults and tests in the fault table be $m$ and $n$ respectively. In order to detect any fault $f_j$, it is necessary and sufficient to include any one of the tests for which there is a 1 in the $j^{th}$ column. If the entry in the $i^{th}$ row and $j^{th}$ column is represented by $a_{ij}$, the minimal test set should satisfy the condition:

$$\sum_{i=1}^{n} a_{ij} x_i = 1$$

Since this condition has to be satisfied for all columns of the fault table, the minimal test set should satisfy the condition:

$$f = \prod_{j=1}^{m} \left( \sum_{i=1}^{n} a_{ij} x_i \right) = 1$$

For small problems, the minimal set is most readily obtained by converting the product-of-sums expression for $f$ obtained as mentioned above to the sum-of-products form and choosing the term containing the least number of variables. This procedure may generate many redundant terms in the sum-of-products form. Some methods which eliminate these terms and are therefore more efficient computationally have been presented by Pyne and McCluskey (1962).

The number of faults for which tests are to be derived can be decreased by taking advantage of the fact that different faults in the circuit may be detected by the same test set. In terms of the fault table, this corresponds to faults which have identical columns, and all columns except one may be deleted from the table. The faults which have identical test sets form an equivalence class and it is sufficient to derive tests for one member of each equivalence class. For example, s-a-0 faults on the inputs and the output of an AND gate form an equivalence class and only one of these need be tested. Similarly, if all tests for detecting a particular fault also detect another fault, it is not necessary to derive tests for the latter. This is the case of column dominance in the fault table. A test for a s-a-1 fault on any input to an AND gate will also detect a s-a-1 fault on its output and the latter need not be tested for explicitly. This technique, called *fault collapsing* (Schertz and Metze, 1968), is useful in test derivation, since some unnecessary tests are not derived at all. Both types of fault collapsing may be used for minimizing fault detection test sets, but only the first type is applicable to diagnosis.

The fault table of any circuit with even a moderate number of inputs becomes too large for practical computations because an $n$-input circuit may require a table with up to $2^n$ rows. Several authors have presented methods for obtaining near-minimal sets of tests without actually constructing the entire fault table.

Galey, Norby and Roth (1964) have proposed a method of obtaining a near-minimal solution by successive intersections of complete sets of tests for individual faults. For any fault $f_i$, let $T_i$ be the complete set of tests that detect it. Starting with the set $T_1$, we intersect it with the set $T_2$. If the intersection is nonempty, it is retained and $T_1$ and $T_2$ are discarded. At every step in the procedure, the complete set of tests for a yet undetected fault is derived and intersected with the sets of tests retained. A pair of sets is replaced by their intersection if it is not empty. The procedure terminates when the test sets for all faults have been derived and intersected with the retained sets of tests. The fault table containing only the tests remaining at the end of the procedure will be considerably smaller than the complete table and may be treated as the starting point for a covering problem. However, the procedure may not yield the true minimal set of tests because tests which should be included in the solution may have been discarded during the intersections. The final result will also be sensitive to the order in which the intersections are performed.

MINIMIZATION OF TEST SETS                                    49

*Near-Minimal Test Sets Using the Equivalent Normal Form*

Armstrong (1966) has proposed a heuristic method of obtaining a near-minimal set of tests without deriving the complete fault table. Using the enf of the circuit and a scoring function, tests are derived, one at a time, so that those tests which are likely to be necessary in the minimal test set are derived first. The scoring function is devised so as to take advantage of the following two desirable properties: (1) The term containing the literal to be tested should contain the fewest number of variables. (2) The literal to be tested should be such that its complement appears the largest number of times in the remaining terms of the enf. The first property assures that several variables will remain unassigned while testing the chosen variable, thereby increasing the chances of being able to assign these variables so as to test other literals simultaneously and hence increase the number of faults detected by the test. When the chosen literal is tested for s-a-1, the second property causes 1's to be assigned to literals in other terms, also making it more likely to be able to test some other literal in one or more of those terms for s-a-1 simultaneously. Recall that a literal in the enf is tested for s-a-1 by assigning the value of 0 to it, 1's to all other literals in the term and additional variables so as to cause all other terms in the enf to be 0. Tests for literals s-a-0 are derived by using the complemented enf. Instead of testing for s-a-1 faults on literals in both the enf and its complement, we may test them for s-a-0. Since all literals in a term will be tested for s-a-0 simultaneously, it is sufficient to specify a scoring function for each term in the enf and complemented enf. Poage's (1963) output propositions may also be used similarly with a scoring function to obtain near-minimal sets of tests.

**Example 2.16:** As an example of the derivation of a near-minimal set of fault-detection tests using Armstrong's method, consider the circuit of Fig. 2.16. The enf and complemented enf of the circuit

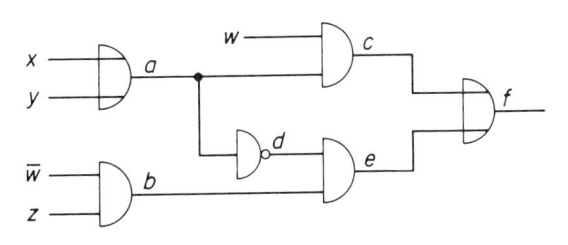

**Figure 2.16**

are:

$$f = w_{cf}x_{acf} + w_{cf}y_{acf} + \bar{w}_{bef}\bar{x}_{adef}\bar{y}_{adef}z_{bef}$$

$$\bar{f} = \bar{w}_{cf}w_{bef} + w_{bef}\bar{x}_{acf}\bar{y}_{acf} + \bar{w}_{cf}x_{adef} + \bar{x}_{acf}x_{adef}\bar{y}_{acf}$$
$$+ \bar{w}_{cf}y_{adef} + \bar{x}_{acf}\bar{y}_{acf}y_{adef} + \bar{w}_{cf}\bar{z}_{bef} + \bar{x}_{acf}\bar{y}_{acf}\bar{z}_{bef}$$

Discarding terms containing a variable and its complement, we obtain the following reduced form of the complemented enf:

$$\bar{f} = w_{bef}\bar{x}_{acf}\bar{y}_{acf} + \bar{w}_{cf}x_{adef} + \bar{w}_{cf}y_{adef}$$
$$+ \bar{w}_{cf}\bar{z}_{bef} + \bar{x}_{acf}\bar{y}_{acf}\bar{z}_{bef}.$$

We shall use the following scoring function proposed by Armstrong for determining the order in which tests for literals in the enf and the complemented enf are to be derived:

$$S_{kj} = \left(1 - \frac{v_j}{v}\right) + \frac{\lambda_{kj}}{L}$$

where $S_{kj}$ = the score for the $k^{\text{th}}$ literal in the $j^{\text{th}}$ term of the enf,
$v_j$ = the number of variables in the $j^{\text{th}}$ term,
$v$ = the total number of variables in the enf,
$L$ = the total number of literal appearances in the enf,
$\lambda_{kj}$ = the number of times the variable corresponding to the literal under consideration appears in the enf, complementary to its appearance in the $j^{\text{th}}$ term.

For our example, $v = 4$ and $L = 8$ for the enf and $L = 12$ for the reduced complemented enf. For the literal $w_{cf}$ in the first term of $f$, $v_1 = 2$ since there are two variables in the first term and $\lambda_{11} = 1$ since $\bar{w}$ appears once in the enf. Therefore $S_{11} = (1 - \frac{2}{4}) + \frac{1}{8} = \frac{5}{8}$. The scores for all the literals in $f$ and $\bar{f}$ are given in Tables 2.4(a) and 2.4(b) respectively. The scores have been multiplied by the common denominator 24, for convenience. The tables also show the tests $T_1$ through $T_7$, which have been derived for the literals starting with the literals with the highest score and proceeding according to descending scores. The subscripts of the test indicate the order in which they were derived. The literals with the highest score are $x_{adef}$ and $y_{adef}$, both of which have a score of 16 in the complemented enf.

# MINIMIZATION OF TEST SETS

Arbitrarily choosing $x_{adef}$ for testing, we set $x_{adef} = 0$ and $\bar{w}_{cf} = 1$. This assignment causes the term $w_{bef}\bar{x}_{acf}\bar{y}_{acf}$ to be 0. We assign $y = 0$ to make the term $\bar{w}_{cf}y_{adef}$ equal to 0. The test $T_1$ shown in Table 2.4(b) is obtained by further assigning $z = 1$ to cause the remaining terms in the enf to be 0. It is also seen that this is a test for a literal appearance in each of the terms of the complemented enf. Next, the test $T_2$ for the literal $w_{cf}$ in the term $w_{cf}x_{acf}$, is derived in the same manner. Table 2.4(c) is the fault table for the circuit. By deleting rows which are covered by other rows, and columns which cover other columns, we obtain the test set $\{T_1, T_2, T_3, T_4\}$, which is sufficient for detecting all s-a-1 and s-a-0 faults. Thus in this example it is unnecessary to test all literals. This set happens to be the minimal test set as can be verified

| enf Score | $w_{cf}\ x_{acf}$ | $w_{cf}\ y_{acf}$ | $\bar{w}_{bef}\ \bar{x}_{adef}\ \bar{y}_{adef}\ z_{bef}$ |
|---|---|---|---|
|  | 15    15 | 15    15 | 6    3    3    0 |
| $T_2$ | 0    1 | 0    0 | 1    0    1    1 |
| $T_3$ | 1    0 | 1    0 | 0    1    1    1 |
| $T_6$ | 0    0 | 0    1 | 1    1    0    1 |
| $T_7$ | 0    0 | 0    0 | 1    1    1    0 |

Table 2.4(a)

| enf Score | $w_{bef}\ \bar{x}_{acf}\ \bar{y}_{acf}$ | $\bar{w}_{cf}\ x_{adef}$ | $\bar{w}_{cf}\ y_{adef}$ | $\bar{w}_{cf}\ \bar{z}_{bef}$ | $\bar{x}_{acf}\ \bar{y}_{acf}\ \bar{z}_{bef}$ |
|---|---|---|---|---|---|
|  | 12    8    8 | 14    16 | 14    16 | 14    12 | 8    8    6 |
| $T_1$ | 0    1    1 | 1    0 | 1    0 | 1    0 | 1    1    0 |
| $T_4$ | 1    0    1 | 0    1 | 0    0 | 0    1 | 0    1    1 |
| $T_5$ | 1    1    0 | 0    0 | 0    1 | 0    1 | 1    0    1 |

Table 2.4(b)

|  | $a_0$ | $b_0$ | $c_0$ | $d_0$ | $e_0$ | $f_0$ | $a_1$ | $b_1$ | $c_1$ | $d_1$ | $e_1$ | $f_1$ |
|---|---|---|---|---|---|---|---|---|---|---|---|---|
| $T_1 = \bar{w}\bar{x}\bar{y}z$ | 0 | 1 | 0 | 1 | 1 | 1 | 1 | 0 | 0 | 0 | 0 | 0 |
| $T_2 = \bar{w}x\bar{y}z$ | 1 | 0 | 0 | 0 | 0 | 0 | 0 | 0 | 1 | 1 | 1 | 1 |
| $T_3 = w\bar{x}\bar{y}z$ | 0 | 0 | 0 | 0 | 0 | 0 | 1 | 1 | 1 | 0 | 1 | 1 |
| $T_4 = wx\bar{y}\bar{z}$ | 1 | 0 | 1 | 0 | 0 | 1 | 0 | 0 | 0 | 0 | 0 | 0 |
| $T_5 = w\bar{x}\bar{y}\bar{z}$ | 1 | 0 | 1 | 0 | 0 | 1 | 0 | 0 | 0 | 0 | 0 | 0 |
| $T_6 = \bar{w}\bar{x}yz$ | 1 | 0 | 0 | 0 | 0 | 0 | 0 | 0 | 1 | 1 | 1 | 1 |
| $T_7 = \bar{w}\bar{x}\bar{y}\bar{z}$ | 0 | 0 | 0 | 0 | 0 | 0 | 0 | 1 | 1 | 0 | 1 | 1 |

Table 2.4(c)

by deriving the complete fault table and obtaining the minimum cover. If after each test was derived, we determined the list of faults already detected by examining the subscripts of the literals tested, we could have terminated the test generation with the test $T_4$. In general, this will yield an efficient but not necessarily minimal set of tests, though in our example the best set was obtained.

*Diagnosing Tree*

An alternative representation of a set of tests in the form of a diagnosing tree is useful for obtaining near-minimal sets of diagnostic tests. The diagnosing tree is a directed graph whose nodes are tests and the outgoing branches from a node represent the different outcomes of the particular test. For a single-output circuit, there will be only two branches emanating from each node, corresponding to the success and failure of the test. Each branch is labeled with the possible sets of single faults that could be in the circuit, as determined by the tests already applied.

If combinational testing is to be used, the test to be applied at any stage of the testing is independent of the results of the past tests. In this case, the diagnosing tree can be arranged in levels and all nodes in the same level represent the same test. The diagnosing tree is continued until there is at most one fault associated with each branch. The problem of finding a minimal set of diagnostic tests becomes that of finding a diagnosing tree with the fewest number of levels.

Even though the number of tests required for diagnosis with combinational testing is independent of the order of tests, the number of levels in the diagnosing tree is dependent on the order of application of tests. This is caused by the masking of certain unnecessary tests by the particular order of testing as shown in the following example.

**Example 2.17:** Let three tests $t_1$, $t_2$ and $t_3$ be used for distinguishing between four possible faults in a circuit. The diagnosing trees starting with $t_1$ and $t_2$ are shown in Fig. 2.17. The tests $t_1, t_2$ and $t_3$ dichotomize the faults as $(f_1; f_2 f_3 f_4)$, $(f_1 f_2; f_3 f_4)$ and $(f_1 f_3; f_2 f_4)$ respectively. In this example, the fact that $t_1$ is unnecessary is masked when it is applied first. In Fig. 2.17, $\varphi$ represents the empty set.

In order to obtain a minimal set of diagnostic tests, it would be necessary to construct the diagnosing tree for every possible ordering of tests.

# REDUNDANCY

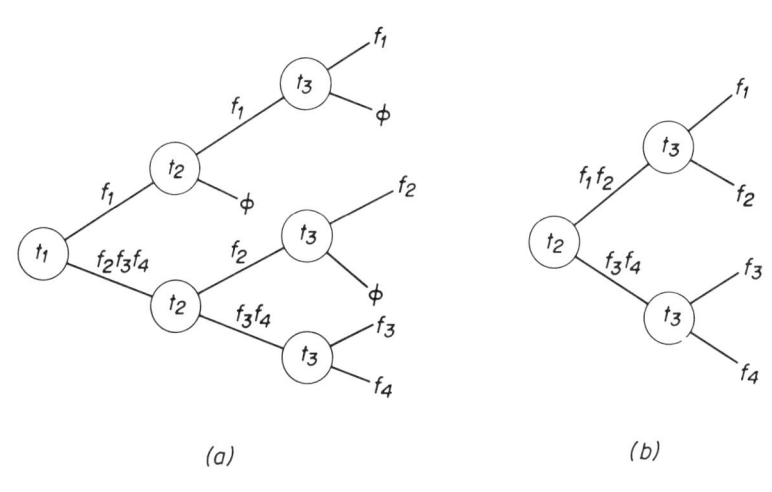

**Figure 2.17**

Since this would be impractical except in very small problems, a heuristic method of choosing the ordering, leading to a good but not necessarily optimal solution can be employed (Chang, 1965). At each step, the test which will distinguish between the largest number of faults not already distinguished is applied. Note that this is exactly what Armstrong's scoring function also endeavors to do (for fault detection only), though in the latter, a test having the desired property is constructed at each step instead of being chosen from a given set of tests.

Near-minimal adaptive schedules of tests can also be derived using the diagnosing tree. Here the tests in each level need not be the same. The heuristic method of choosing the locally optimal test at each step remains valid. Adaptive testing often requires shorter sequences of tests than are necessary for combinational testing.

## REDUNDANCY

A connection in a circuit is said to be *redundant* if no output function of the circuit is changed as a result of cutting the connection. Cutting an input to a gate has the same effect on its output as assigning a fixed value to that input such that the output is independent of the fixed input. For example, cutting an input wire of an AND or NAND gate is equivalent to assigning the fixed value of 1 to that wire. Similarly, cutting an input to an OR or NOR gate is equivalent to setting it to 0. Since cutting a redundant connection does not affect any output of the circuit, it follows that the equivalent s-a-1 or s-a-0 fault will not affect any output for all input combinations. Thus, depending upon the type of gate to whose input the redundant wire is connected, a s-a-0 or s-a-1 fault on it cannot be detected. If the circuit is irredundant, for every connection in it, there exists some output terminal and some input combination such that the signal on the output wire is dependent on the signal on the connection under consideration.

Redundancy is undesirable in combinational circuits from the point of view of testing, because some faults on the redundant connections in a circuit are undetectable. This, in turn, invalidates the single-fault assumption which is frequently used in deriving tests. The presence of an undetectable fault may cause some other detectable fault to become undetectable by a complete set of tests derived under the single-fault assumption (Friedman, 1967).

**Example 2.18**

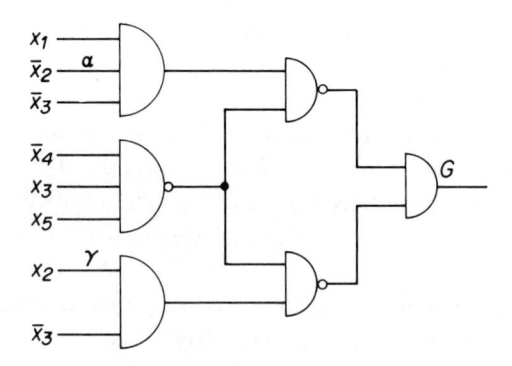

**Figure 2.18**

In Fig. 2.18, the fault $\alpha$ s-a-1 is not detectable. The set of tests $T = \{x_1\bar{x}_2 x_3 x_4, \bar{x}_1 \bar{x}_2 \bar{x}_3, x_1 \bar{x}_2 \bar{x}_3 \bar{x}_4 x_5, x_1 x_2 \bar{x}_3 \bar{x}_4 x_5, x_2 x_3 x_4\}$ detects all detectable single faults in the circuit. Thus, $\gamma$ s-a-0 is detected by $x_1 x_2 \bar{x}_3 \bar{x}_4 x_5$ which is a member of T. However, this test will not detect the fault in the presence of the fault $\alpha$ s-a-1 because the effect of the fault cannot be made to propagate through the gate $G$ when $x_1 = \bar{x}_3 = 1$. Under these circumstances $\gamma$ s-a-0 is detectable by $\bar{x}_1 x_2 \bar{x}_3$, which is not included in T. Thus the test set T is not sufficient for detecting all detectable faults, in the presence of an undetectable fault. In deriving tests for redundant circuits, it is necessary to verify that the tests are such that the occurrence of any sequence of undetectable faults does not invalidate any of them.

REDUNDANCY

The occurrence of an undetectable fault may also make two distinguishable faults indistinguishable as shown in the following example.

**Example 2.19**

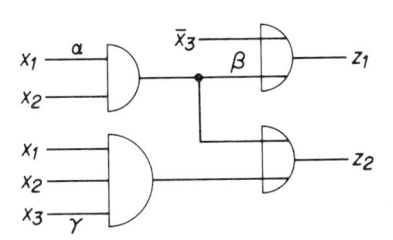

Figure 2.19

In Fig. 2.19, the fault $\gamma$ s-a-1 is not detectable. The fault $\alpha$ s-a-0 is detectable on output $z_2$ by $x_1 x_2 \bar{x}_3$ and on output $z_1$ by $x_1 x_2 x_3$. The fault $\beta$ s-a-0 is detected only on $z_1$ by $x_1 x_2 x_3$. Hence $\alpha$ s-a-0 and $\beta$ s-a-0 are distinguishable. However, if the fault $\gamma$ s-a-1 occurs, these two faults become indistinguishable since they are both detectable only on $z_1$ by $x_1 x_2 x_3$.

Though redundancy, in general, complicates the derivation of tests, certain types of redundancy do not have this effect. For example, certain types of combinational hazards can be eliminated by the introduction of redundant terms. Eichelberger (1964) has shown that a sum-of-products realization of a combinational function will be free of all logic hazards if and only if the realization contains all prime implicants of the function. For a two-level sum-of-products realization containing all prime implicants of a combinational function, a complete set of tests derived under the single-fault assumption will detect all detectable faults in the circuit even if it is preceded by the occurrence of any sequence of undetectable faults. In such a circuit, the only undetectable faults are s-a-0 faults on some AND gate, such as $G_1$, such that whenever the output of the gate is 1, the output of another AND gate in the circuit is also 1 in the normal circuit. However, the occurrence of a s-a-0 fault on $G_1$ will not invalidate any test for any other gate, because in such a test, the normal output of $G_1$ will also be 0. On the other hand, the occurrence of a s-a-0 fault on $G_1$ may cause a previously undetectable fault to become detectable, because the occurrence of the s-a-0 fault is equivalent to removing a redundant term from the realization.

**Example 2.20:** In the circuit of Fig. 2.20, $\alpha$ s-a-0 and $\beta$ s-a-0 are both undetectable. However, in the presence of one of the above two faults, the other fault is detectable by $\bar{x}_1 x_2 \bar{x}_3$. Thus, the complete set of tests for a redundant circuit should also include tests for faults which may become detectable in the presence of undetectable faults.

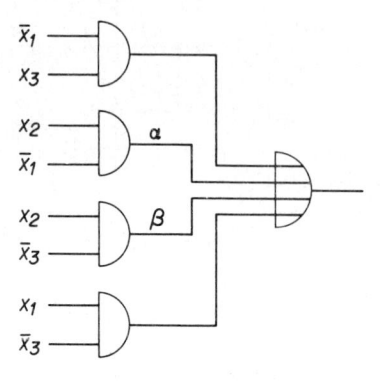

**Figure 2.20**

## SUMMARY

In this chapter we have presented various procedures for generating fault-detection tests for combinational circuits. The most effective procedure for generating test sets for large circuits seems to be the path-sensitizing algorithm and its formal version, the D-algorithm. We have shown how these procedures can be extended to generate tests for multiple faults. Some minimization techniques for obtaining near-minimal test sets have been considered. Finally, we have shown how tests derived under the single-fault assumption may not be valid for redundant circuits.

## REFERENCES

Armstrong, D. B., "On Finding a Nearly Minimal Set of Fault Detection Tests for Combinational Logic Nets", *IEEE Trans. on Electronic Computers* EC-15, 66–73, 1966.

Chang, H. Y., "An Algorithm for Selecting an Optimum Set of Diagnostic Tests", *IEEE Trans. on Electronic Computers* EC-14, 706–711, 1965.

Chang, H. Y., Manning, E. G. and Metze, G., *Fault Diagnosis in Digital Systems*, Wiley-Interscience, 1970.

Eichelberger, E. B., "Sequential Circuit Synthesis Using Hazards and Delays", *Ph.D. Dissertation*, Princeton University, 1963.

Friedman, A. D., "Fault Detection in Redundant Circuits", *IEEE Trans. on Electronic Computers* EC-16, 99–100, 1967.

Galey, J. M., Norby, R. E. and Roth, J. P., "Techniques for the Diagnosis of Switching Circuit Failures", *IEEE Trans. on Commun. Electronics* 83, 509–514, 1964.

Gimpel, J. F., "A Reduction Technique for Prime Implicant Tables", *IEEE Trans. on Electronic Computers* EC-14, 535–541, 1965.

McCluskey, E. J., Jr., "Minimization of Boolean Functions", *Bell System Tech. J.* 35, 1417–1444, 1956.

Poage, J. F., "Derivation of Optimum Tests to Detect Faults in Combinational Circuits", *Proc. Symposium on Mathematical Theory of Automata*, Polytechnic Institute of Brooklyn, 483–528, 1963.

Pyne, I. B. and McCluskey, E. J., Jr., "The Reduction of Redundancy in Solving Prime Implicant Tables", *IRE Trans. on Electronic Computers* EC-11, 473–482, 1962.

Roth, J. P. (1966), "Diagnosis of Automata Failures: a Calculus and a Method", *IBM J. of Res. and Dev.* 10, 278–291, 1966.

Schertz, D. R. and Metze, G. A., "On the Distinguishability of Faults in Digital Systems", *Proc. 6th Annual Allerton Conference on Circuit and Systems Theory*, 752–760, 1968.

Sellers, F. F., Hsiao, M. Y. and Bearnson, L. W., "Analyzing Errors with the Boolean Difference", *IEEE Trans. on Computers* C-17, 676–683, 1968.

## PROBLEMS

1. Prove the following relations

    a) $$\frac{d\bar{F}(\mathbf{x})}{dx_i} = \frac{dF(\mathbf{x})}{dx_i}$$

b) $$\frac{dF(\mathbf{x})}{dx_i} = \frac{dF(\mathbf{x})}{d\bar{x}_i}$$

c) $$\frac{d}{dx_i}\left(\frac{dF(\mathbf{x})}{dx_j}\right) = \frac{d}{dx_j}\left(\frac{dF(\mathbf{x})}{dx_i}\right)$$

d) $$\frac{d(F(\mathbf{x})G(\mathbf{x}))}{dx_i} = F(\mathbf{x})\frac{dG(\mathbf{x})}{dx_i} \oplus G(\mathbf{x})\frac{dF(\mathbf{x})}{dx_i} \oplus \frac{dF(\mathbf{x})}{dx_i}\frac{dG(\mathbf{x})}{dx_i}$$

e) $$\frac{d[F(\mathbf{x}) \oplus G(\mathbf{x})]}{dx_i} = \frac{dF(\mathbf{x})}{dx_i} \oplus \frac{dG(\mathbf{x})}{dx_i}$$

f) $$\frac{d[F(\mathbf{x}) + G(\mathbf{x})]}{dx_i} = \bar{F}(\mathbf{x})\frac{dG(\mathbf{x})}{dx_i} \oplus \bar{G}(\mathbf{x})\frac{dF(\mathbf{x})}{dx_i} \oplus \frac{dF(\mathbf{x})}{dx_i}\frac{dG(\mathbf{x})}{dx_i}$$

2. For the following combinational circuit find the *complete* set of tests using the path sensitizing procedure and Poage's method.
   a) the fault $\alpha$ s-a-1
   b) the fault $\beta$ s-a-0
   c) the multiple fault $\alpha$ s-a-1, $\beta$ s-a-0.

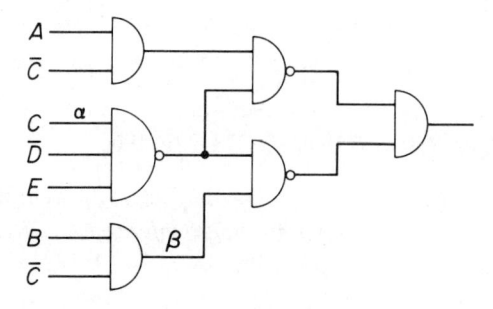

Figure 2.21

3. Derive a near-minimal set of tests to detect all single s-a-0 and s-a-1 faults in the circuit of Fig. 2.21, using the enf method.

4. For the following circuit find the *complete* set of tests to detect the fault $\alpha$ s-a-0 using:
   a) Poage's method
   b) the D-algorithm.

PROBLEMS 59

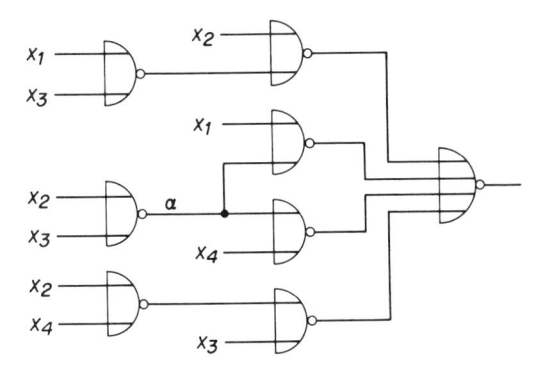

**Figure 2.22**

5. a) For the following circuit find a complete set of tests for all single detectable s-a-0 and s-a-1 faults using the path-sensitizing procedure.
   b) The fault $\alpha$ s-a-1 is not detectable. Find a complete set of tests for all single detectable s-a-0 and s-a-1 faults in the presence of this undetectable fault.

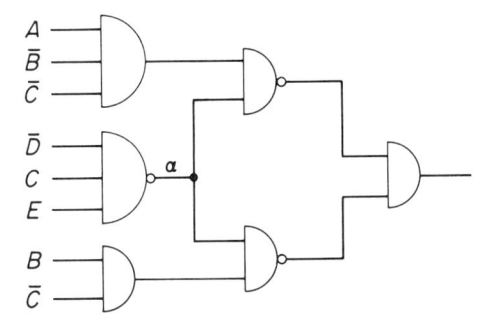

**Figure 2.23**

6. Consider a fault which causes a NOR gate to behave as a gate which produces a 1-output if and only if an even number of its inputs are 1. For the circuit of Fig. 2.9 find a complete set of tests to detect all detectable faults of this type.

7. For the following circuit find a minimal set of tests to detect all single s-a-0 and s-a-1 faults, assuming that the exclusive-OR's are realized in the minimal two level sum-of-products form.

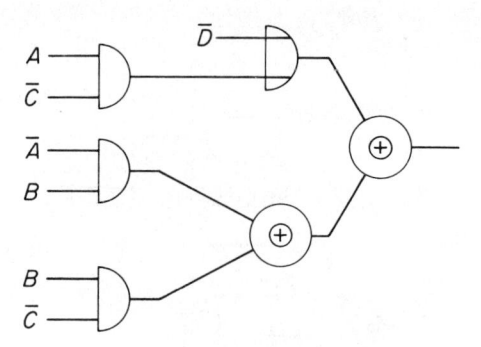

**Figure 2.24**

8. Assuming that the circuit of Fig. 2.3 is realized using diode-transistor logic, derive a test for detecting a shorted input diode connected to the $x_3$ input of gate $B$. Assume negative logic.

9. Prove or disprove the following: The presence of a shorted diode can be detected in an irredundant circuit (in which all single s-a-0 and s-a-1 faults are detectable) provided that there is at least one fan-out lead connected to the shorted diode.

10. Prove or disprove the following statements:
    a) In a circuit in which all gates have unity fan-out, any set of tests which detect all single faults on input wires detects all single faults in the circuit.
    b) In any combinational circuit, any set of tests which detect any single fault on input wires and all fan-out leads from points with fan out exceeding one, detects all single faults in the circuit.

11. From the following fault table:
    a) Find a minimal set of tests to detect all single faults.
    b) Find a minimal set of tests to detect and distinguish all faults which are distinguishable.

# PROBLEMS

|       | $f_1$ | $f_2$ | $f_3$ | $f_4$ | $f_5$ | $f_6$ | $f_7$ |
|-------|-------|-------|-------|-------|-------|-------|-------|
| $t_1$ | 1 | 1 | 0 | 0 | 1 | 0 | 0 |
| $t_2$ | 0 | 1 | 1 | 1 | 0 | 0 | 0 |
| $t_3$ | 0 | 0 | 1 | 0 | 0 | 0 | 1 |
| $t_4$ | 0 | 0 | 0 | 1 | 1 | 0 | 0 |
| $t_5$ | 1 | 0 | 1 | 0 | 1 | 0 | 1 |
| $t_6$ | 0 | 0 | 0 | 0 | 0 | 1 | 1 |

Table 2.5

12. Assuming that Armstrong's conjecture is true, show that the terms of the enf which are discarded are not necessary for deriving tests for all s-a-0 and s-a-1 faults.

13. Prove or disprove the following: "Any irredundant realization of a given function can be tested for all single s-a-0 and s-a-1 faults by the set of tests consisting of all 1-vertices in its map adjacent to 0-vertices ond 0-vertices adjacent to 1-vertices."

14*. Derive least upper and greatest lower bounds for the number of tests required for detecting all s-a-0 and s-a-1 faults in any irredundant realization of a function.

---

* Research problems are indicated by asterisks throughout the book.

CHAPTER 3

# SEQUENTIAL CIRCUITS

As discussed in Chapter 1, the outputs of a sequential circuit are dependent not only on its inputs but also on its internal state. The internal state is represented by the combination of signals on feedback leads. The derivation of fault-detection and diagnostic tests for sequential circuits is greatly complicated by the fact that these signals are usually neither observable nor directly controllable. Whereas a test for a combinational circuit is a single combination of inputs, a test for a sequential circuit must generally be a sequence of inputs.

In this chapter, we shall be concerned with methods for deriving test sequences for detecting faults in sequential circuits. Two different approaches to the problem will be considered. In the first, which we shall refer to as the circuit-testing approach, the circuit realization and the class of faults that can occur are assumed to be known. In the second approach, the flow table of the machine to be tested is given, but the circuit realization is unknown. We shall be interested in deriving *checking sequences* to determine whether the given circuit realizes the given flow table. This approach, called the machine-identification approach, covers a larger class of faults.

**CIRCUIT-TESTING APPROACH**

The following example demonstrates a direct procedure for deriving tests for specified faults in a sequential circuit.

# CIRCUIT-TESTING APPROACH 63

**Example 3.1:** The flow table, state assignment and circuit realization of a machine are given in Fig 3.1. The normal and faulty machines are assumed to operate in a synchronous manner, i.e., there are no races or hazards.

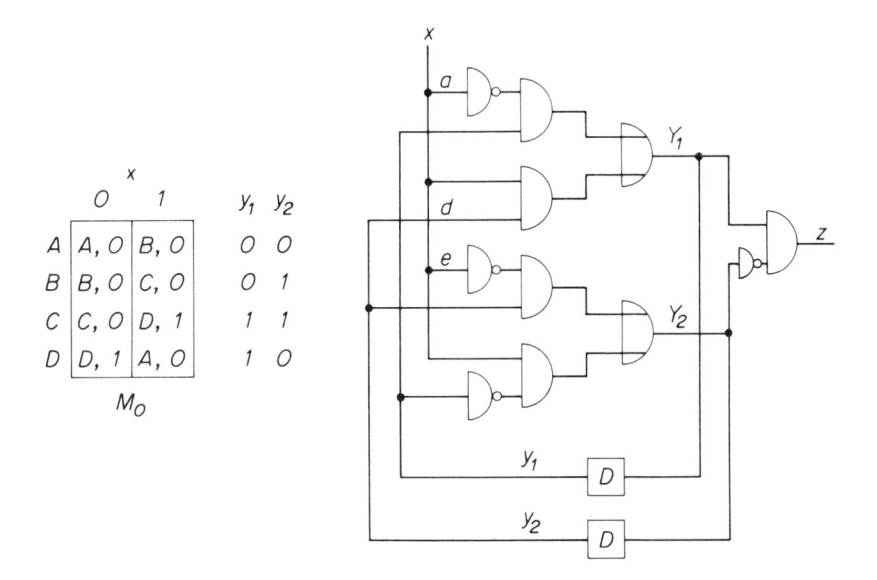

|   | x        |          | $y_1$ $y_2$ |
|---|----------|----------|-------------|
|   | 0        | 1        |             |
| A | A, 0     | B, 0     | 0  0        |
| B | B, 0     | C, 0     | 0  1        |
| C | C, 0     | D, 1     | 1  1        |
| D | D, 1     | A, 0     | 1  0        |

$M_0$

Figure 3.1

In the above circuit, if the input wire labeled $a$ is s-a-1, the operation of the faulty circuit can be represented by the following flow table $M_{a_1}$:

|   | 0    | 1    |
|---|------|------|
| A | A, 0 | B, 0 |
| B | B, 0 | C, 0 |
| C | B, 0 | D, 1 |
| D | A, 0 | A, 0 |

$M_{a_1}$

We must now derive a sequence of inputs which will distinguish this flow table from that of the normal machine ($M_0$) regardless of the initial state.

If we apply a test sequence T to $M_0$, in general, we get one of four different output sequences depending on the initial state. In order for T to detect the fault $a$ s-a-1, each of the four sequences which we may get from applying T to $M_{a_1}$ must be different from all the sequences we get from applying T to $M_0$.

If T starts with a 0, the first output will be 0 for all sequences under consideration except $M_0$, initial state D. Thus this sequence is distinguished from all the $M_{a_1}$ sequences. If the second input is a 1 the output will be 0 for all sequences except $M_0$, initial state C. It remains to distinguish $M_0$ initial state A or B from the four $M_{a_1}$ sequences. If the next two inputs are 10, only the sequence generated by $M_0$ with initial state B produces a 11 output. Finally if the fifth input is 1, the sequence from $M_0$, initial state A produces a 1 output while all of the $M_{a_1}$ sequences produce a 0 output. Thus the test sequence T = 01101 detects $a$ s-a-1. The eight responses to T are shown below:

|       | Initial State | Response to T = 01101 |
|-------|---------------|-----------------------|
| $M_0$ | A | 0 0 0 0 1 |
|       | B | 0 0 1 1 0 |
|       | C | 0 1 0 0 0 |
|       | D | 1 0 0 0 0 |

|           | Initial State | Response to T = 01101 |
|-----------|---------------|-----------------------|
| $M_{a_1}$ | A | 0 0 0 0 0 |
|           | B | 0 0 1 0 0 |
|           | C | 0 0 1 0 0 |
|           | D | 0 0 0 0 0 |

Considering a second fault $e$ s-a-1, we form the faulty table $M_{e_1}$:

|   | 0 | 1 |
|---|-----|-----|
| A | A, 0 | B, 0 |
| B | A, 0 | C, 0 |
| C | D, 1 | D, 1 |
| D | D, 1 | A, 0 |

$M_{e_1}$

For the test sequence T = 01101 just derived, $M_{e_1}$ will produce the four output sequences shown below:

|           | Initial State | Response to T = 01101 |
|-----------|---------------|-----------------------|
| $M_{e_1}$ | A | 0 0 0 1 0 |
|           | B | 0 0 0 1 0 |
|           | C | 1 0 0 0 0 |
|           | D | 1 0 0 0 0 |

# CIRCUIT-TESTING APPROACH

Since the sequence produced by $M_{e_1}$ with initial state $D$ or $C$ is not distinct from the sequence of $M_0$ in initial state $D$, T does not detect the fault $e$ s-a-1. However adding a 1 to T will distinguish $M_0$ from $M_{e_1}$. Furthermore, since the four $M_{e_1}$ sequences are then distinct from the four $M_{a_1}$ sequences, the resultant test sequence distinguishes between the two faults.

*Successor Tree*

One way to derive a test to detect a class of faults is to obtain the complete class of faulty flow tables and then derive a test T such that the sequences generated by $M$ in response to T from any initial state are distinct from those of the faulty tables from any initial state. In fact, a minimal length sequence can be found by exhaustively examining all sequences of length 1, 2, 3, ... , till we find a sequence which detects all faults. This can be done most simply by constructing a successor tree (Poage and McCluskey, 1964) of the type shown in Fig. 3.2.

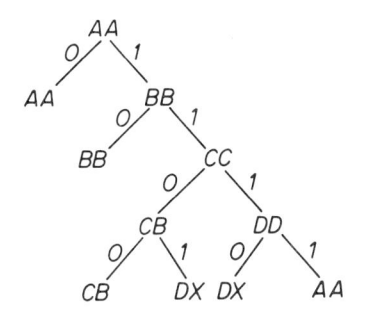

**Figure 3.2**

In Fig. 3.2, machines $M_0$ and $M_{a_1}$ are both started in state $A$. Each node in the tree represents the states of the two machines and each branch represents the application of an input symbol. $X$ indicates that the output of the faulty machine is different from that of the normal machine. The state of the faulty machine is no longer of interest because the fault is already detected. If the label of a node is the same as the label of some node in an earlier level it is treated as a terminal node and its successors are not determined. If two or more nodes in the same level have identical labels, the successors of only one of these are included in the tree.

From the successor tree of Fig. 3.2, it is seen that the only input sequences of length 4 that can distinguish $M_{a_1}$ from $M_0$ when both start in state $A$ are 1110 and 1101. However, it can be verified by making use of the flow tables, that neither sequence distinguishes $M_{a_1}$ from $M_0$, when both start in state $C$, since the output sequence will be 1000 in both cases. Thus there exists no sequence of length 4 to detect the fault $a$ s-a-1 and the sequence of length 5 derived earlier is indeed a minimal length test sequence.

The above method can be generalized in an obvious manner so that several faulty machines (or the same machine in several different initial states) can be included in the same successor tree. Thus, the general fault-detection problem for sequential circuits can be solved by constructing a successor tree for each combination of the initial states of the normal and faulty circuits. The procedure is finite but requires a tremendous amount of computation.

These procedures can also be extended to detecting multiple faults and to fault location. By making some simplifying assumptions it is possible to significantly reduce the amount of work. One assumption which has been made in the literature is that both the normal and faulty machines can be reset to a known initial state. Under this assumption it is simple to construct a successor tree which reveals a minimal-length test sequence. For the previous example, to derive a test to detect both single faults $a$ s-a-1 and $e$ s-a-1 from initial state $A$, the tree derived from the individual tables is as shown below, and the only minimal length test sequence is 1101. Whether it is reasonable to assume a reset signal would depend on the circuit being tested.

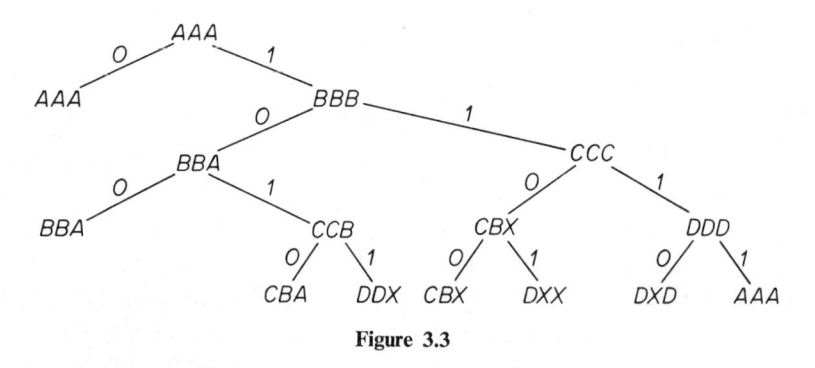

Figure 3.3

In order to construct the successor tree for deriving test sequences, it is not necessary to derive the complete flow tables of the faulty machines. Instead, it is sufficient to determine the next state and output entries for the inputs and states that lead to incorrect operation. This can be done using path-sensitizing techniques on the sequential circuit with the loops opened as shown in the following example.

# CIRCUIT-TESTING APPROACH

**Example 3.2:** The circuit of Fig. 3.1 is redrawn in Fig. 3.4 with feedback loops opened. Treating $x$, $y_1$ and $y_2$ as inputs and $z$, $Y_1$ and $Y_2$

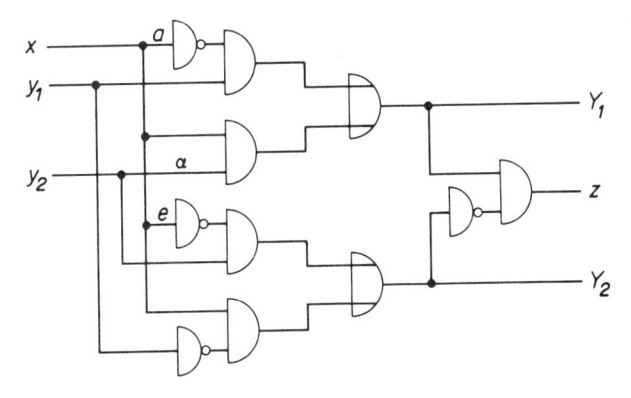

Figure 3.4

as outputs, the complete set of tests for $a$ s-a-1 and $e$ s-a-1 are derived using the path-sensitizing technique (or any other method discussed in Chapter 2). These test sets are $\bar{x}y_1$ and $\bar{x}y_2$ respectively. The only entries that will be affected are in the $x = 0$ column, states $C$ and $D$ in $M_{a_1}$ and $x = 0$, states $B$ and $C$ in $M_{e_1}$. These entries of the faulty table are shown below:

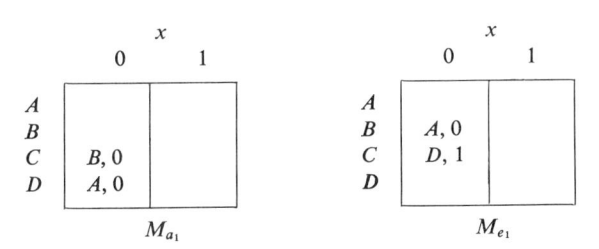

|   | $x$ 0 | 1 |
|---|---|---|
| $A$ |  |  |
| $B$ |  |  |
| $C$ | $B, 0$ |  |
| $D$ | $A, 0$ |  |

$M_{a_1}$

|   | $x$ 0 | 1 |
|---|---|---|
| $A$ |  |  |
| $B$ | $A, 0$ |  |
| $C$ | $D, 1$ |  |
| $D$ |  |  |

$M_{e_1}$

Poage and McCluskey (1964) have presented a procedure for deriving minimal-length test sequences for sequential machines. It assumes that both the normal and faulty machines can be reset. The method uses the successor tree for deriving a minimal-length test sequence, but certain branches of the tree that cannot lead to minimal sequences are identified and terminated using properties similar to the row and column dominance discussed in Chapter 2. Though the size of the successor tree to be constructed is reduced somewhat by this procedure, the method seems to be practical only for machines with a few states.

## Path Sensitization and the D-Algorithm

For large circuits, a direct method not involving the flow table of the normal circuit and the erroneous entries corresponding to each fault may be preferable. Extensions of the path-sensitizing technique or the D-algorithm may be effective in such cases. However, the minimality of the length of test sequences obtained by these methods cannot be guaranteed.

In extending these procedures to sequential circuits, it is convenient to treat the given sequential circuit as a semi-infinite one-dimensional array of identical combinational cells as shown in Fig. 3.5. Here $x(i)$, $y(i)$ and $z(i)$

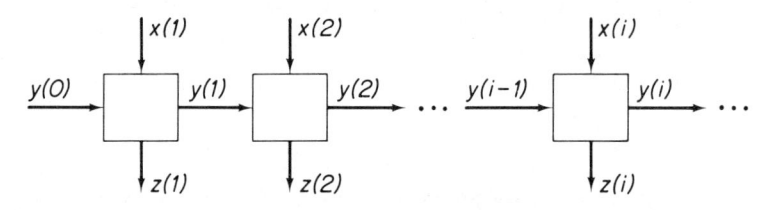

**Figure 3.5**

associated with the $i^{th}$ cell of the array correspond to the input, the next state and the output of the sequential circuit at the $i^{th}$ instant of time. The combinational logic in each cell is identical to that of the sequential circuit, and a fault in the sequential circuit is represented by the same fault in every cell of the array.

The derivation of a test for a given fault consists of propagating a D or $\bar{D}$ to a $z$ output. If this is not possible, we attempt to propagate it to a $y$ output. This results in D or $\bar{D}$ on one or more of the $y$ inputs of the next cell. The problem of propagating a D or $\bar{D}$ to some output of this cell in the presence of the fault is the same as that of deriving a test for a combinational circuit with multiple faults. The D-algorithm for multiple faults discussed in Chapter 2 may be used for accomplishing this.

The states of the normal and faulty circuits may be represented conveniently by a vector **y**, with components $y_i = 0, 1, D$ or $\bar{D}$; $i = 1, \ldots, n$. If the normal and faulty circuits are in the same internal state, the state vector will not contain any D's or $\bar{D}$'s. The following algorithm will yield a test sequence for any detectable fault, but the sequence may not be of minimal length.

    **1.** With the $y$ inputs specified by the present state vector, determine a combination of $x$ inputs using the D-algorithm (or the multiple-

# CIRCUIT-TESTING APPROACH

fault D-algorithm, if necessary), such that a D or $\bar{D}$ appears at some $z$ output. If such an input exists, it will be the last input in the test sequence that will detect the fault. If no such input exists, go to 2.

2. Obtain an input combination which produces a next-state vector that has not been produced before, preferring an input whose next-state vector has a D or $\bar{D}$. (This is based on the heuristic that a shorter test sequence may be obtained if the normal and faulty circuits are in different states). Make an arbitrary choice, if necessary, and go to 1. If no new next-state vector can be produced, go to 3.

3. If an arbitrary choice has been made, delete the last arbitrarily chosen input and all succeeding inputs. Make another choice and go to 1. If all choices have been exhausted, the fault is undetectable.

**Example 3.3:** Consider the circuit of Fig. 3.4 with the fault, $a$ s-a-1, in the initial state $y_1 = 0$, $y_2 = 1$. Assigning $\bar{D}$ to the faulty wire, we see that it cannot be propagated to the $z$ output, nor can it be propagated to $Y_1$ or $Y_2$. We also note that $x = 0$ will not cause any change in the state vector. However, $x = 1$ makes $Y_1 = Y_2 = 1$, and it is chosen as the first input in the test sequence. With $y_1 = y_2 = 1$, we cannot propagate a D or $\bar{D}$ to the $z$ output. Since $x = 0$ produces $Y_1 = D$, $Y_2 = 1$, we choose it as the second input to the sequence. We choose $x = 1$ as the third and final input in the sequence since it produces $z = D$, detecting the fault. The fault $a$ s-a-1 is detected by the sequence 101, if both the normal and faulty machines are initially in the state, $y_1 = 0$, $y_2 = 1$. This happens to be one of the minimal-length test sequences for the given fault and initial state, as can be verified from the successor tree of Fig. 3.2. The other minimal-length sequence 110, obtainable from the successor tree, was not obtained by the algorithm because the branch from the node *CC* to *CB* was preferred by the algorithm over the branch to the node *DD* in Fig. 3.2.

The algorithm presented in this section *may* yield test sequences for some faults, when the initial state of the circuit is unknown. The test sequence obtained will be such that some output of the normal circuit becomes independent of the initial state after some length of time and the same output of the faulty circuit also becomes independent of the initial state and opposite in value to the normal circuit. This condition is sufficient for detecting the fault, independent of the initial state, but not necessary. If there exists an input sequence such that for any possible initial state, the output sequences produced by the normal and faulty circuits are different, that sequence will detect the fault independent of the initial state. In applying our algorithm to obtain such test sequences, it becomes necessary to derive test sequences for all possible initial states and then construct a sequence from those that will detect the fault in all cases. However, this procedure may not be computationally feasible. In Example 3.4, test sequences for $a$ s-a-1 cannot be derived treating the initial state as unknown, although the fault can be detected by a sequence of length 5, independent of the initial state, as shown in Example 3.1. This is because the values of $Y_1$, $Y_2$, or z cannot be determined without any knowledge of the initial state.

*Sequential Analyzer*

Construction of parts of the successor tree is also implicit in the test generation method using the Sequential Analyzer developed by Seshu and Freeman (1962). The Sequential Analyzer, which will be described in greater detail in Chapter 5, is a program which simulates the behavior of the normal machine and several faulty machines simultaneously. At each step in the derivation of the test sequence, the input which maximizes one of several criteria of optimality is selected. If diagnosis is desired, "information gain" is used as the criterion for selecting the next input to be applied. For fault detection, the input which detects the largest number of previously undetected faults is chosen. If no input is found to be useful, the next input is chosen randomly and the procedure repeated. The method is applicable to large circuits and is capable of detecting and locating a large fraction of all possible faults. However, it may not yield tests for some detectable and locatable faults in the circuit.

## MACHINE IDENTIFICATION

In all of the procedures discussed so far it has been assumed that the normal machine can be represented by a flow table $M_0$ and each physical fault transforms $M_0$ into some other flow table $M_i$. The problem thus becomes that of deriving a sequence of inputs which distinguishes $M_0$ from each of the $M_i$ defined by a fault.

Another approach to the problem is to derive a sequence of inputs

# MACHINE IDENTIFICATION

which distinguishes $M_0$ from *all* other flow tables with the same number of states, inputs and outputs. This includes distinguishing $M_0$ from some flow tables which cannot result from any single s-a-1 or s-a-0 fault in the circuit realizing $M_0$. Although this may seem wasteful, the test sequences may be much easier to derive and may also detect multiple faults. The method has the added advantage that the test sequences are applicable to any realization of a flow table. Since the sequence distinguishes the given flow table from all other tables with the same number of states, it is especially useful when the types of faults that may occur in the circuit are not known. The input-output sequence which distinguishes a given machine from all other machines with the same number of states, inputs and outputs is referred to as a *checking experiment* or a *checking sequence*.

Checking experiments can be adaptive or preset depending upon whether or not the next input to be applied is based on the outputs previously produced by the machine. Except where otherwise noted, we shall be concerned with preset experiments. Experiments are also classified as simple, requiring only one copy of the machine or multiple, requiring more than one copy. We shall consider only experiments belonging to the former class.

The following definitions from partition theory (Hartmanis and Stearns, 1966) will be useful in the material we shall be considering later in this chapter. A *partition* $\pi$ on the set of states of a machine is a grouping of all the states into disjoint subsets called *blocks*. The product of two partitions $\pi_1$ and $\pi_2$, denoted by $\pi_1 \cdot \pi_2$, is the partition in which two states are in the same block if and only if they are in the same block of both $\pi_1$ and $\pi_2$. A partition $\pi_2$ is a *proper refinement* of a partition $\pi_1$ if $\pi_1 \cdot \pi_2 = \pi_2$ and $\pi_1 \neq \pi_2$. A partition with one member in each block is called the 0-partition. For a machine $M$ and an input sequence $X$, the partition in which two states $s_i$ and $s_j$ are in the same block, if and only if the output sequences produced by $M$ for the input sequence $X$ and initial states $s_i$ and $s_j$ are identical, is called the partition induced by the input sequence $X$ and is denoted by $\pi_X$.

The earliest published work on the construction of checking experiments is by Moore (1956). He showed that any machine $M_v$ with $n$ states, $m$ input symbols and $p$ output symbols, referred to as an $(n, m, p)$-machine, can be distinguished from all other $(n, m, p)$-machines by a simple experiment. In order to prove this result the following preliminary results are required.

***Lemma 3.1:*** *Given any reduced* n-*state sequential machine* $M_0$ *there exists an experiment of length* $n(n - 1)/2$ *which can determine the state of* $M_0$ *at the end of the experiment.*

**Proof:** Initially the machine can be in any one of $n$ states. Since the machine is reduced, there must be some input for which it produces at least two different responses depending upon the initial state. This input, therefore, partitions the next state into at least two blocks, none of which contains more than $n - 1$ states. If this input is applied to the machine, the number of possible final states is at most $n - 1$. We now show by induction that the number of possible final states can be reduced to $n - k$ by a sequence of length $k(k + 1)/2$, as follows:

Assume that the statement is true for $k - 1$; that is, the set of possible final states is $G_{k-1}$ and it contains $n - (k - 1)$ states after applying some input sequence of $k(k - 1)/2$ inputs. Define $\pi_k$ to be a partition on the states of $M_0$ such that $S_i$ and $S_j$ are in the same block of $\pi_k$ if and only if there is no input sequence of length $\leq k$ which distinguishes $S_i$ and $S_j$. It can be shown that $\pi_{i+1}$ is a proper refinement of $\pi_i$. Therefore $\pi_k$ partitions the set of states into at least $k + 1$ blocks, and hence has no block with more than $n - k$ states. Therefore $G_{k-1}$ must have two states $S_a$ and $S_b$ which are in different blocks of $\pi_k$ and thus the set of possible states can be reduced to $n - k$ by an experiment of length $k + (k - 1)(k)/2 = k(k + 1)/2$. $G_{n-1}$ contains one state and therefore there exists an input sequence of length $n(n - 1)/2$ which determines the final state.

*Lemma 3.2:* *If* M *is an* n-*state,* m-*input,* p-*output* (n, m, p)-*machine such that any two of its states are distinguishable, then they are distinguishable by a sequence of length* n − 1.

**Proof:** Define $\pi_k$ as in the previous lemma. Since $\pi_{k+1}$ is a refinement of $\pi_k$ and the identity partition on $n$ states (all states in the same block) can be refined at most $n - 1$ times, the lemma follows.

*Lemma 3.3:* *If* $M_0$ *and* $M_1$ *are* (n, m, p)-*machines and state* $q_i$ *of* $M_0$ *can be distinguished from state* $q_j$ *of* $M_1$ *then there exists such an experiment of length* $\leq$ 2n − 1.

**Proof:** Define a $(2n, m, p)$-machine $M_0 + M_1$ with states 1 to $n$ defining the transitions of $M_0$, and states $n + 1$ to $2n$ defining the transitions of $M_1$. By Lemma 3.2 we can distinguish the state of $M_0 + M_1$ by an experiment of length $\leq 2n - 1$ and hence state $q_i$ of $M_0$ can be distinguished from state $q_j$ of $M_1$ by this experiment.

# MACHINE IDENTIFICATION

***Theorem 3.1:*** *Given any strongly connected reduced* (n, m, p)-*machine* $M_0$ *there exists a simple experiment of length* $< n^2(np)^{nm}$, *which distinguishes* $M_0$ *from all other* (n, m, p)-*machines.*

**Proof:** There are $(np)^{nm}$ possible $(n, m, p)$-machines. Since these include machines isomorphic to $M_0$ obtained by permuting the state labels of each machine, the number of distinguishable machines is less than $N = (np)^{nm}$.* Define the composite machine $\sum$ for all of these as in Lemma 3.3, and consider the subsets of states of $\sum$ obtained from each of the original machines. By Lemma 3.1 there exists an experiment of length $\leq n(n-1)/2$ which will distinguish the state of each subset. Thus all but one of the members of each subset can be eliminated by an experiment of length $\leq Nn(n-1)/2$. Considering pairs of machines containing $M_0$ and each of the remaining $N-1$ machines, it follows from Lemma 3.3 that a sequence of length $\leq (N-1)(2n-1)$ is sufficient to determine whether the machine $\sum$ is in one of the states of $M_0$. Thus the entire experiment to distinguish $M_0$ is of length $L$

where
$$L < Nn(n-1)/2 + (N-1)(2n-1)$$
$$< [n(n-1)/2 + 2n - 1](np)^{nm}$$
$$\leq n^2(np)^{nm}$$

Note that the above bound is for a Mealy machine, where the output is a function of the present state and input. If we consider a Moore machine, whose output is a function of the present state only, the bound for the length of the experiment becomes $n^2[n^{mn}p^n]$ (Moore, 1956).

Although the bound is very high, this result provides the motivation behind a different philosophy of testing sequential circuits, which has been developed by Hennie (1964).

*Hennie's Procedure*

Whereas Poage's approach consisted of deriving an input sequence which distinguishes the normal flow table from each of the faulty flow tables,

---

*Not all permutations of a machine lead to indistinguishable machines. The number of distinguishable machines has been shown (Harrison, 1966) to approach $(np)^{nm}/n!$ asymptotically.

Hennie has developed a procedure which is computationally simpler than Poage's but in general leads to longer test sequences. For a given strongly connected $n$-state flow table $M$, Hennie develops an input-output sequence which distinguishes this machine $M$ from all machines with $n$ (or fewer) states. This sequence can then be used to detect all faults in the circuit assuming that the number of states in the faulty table does not exceed $n$.

**Example 3.4:** Suppose the following input-output sequence is observed from a 4-state machine:

```
Input   1 1 1 1 1 1 1 0 1  1  1  0  1  1  0  1  1  1  1  0  1  1
Output  0 0 1 0 0 0 1 1 0  0  0  0  1  0  0  0  0  1  0  0  0  0  1
t       1 2 3 4 5 6 7 8 9 10 11 12 13 14 15 16 17 18 19 20 21 22 23
```

There is only one 4-state machine which could generate this sequence as we shall now show. Let us label the state at $t = 1$ as $A$. If $M$ is in state $A$, it responds to the input sequence 111 with output 001. Thus at time $t = 2$, $M$ must be in some other state $B$ since it responds to 111 with 010. Similarly at $t = 3$, $M$ is in $C$ and at $t = 4$, $M$ is in $D$. Since $M$ has only 4 states, at $t = 5$ it must be back in $A$. We are thus able to construct the following part of the table $M$.

|   | 0 | 1 |
|---|---|---|
| $A$ |   | $B, 0$ |
| $B$ |   | $C, 0$ |
| $C$ |   | $D, 1$ |
| $D$ |   | $A, 0$ |

Since only state $C$ responds to a 1 input with a 1 output we can conclude that at $t = 7$ we were in state $C$ and at $t = 8$ we are in state $D$. At $t = 9$ we must be in state $D$ since only that state responds to 111 with 000. We can thus conclude that $N(D, 0) = D, Z(D, 0) = 1$. ($N(D, 0)$ and $Z(D, 0)$ are the next-state and output respectively, when the input 0 is applied to the machine in state $D$.) Similarly at $t = 12$ we must be in state $C$ and at $t = 13$ we must be in state $C$ since a 1 input yields a 1 output. Thus $N(C, 0) = C, Z(C, 0) = 0$. Finally, at $t = 15$ we must be in state $A$ and at $t = 16$ in state $A$ since only $A$ responds to 111 with 001. Thus $N(A, 0) = A, Z(A, 0) = 0$. And at $t = 21$ we must be in $B$ and at $t = 22$ we must be in $B$ since only

# MACHINE IDENTIFICATION

*B* responds to 11 with 01. We can thus complete the table as shown below.

|   | 0    | 1    |
|---|------|------|
| A | A, 0 | B, 0 |
| B | B, 0 | C, 0 |
| C | C, 0 | D, 1 |
| D | D, 1 | A, 0 |

If we apply the above input sequence to a 4-state machine and obtain the above output sequence then we can conclude that the machine is *M*. However the converse is not true, for *M* will give that output sequence only if started in state *A*. To start the machine in state *A* we apply a string of 1 inputs until we get a 1 output and then we apply one more 1 input. This initializing sequence followed by the above input sequence constitutes a test for *M* under the assumption that no fault will increase the number of states, and *M* is strongly connected. We shall now present general procedures for deriving such checking sequences.

The derivation of checking sequences is greatly simplified for machines having *distinguishing sequences* (also called diagnosing sequences (Gill, 1962)), so we shall consider this case first. A distinguishing sequence (DS) for a flow table *M* is an input sequence which when applied to *M* in any state $S_i$ yields a different output sequence than when applied to *M* in a different state $S_j$. Thus, it is possible to determine the initial state by observing the output response to the distinguishing sequence. In the previous flow table, the input sequence 111 is a distinguishing sequence.

If an *n*-state table has a distinguishing sequence $X_0$ and *n* different responses to the DS appear in the checking sequence, then we can conclude that the machine was in a distinct state when each of the responses was produced. We can then use the DS for checking the various transitions in the table. If our checking sequence contains the two subsequences

$$X_0 X' X_0 \quad \text{and} \quad X_0 X' x_i X_0$$
$$Z_a Z' Z_b \qquad \qquad Z_a Z' z_i Z_c$$

where $Z_a$ is the response of *M* to $X_0$ in initial state *a*, we can conclude from the outputs, that at the beginning of *both* subsequences the machine was in state $a$. From the first subsequence we can conclude that the input sequence $X_0X'$ takes the machine from $a$ to $b$, and from the second subsequence we can conclude that the input sequence $X_0X'x_i$ takes the machine from $a$ to $c$. Thus it is evident that $N(b, x_i) = c$, $Z(b, x_i) = z_i$, and this transition in the table has been checked.

The essential idea is to use the information obtained from the distinguishing sequences to verify that at certain points in the experiment the circuit must be in some specific state $k$. The transition from state $k$ with input $x_i$ can then be checked by applying input $x_i$ followed by $X_0$. This can be done for all transitions. In the previous example, the first seven inputs displayed the four responses to the distinguishing sequence and also enabled us to conclude that since the states at $t = 1$ and $t = 5$ were identical and the state at $t = 8$ was identical to the state at $t = 4$ which we called $D$. We could then check the 0-transition from state $D$, by applying 0111. The other transitions were similarly checked.

There are no algorithms at present to enable the derivation of an *optimum-length* checking sequence (other than enumerative procedures which are computationally unfeasible). However the following procedure for deriving a checking sequence gives us an upper bound on the length of a checking sequence.

Let $Q_i \equiv N(S_i, X_0)$, i.e., $Q_i$ is the next state of $M$ when the distinguishing sequence $X_0$ is applied to state $S_i$. Let $T(Q_i, S_j)$ be an input sequence which takes the correct machine from state $Q_i$ to $S_j$. Such sequences will be called *transfer sequences*. (Although more than one such sequence may exist, $T(Q_i, S_j)$ always refers to one specific sequence from this set.) Then consider the application of the following sequence, which we shall refer to as Part 1 of the checking experiment, to the machine in state $S_1$:

$$X_0T(Q_1, S_2)X_0T(Q_2, S_3) \ldots X_0T(Q_n, S_1)X_0$$

This sequence displays all the responses to the distinguishing sequence and also verifies some transfer sequences which may then be used for checking transitions. For example, if the last transition checked takes the machine to $S_m$, application of $X_0$ leaves it in $Q_m$. If we wish to check a transition from state $S_i$ under input $x_k$, we apply the subsequence $T(Q_m, S_{i-1})X_0T(Q_{i-1}, S_i)x_kX_0$. $T(Q_m, S_{i-1})$ takes the machine to state $S_{i-1}$, but since this transfer sequence has not been checked previously, we apply $X_0$ to verify that it is in fact in $S_{i-1}$. We can be certain the machine will be in state $S_i$ after the application of $T(Q_{i-1}, S_i)$, since this transfer sequence was verified in Part 1. In Part 2 of the experiment, each transition in the flow table is checked using this method.

# MACHINE IDENTIFICATION

Each of the transfer sequences is of length $\leq n - 1$. If $X_0$ is of length $L$ then Part 1 of the checking sequence is of length $\leq (n + 1)L + n(n - 1)$. Each transition is checked in Part 2 in at most $2(n - 1 + L) + 1$ inputs. Thus an $m$-input $n$-state machine has a checking sequence of at most $nm(2n + 2L - 1) + (n + 1)L + n(n - 1) < 2n(m + 1)(n + L)$. For the previous example this bound is 168, whereas a sequence of length 22 actually exists.

Checking experiments which are considerably shorter than the bound can be constructed by taking advantage of the properties of the specific machine under consideration. By checking the transitions in a suitable order, several transfer sequences may be omitted. Transfer sequences may also be omitted from Part 1 of the sequence by a suitable choice of the order in which the states are visited. Different subsequences may be overlapped to reduce the length of the experiment. The division of the experiment into two parts was previously done only for deriving the bound. In practice, the two parts may in fact overlap. It is sufficient if all the responses to the distinguishing sequence are displayed and all the transfer sequences verified somewhere in the experiment.

The checking experiments discussed in this chapter require that the machine under test be in a specified initial state. Some machines have synchronizing sequences, which may be used for this purpose. A *synchronizing sequence* is an input sequence which takes the machine to a unique final state, independent of its initial state. For machines that do not have synchronizing sequences, homing sequences may be used for initialization. A *homing sequence* is an input sequence, the response to which uniquely determines the *final* state of the machine. An appropriate transfer sequence may then be applied to take it to the desired state. Note that this part of the experiment is adaptive, since the transfer sequence to be applied depends on the response to the homing sequence.

It follows from Lemma 3.1 that every reduced sequential machine has a homing sequence. A homing sequence can be derived by constructing a modified successor tree, which we shall refer to as a *homing tree*. The initial node of the tree contains all the states of the machine. From each node emanates a branch corresponding to each input symbol that may be applied. These branches terminate at nodes containing the next states, grouped according to the outputs, without repeated states in any group. If a node is identical to a node at an earlier level, that branch of the tree is terminated. In such a tree, the branches from the initial node to a node in which each group contains a single state defines a homing sequence.

**Example 3.5**

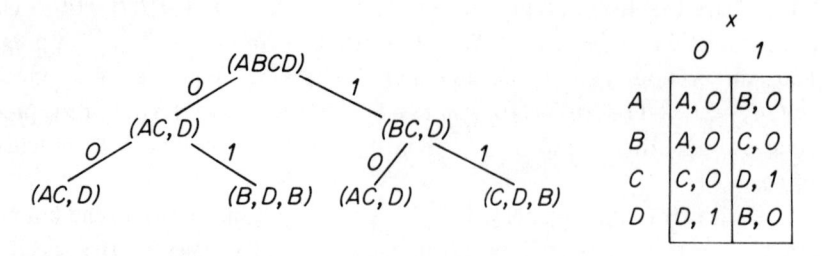

```
            (ABCD)
          0/      \1
      (AC,D)      (BC,D)
      0/  \1      0/  \1
  (AC,D) (B,D,B) (AC,D) (C,D,B)
```

|   | x      |      |
|---|--------|------|
|   | 0      | 1    |
| A | A, 0   | B, 0 |
| B | A, 0   | C, 0 |
| C | C, 0   | D, 1 |
| D | D, 1   | B, 0 |

**Figure 3.6**

01 is a homing sequence as is 11.

A successor tree with slightly different terminating rules may be used for determining whether a given machine has a distinguishing sequence and deriving a distinguishing sequence. We shall refer to such a tree as a *distinguishing tree*. As before, the initial node contains all states of the machine. For each input, there is a branch to the set of next states. The next states are grouped according to the outputs associated with the transition, never grouping together states which have been separated at a preceding node. If two states in a group have identical next states and output for some input, that branch is terminated. A node in which each group contains a single state is also a terminal node, and the branches from the initial node to such a node define a distinguishing sequence. If no such node exists, the machine does not have a distinguishing sequence.

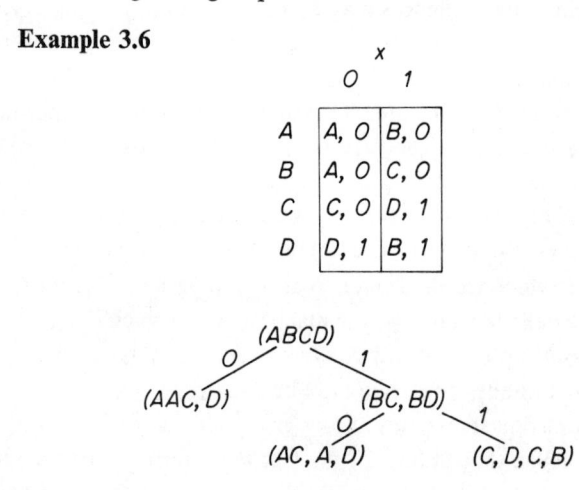

**Example 3.6**

|   | x    |      |
|---|------|------|
|   | 0    | 1    |
| A | A, 0 | B, 0 |
| B | A, 0 | C, 0 |
| C | C, 0 | D, 1 |
| D | D, 1 | B, 1 |

```
            (ABCD)
          0/      \1
      (AAC,D)    (BC,BD)
                 0/    \1
            (AC,A,D)  (C,D,C,B)
```

**Figure 3.7**

11 is a distinguishing sequence.

# MACHINE IDENTIFICATION

Not all sequential machines have distinguishing sequences as Fig. 3.8 illustrates.

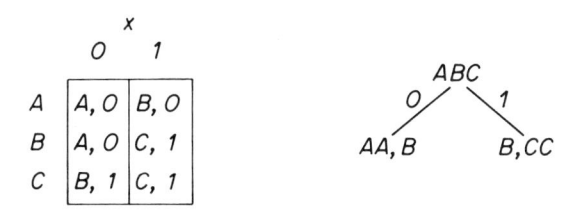

|   | x |   |
|---|---|---|
|   | 0 | 1 |
| A | A, 0 | B, 0 |
| B | A, 0 | C, 1 |
| C | B, 1 | C, 1 |

ABC
0 / \ 1
AA, B     B, CC

**Figure 3.8**

Hennie has generalized his procedure for machines that do not have distinguishing sequences. Before presenting the procedure for constructing checking experiments for such machines, let us analyze an example of such an experiment.

**Example 3.7:** Consider the following input-output sequence for a 3-state circuit.

```
x  1 1 0 0 1 0 1 0 1 1  1  1  1  0  0  0  1  1  0  0  1  0  1
z  1 0 0 0 0 0 0 0 0 1  0  1  0  0  0  0  1  1  1  0  0  0
t  1 2 3 4 5 6 7 8 9 10 11 12 13 14 15 16 17 18 19 20 21 22 23
```

From the response at $t = 19$, the circuit has at least one state that responds to a 0 input with a 1 output and hence at most two states that respond to a 0 input with a 0 output. Therefore the states at $t = 4$, 6, 8 cannot all be different. If the state at $t = 4$ equals the state at $t = 6$ then the state at $t = 6$ equals the state at $t = 8$. Thus $S(8)$ (the state at $t = 8$) $= S(4)$ or $S(6)$. And hence $S(10) = S(6)$. Therefore $S(10)$ which we shall call $A$ produces a 0 output for a 0 input and a 1 output for a 1 input. We shall refer to the technique used here for identifying the state $A$ as the "*nesting technique*".

In a similar manner it can be shown that $S(17) = S(16)$ or $S(15)$, and $S(17) \neq S(10)$. $S(17)$ which we shall call $B$ responds to a 0 or 1 input with a 0 output. Therefore the third state $C$ must respond to a 0 input with a 1 output. Thus $S(19) = C$ and $S(20) = C$, and the following part of the table can be filled.

| | | |
|---|---|---|
| A | , 0 | , 1 |
| B | , 0 | , 0 |
| C | C, 1 | , 0 |

Since $A$ is the only state which produces a 1 output for a 1 input, $S(18) = A$ and the machine has a transition from $A$ to $C$ for a 1 input. Since $S(17) = B$, the 1-transition from B to A can be determined.

We can now determine that $S(11) = C$ and $S(12) = A$ so we can fill in the table as shown below.

|      |      |
| ---- | ---- |
| , 0  | C, 1 |
| , 0  | A, 0 |
| C, 1 | A, 0 |

Since $S(14) = S(22) = A$, $S(15) = S(23)$. But $S(15)$ produces a 0 in response to a 0 and $S(23)$ produces a 0 in response to a 1. Therefore $S(15) = S(23) = B$ and a 0 input causes a transition from $A$ to $B$. Similarly $S(5) = S(16) = B$ and the table is completed as shown below.

|      |      |
| ---- | ---- |
| B, 0 | C, 1 |
| B, 0 | A, 0 |
| C, 1 | A, 0 |

Thus the proposed input-output sequence is a checking experiment for the above 3-state machine. Although this machine has no distinguishing sequence, knowledge of the outputs produced by the machine to each of the inputs 0 and 1 is sufficient to identify the state. The input sequences 0 and 1 are said to consitute a set of *characterizing sequences* for the given machine.

In the above example, states were identified by locating two points in the sequence where the machine is in the same state and a different one of the characterizing sequences was applied at each of those points. Subsequences which have this property are referred to as *locating sequences*. We now present a systematic method of constructing locating sequences for a machine with a set of two characterizing sequences.

Let $X_1$ and $X_2$ constitute a set of characterizing sequences for an $n$-state machine. If the machine is in state $S_i$ let the responses to the sequences be denoted as $Z_1(i)$ and $Z_2(i)$ and let the final states be $P_i$ and $Q_i$ respectively. Now suppose that the checking sequence contains $[X_1 T(P_i, S_i)]^n X_2$, applied when the machine is in state $S_i$, where $[X]^n$ indicates the sequence $X$ repeated $n$ times. Since there can be at most $n - 1$ states that produce the response of

# MACHINE IDENTIFICATION

$Z_1(i)$ to the sequence $X_1$, (provided that the machine responds correctly to the locating sequences of all the other states), the state of the machine immediately prior to the application of $X_2$ must be identical to one of the states that responded to $X_1$ with $Z_1(i)$. Thus this state responds to $X_1$ with $Z_1(i)$ and $X_2$ with $Z_2(i)$ and therefore may be labeled $S_i$. This sequence is a locating sequence for the state $S_i$. Similar locating sequences may be derived for all states in the machine. The following example from Hennie (1964) shows the locating sequences for a given 4-state machine and how these sequences can be shortened for the specific flow table.

**Example 3.8:** The sequences 0, 10 constitute a set of characterizing sequences for the machine shown below.

|   | 0    | 1    |
|---|------|------|
| A | B, 0 | D, 0 |
| B | A, 0 | B, 0 |
| C | D, 1 | A, 0 |
| D | D, 1 | C, 0 |

For the given flow table, $P_A = B$, $T(B, A) = 0$; $P_B = A$, $T(A, B) = 0$; $P_C = D$, $T(D, C) = 1$; $P_D = D$, $T(D, D) = \lambda$, where $\lambda$ is the null input. This leads to the following set of locating sequences and their responses:

$$L_A = [00]^4 10 \qquad L_B = [00]^4 10$$

$$Z_A = [00]^4 01 \qquad Z_B = [00]^4 00$$

$$L_C = [01]^4 10 \qquad L_D = [0]^4 10$$

$$Z_C = [10]^4 00 \qquad Z_D = [1]^4 01$$

If the machine responds correctly to $L_A$ and $L_B$, we can conclude that there are at most two states that produce a 1 output in response to a 0 input and three repetitions are sufficient in $L_C$ and $L_D$. Similarly, we can conclude from $L_C$ and $L_D$ that there are at most two states that respond to a 0 input with a 0 output, and three repetitions are sufficient in $L_A$ and $L_B$ also. Thus we get the following shortened locating sequences: $L_A = L_B = [00]^3 10$; $L_C = [01]^3 10$; $L_D = [0]^3 10$.

The above method of obtaining shorter locating sequences can be generalized as follows:

**Theorem 3.2:** *Let the set of characterizing sequences of an n-state machine consist of two sequences* $X_1$ *and* $X_2$ *and let the machine produce m different responses* $Z_i$, $i = 1, \ldots, m$ *to* $X_1$. *Let* $n_i$ *be the number of states that produce the response* $Z_i$, *where*

$$\sum_{i=1}^{m} n_i = n$$

*The following is a locating sequence for a state* $S_j$ *which responds to* $X_1$ *with* $Z_i$, *provided that the checking sequence contains locating sequences for all states:*

$$L_{S_j} = \begin{cases} [X_1 T(P_j, S_j)]^{n_i+1} X_2, & \text{for } n_i > 1 \\ X_1, & \text{for } n_i = 1. \end{cases}$$

**Proof:** If the fault does not change $n_i$, for all $i = 1, 2, \ldots, m$, then the theorem is obviously true because the state prior to the application of $X_2$ is the same as a state that produces the response of $Z_i$ to $X_1$. Let the number of states in the faulty machine that produce $Z_i$ be $n'_i$ and let $n'_i > n_i$. Now, the state before the application of $X_2$ may not be a state that produced $Z_i$ and the locating sequence is not valid. However, if the number of states in the machine does not increase, $n'_i > n_i$ implies that $n'_k < n_k$ for some $k \neq i$. But if $n_k$ different states are shown to produce the response of $Z_k$, then $n'_k \not> n_k$. Also $n'_i \not< n_i$, since $n_i$ different states are shown to produce $Z_i$. The case $n_i = 1$ is obvious.

In designing checking experiments using characterizing sequences, a subsequence containing a locating sequence for each state of the machine constitutes Part 1. Part 2 of the experiment checks each transition of the machine, using one or more locating sequences and the characterizing sequences used in Part 1. To check a transition from state $S_i$ under input $x_j$, using a locating sequence $L_a$ and the characterizing sequences $X_1$ and $X_2$, the checking experiment should contain the following subsequences:

$$L_a T(Q_a, S_i) X_1, \quad L_a T(Q_a, S_i) X_2$$

and

$$L_a T(Q_a, S_i) x_j X_1, \quad L_a T(Q_a, S_i) x_j X_2,$$

# MACHINE IDENTIFICATION

The first two subsequences verify that the subsequence $L_aT(Q_a, S_i)$ does indeed take the machine to state $S_i$. The last two subsequences use the verified subsequence to take the machine to $S_i$, apply the input $x_j$ and check the final state by applying the two characterizing sequences. Note that the machine will be in state $Q_a$ at the end of each application of the locating sequence $L_a$. In our example, if we use $L_B$ for checking the transition from state $D$ under input 0, the following subsequences may be used:

$$L_B10, \ L_B110 \quad \text{and} \quad L_B100, \ L_B1010.$$

At the end of the sequence $L_B$, the machine is in state $A$ and the transfer sequence 1 is used to take it to state $D$. A set of subsequences may be derived for every transition in the flow table. Any sequence containing a sufficient set of subsequences for checking every transition in the machine will constitute Part 2 of the checking experiment. However, the experiments obtained by this method will be rather long. These experiments could be shortened somewhat by overlapping subsequences and by making use of transitions which have been checked in taking the machine to desired states.

Not all machines have a set of two characterizing sequences. However, it can be shown that every $n$-state machine has a set of at most $n-1$ characterizing sequences of length not more than $n-1$. Hennie has shown how locating sequences may be constructed using three or more characterizing sequences. For three characterizing sequences $X_1$, $X_2$ and $X_3$ the sequence

$$(Y_1^n Y_2)^n X_3 \quad \text{where} \quad Y_1 = X_1 T(P_i, S_i) \quad \text{and} \quad Y_2 = X_2 T(Q_i, S_i)$$

is a locating sequence for the state $S_i$. Methods similar to those of Theorem 3.2 may be used to shorten these sequences. The generalization to sets of more than three characterizing sequences is obvious. The method of checking transitions with a set of $k$ characterizing sequences is similar to the case where two sequences are sufficient, except that $2k$ subsequences of the type discussed earlier are used.

A set of characterizing sequences for a machine can be derived by finding a set of input sequences, such that the product of the partitions induced by these sequences is the 0-partition. This can be accomplished by an enumerative procedure in which we start with sequences of length 1, list the partitions induced by them and continue with longer sequences until a set of sequences with the desired property is obtained. For an $n$-state strongly connected machine, it is sufficient to consider sequences of length up to $n-1$. A modified form of the successor tree may be used for deriving the partitions induced by different input sequences, as shown in the following example.

**Example 3.9:** The successor tree showing the partitions induced by input sequences of length up to 3 for the machine of Example 3.8 is shown below. From Fig. 3.9, it is seen that the partitions induced by the sequences 0 and 10 are $\pi_0 = (AB, CD)$ and $\pi_{10} = (AD, BC)$ and $\pi_0 \cdot \pi_{10} = 0$. Thus (0, 10) is a set of characterizing sequences for the machine.

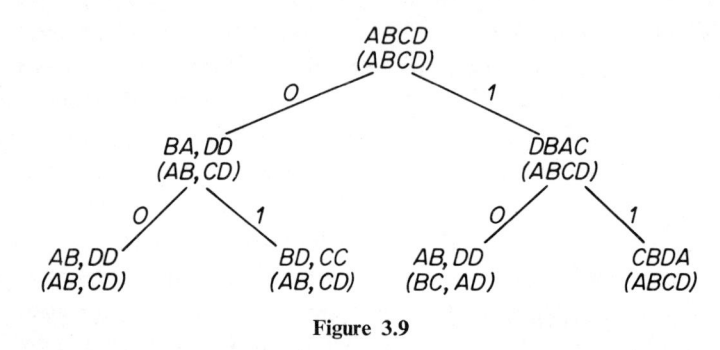

```
              ABCD
             (ABCD)
           0/      \1
      BA,DD          DBAC
     (AB,CD)        (ABCD)
     0/   \1        0/   \1
  AB,DD   BD,CC   AB,DD   CBDA
 (AB,CD) (AB,CD) (BC,AD) (ABCD)
```

Figure 3.9

Our discussions so far have assumed that the fault does not cause the number of states to increase. This assumption may not be valid in many practical circuits. Although it may be reasonable to assume that the fault does not cause an increase in the number of memory elements, the number of states in the faulty machine may increase when the number of states in the machine is not an integral power of 2. In such a case, the normal machine realized by the circuit may not be reduced or it may not be strongly connected. However, it is reasonable to assume that the number of states in the faulty machine does not exceed $2n - 1$, where $n$ is the number of states in the reduced normal machine. Under these conditions, we can derive an experiment to determine whether the machine under test is equivalent to that defined by the reduced table.

The first step is to select a set of characterizing sequences for the reduced table. Locating sequences are then derived. However, in deriving these sequences, subsequences are repeated $n_i + n$ times instead of $n_i + 1$ times as discussed earlier.

If the number of states in the faulty machine is greater than $n$, in general, one cannot guarantee that the actual circuit has visited all its states. Therefore two different appearances of a locating sequence with the correct output sequence do not necessarily leave the machine in the same state. However the sequence $L_aT(a, b)L_bT(b, c)L_c \ldots L_n$ is guaranteed to leave the machine in the same state whenever it appears with the correct output sequence. This is because the faulty circuit has at most $2n - 1$ states and cannot have two different states responding correctly to each of $L_a, L_b, \ldots L_n$.

Knowing the response of a single state in the circuit to each input sequence of length $3n - 2$ is sufficient to determine whether or not that state is equivalent to a given state of the reduced table. (This result follows from applying Lemma 3.2 to the machine $M + M'$ where $M'$ is the faulty circuit with $2n - 1$ states and $M$ has $n$ states). Thus a checking sequence can be formed by repeating the compound locating sequence $m^{3n-2}$ times, each time following it with a different sequence of length $3n - 2$. In general, such sequences can be shortened considerably.

*Hsieh's Procedure*

Hennie's procedure is very inefficient for machines that do not have distinguishing sequences. Hsieh (1969) has shown how more efficient checking experiments can be derived for machines which have an input sequence that produces a unique output sequence for one state of the machine. This class of machines properly contains the class of machines with distinguishing sequences.

It is convenient to represent the state of a machine by an *input/output (I/O) pair*, using subscripts to distinguish between identical I/O pairs associated with different states. The table obtained by replacing output entries in a flow table by the corresponding I/O pairs is called the *I/O canonical form* of the table. *An input/output (I/O) sequence I/Z* will be used to denote an input sequence $I$ and the output sequence $Z$ produced by the machine, when $I$ is applied. Note that an I/O sequence is a string of I/O pairs. We shall use single Greek letters to represent I/O sequences. If the machine is in state $S_0$ when the I/O sequence $\pi$ is generated, we shall refer to $\pi$ as the I/O sequence *generated* by the state $S_0$. A *simple I/O* sequence is an I/O sequence that can be generated by only one state. Thus a machine with a distinguishing sequence has a simple I/O sequence for each state. The method we shall now discuss is applicable to machines with at least one simple I/O sequence.

As in Hennie's method, the checking experiment can be divided into two parts, excluding the initializing part. In the first part, called the validating part and denoted by $T_v$, a simple I/O sequence of the machine is verified to be valid for the machine under test. The second part, called the diagnosing part $T_d$, verifies the transitions of the machine, using the simple I/O sequence verified in $T_v$ in much the same manner that Hennie uses locating sequences. The subsequences required in $T_v$ and $T_d$ are derived and merged in an efficient manner to obtain a checking experiment.

In order to verify the validity of a simple I/O sequence $I/Z$, it is necessary to display $n - 1$ other states which respond to the input sequence $I$ with output sequences other than $Z$. This can be done by using locating sequences for the different states of the machine. If the set of characterizing sequences consists of two sequences $X_1$ and $X_2$, the following subsequences may be used to display the response to the input sequence $I$ for some state $S_i$, using a locating sequence $L_{S_i}$:

$$L_{S_i}T(Q_j, S_i)X_1, \quad L_{S_i}T(Q_j, S_i)X_2, \quad L_{S_i}T(Q_j, S_i)I$$

The machine must be in state $S_j$ before each of the above sequences is applied. If the characterizing set contains more sequences, the corresponding locating sequences can be used in a similar way. However, the validating part of the experiment becomes very long.

The validating part of the experiment can be shortened considerably if the machine possesses a *valid homing sequence*. A valid homing sequence is an I/O sequence whose occurrence in an experiment ensures that the *machine under test* is in a unique final state. An I/O sequence $\pi$ is said to *display* k distinct states if $\pi$ can be written in the form $\pi = \pi_1\pi_2 \ldots \pi_k$, where the I/O sequences $\pi_1, \pi_2, \ldots, \pi_k$ distinguish $k$ distinct states of the machine. The following theorem (Hsieh, 1969) is useful in constructing the validating part of the experiment in this case.

**Theorem 3.3:** *If $\pi$ is an I/O sequence displaying* k *distinct states and* M *is a machine with* 2k $-$ 1 *or fewer states that can generate* $\pi$, *then* $\pi$ *is a valid homing sequence for* M.

The proof of this theorem is left as an exercise.

A valid homing sequence can be used instead of locating sequences to validate a simple I/O sequence. If the valid homing sequence $\pi$ takes the machine to state $S_0$, the following subsequences display the response of the machine in state $S_i$ to the input sequence $I$:

$$\pi T(S_0, S_i)I, \pi T(S_0, S_i)X_1, \ldots, \pi T(S_0, S_i)X_p$$

# MACHINE IDENTIFICATION

where $X_1, \ldots, X_p$ are the characterizing sequences of the machine and $T(S_0, S_i)$ is a transfer sequence. These subsequences may appear anywhere in the checking experiment. Since the valid homing sequence is likely to be much shorter than the locating sequences, especially when several characterizing sequences are necessary, the validating part of the experiment using the former will be correspondingly shorter. If a simple I/O sequence is verified somewhere in the experiment, it can be used in place of locating sequences in Hennie's experiments.

If $\lambda$ is a valid (verified) simple I/O sequence which leaves the machine in state $S_0$, it can be used to check a 0-transition from $S_i$ by including the following subsequences in the checking sequence.

$$\lambda T(S_0, S_i)X_1, \quad \lambda T(S_0, S_i)X_2 \ldots \lambda T(S_0, S_i)X_p$$

$$\lambda T(S_0, S_i)0X_1, \quad \lambda T(S_0, S_i)0X_2 \ldots \lambda T(S_0, S_i)0X_p$$

where $\{X_1, X_2, \ldots, X_p\}$ is a set of characterizing sequences for the machine under test.

Hsieh's test derivation procedure can be summarized in the following steps:

1. Find a sufficient set of I/O sequences to verify a simple I/O sequence (or a set of simple I/O sequences).

2. Using the valid simple I/O sequence, find the I/O sequences necessary to verify all transitions of the flow table.

3. Find a sequence containing all the subsequences of steps 1 and 2 using overlap wherever possible to shorten the sequence.

**Example 3.10:** Consider the following flow table (Hennie, 1964) and the I/O canonical form of the table where $a = 0/0$, $b = 0/1$ and $c = 1/0$.

|   | 0    | 1    |
|---|------|------|
| A | B, 0 | D, 0 |
| B | A, 0 | B, 0 |
| C | D, 1 | A, 0 |
| D | D, 1 | C, 0 |

|   | 0       | 1       |
|---|---------|---------|
| A | B, $a_1$ | D, $c_1$ |
| B | A, $a_2$ | B, $c_2$ |
| C | D, $b_1$ | A, $c_3$ |
| D | D, $b_2$ | C, $c_4$ |

By constructing the distinguishing tree, we see that states $A$ and $B$ can be identified by applying the input sequence 010 and that $\{0, 10\}$

is a characterizing set. The response to the input sequence 010 for the four states are:

$A$: 000,    $B$: 001;    $C$ and $D$: 101.

Thus the machine has two simple I/O sequences: $a_1c_2a_2$ and $a_2c_1b_2$. The input sequence 01010 when applied to the machine in state $A$ displays three distinct states and is a valid homing sequence, by Theorem 3.3. This sequence can be written as $a_1c_2a_2c_1b_2$. Since this sequence displays two different responses to the input sequence 010, the validity of the simple I/O sequences can be established by displaying two states that respond differently to this input sequence. Representing the valid homing sequence by $\pi$, the following subsequences are sufficient for the validation of the simple I/O sequences: $\pi b_2$, $\pi c_4 b_1$ and $\pi b_2 c_4 b_1$ to display state $D$ and $\pi c_4 b_1$, $\pi c_4 c_3 a_1$ and $\pi c_4 b_1 c_4 b_1$ to display state $C$. The first two subsequences of each set display the responses to the characterizing sequences and the last subsequence displays the response to the input sequence 010. Since these states are seen to respond differently from $A$ and $B$ to input 0, they will respond differently to the input sequence 010 and the last subsequence may be omitted from both sets. Ignoring subsequences contained in other subsequences, we have the following set which must be displayed: $\pi b_2$, $\pi c_4 c_3 a_1$ and $\pi c_4 b_1$.

Using the simple I/O sequences $a_1c_2a_2$ and $a_2c_1b_2$ which are verified somewhere in the experiment as discussed above, the transitions in the flow table are checked by the sequences given in Table 3.1. The

| Transition | Set 1 | Set 2 |
|---|---|---|
| $(A, 0)$ | $(a_1c_2a_2)(a_1c_2a_2)$ | $(a_1c_2a_2)a_1(a_2c_1b_2)$ |
| $(A, 1)$ | " | $(a_1c_2a_2)c_1b_2, (a_1c_2a_2)c_1c_4b_1$ |
| $(B, 0)$ | $(a_1c_2a_2)a_1(a_2c_1b_2)$ | $(a_1c_2a_2)a_1a_2(a_1c_2a_2)$ |
| $(B, 1)$ | " | $(a_1c_2a_2)a_1c_2(a_2c_1b_2)$ |
| $(C, 0)$ | $(a_2c_1b_2)c_4b_1,$ $(a_2c_1b_2)c_4c_3a_1$ | $(a_2c_1b_2)c_4b_1b_2,$ $(a_2c_1b_2)c_4b_1c_4b_1$ |
| $(C, 1)$ | " | $(a_2c_1b_2)c_4c_3(a_1c_2a_2)$ |
| $(D, 0)$ | $(a_2c_1b_2)b_2, (a_2c_1b_2)c_4b_1$ | $(a_2c_1b_2)b_2b_2, (a_2c_1b_2)b_2c_4b_1$ |
| $(D, 1)$ | " | $(a_2c_1b_2)c_4b_1, (a_2c_1b_2)c_4c_3a_1$ |

Table 3.1

MACHINE IDENTIFICATION

sequences in Set 1 verify that the application of a simple I/O sequence followed by an appropriate transfer sequence does take the machine to the desired state. In Set 2, the desired input is applied and the state resulting from the application of the input is identified. Identification of the state is done by means of a simple I/O sequence or the set of characterizing sequences. Simple I/O sequences within each I/O sequence are parenthesized in Table 3.1.

Eliminating repetitions and sequences contained in other sequences we obtain the following set of I/O sequences required for checking all transitions in the machine.

1. $a_1c_2a_2a_1a_2c_1b_2$
2. $a_1c_2a_2c_1c_4b_1$
3. $a_1c_2a_2a_1a_2a_1c_2a_2$
4. $a_1c_2a_2a_1c_2a_2c_1b_2$
5. $a_2c_1b_2c_4b_1b_2$
6. $a_2c_1b_2c_4b_1c_4b_1$
7. $a_2c_1b_2c_4c_3a_1c_2a_2$
8. $a_2c_1b_2b_2b_2$
9. $a_2c_1b_2b_2c_4b_1$

To this set we must add the following sequences derived earlier for verifying the simple I/O sequences:

10. $a_1c_2a_2c_1b_2b_2$
11. $a_1c_2a_2c_1b_2c_4c_3a_1$
12. $a_1c_2a_2c_1b_2c_4b_1$

Merging these sequences by overlapping wherever possible, we obtain the following sequences.

4–11–7–2: $a_1c_2a_2a_1c_2a_2c_1b_2c_4c_3a_1c_2a_2c_1c_4b_1 = X_1$
3–12–6 : $a_1c_2a_2a_1a_2a_1c_2a_2c_1b_2c_4b_1c_4b_1 = X_2$
1–5 : $a_1c_2a_2a_1a_2c_1b_2c_4b_1b_2 = X_3$
10–8 : $a_1c_2a_2c_1b_2b_2b_2 = X_4$
9 : $a_2c_1b_2b_2c_4b_1 = X_5$

To obtain the checking sequence, the above sequences should be joined together by appropriate transfer sequences. All the sequences end in $b_1$ or $b_2$ and the final state is $D$. The I/O pair $a_1$ corresponds to state $A$. From the I/O canonical table, $c_4c_3$ is a transfer sequence from $D$ to $A$. Similarly $a_2$ is produced by state $B$ and $c_4c_3a_1$ is a transfer sequence from $D$ to $B$. With the machine initially in state $A$, the following checking experiment for it requires 62 inputs.

$$X_1 c_4 c_3 X_2 c_4 c_3 X_3 c_4 c_3 X_4 c_4 c_3 a_1 X_5.$$

The length of the sequence can be reduced by 1 if the initial state is $B$. Now the checking sequence can be started with $X_5$. However, the initializing part may be longer for this initial state.

*Ad Hoc Methods*

Experiments which are considerably shorter than those obtainable using the algorithms of Hennie and Hsieh may be derived for machines, with distinguishing sequences or simple I/O sequences, using what are, at present, *ad hoc* methods. These sequences first display all states (thus verifying the distinguishing sequences or simple I/O sequence) and then check all transitions. However, in the course of checking transitions use is made of information obtained from previously checked transitions. The following example illustrates the procedure on the machine of Example 3.10.

**Example 3.11**

|   | 0    | 1    |
|---|------|------|
| $A$ | $B, 0$ | $D, 0$ |
| $B$ | $A, 0$ | $B, 0$ |
| $C$ | $D, 1$ | $A, 0$ |
| $D$ | $D, 1$ | $C, 0$ |

From Example 3.10, we know that the machine has no distinguishing sequence but that states $A$ and $B$ can be identified by their responses to the input sequence 010. We shall derive a checking experiment by first displaying all the states of the machine and then checking each transition.

Assuming that the machine is initially in state $A$, we can exhibit states $A$ and $B$ by the sequence:

# MACHINE IDENTIFICATION

```
t    0  1  2  3  4
x    0  1  0  1  0
z    0  0  0  0  1
```

$S(0) \neq S(2)$ (where $S(i)$ is the state of $M$ at time $t = i$), since they respond differently to the sequence 010. We can label $S(2) = B$. To distinguish $C$ and $D$ from each other and from $A$ and $B$, we make use of the two characterizing sequences 0 and 10. We extend the sequence as shown below:

```
t    4  5  6  7  8
x    0  0  0  1  0
z    1  1  1  0  1
```

By Hennie's nesting technique, we can verify that $S(7)$ is a state that responds to a 0 input with a 1 output and 10 with 01. Let $S(7) = D$. Extending the sequence as shown below

```
t    8  9  10  11  12  13
x    0  1   0   1   1   0
z    1  0   1   0   0   0
```

and again using the nesting argument we can identify $S(12)$ as a state which responds to the characterizing sequences 0 and 10 with 1 and 00, which we label as $C$. At this stage, the following portions of the flow table and checking sequence can be filled in (using $A/B$ to indicate $A$ or $B$):

|   | 0   | 1       |
|---|-----|---------|
| A | , 0 |         |
| B | , 0 |         |
| C | , 1 | $A/B$, 0 |
| D | , 1 | $C/D$, 0 |

```
t   0  1  2  3  4  5  6  7  8  9  10  11  12  13
x   0  1  0  1  0  0  0  1  0  1   0   1   1   0
    A  B           D C/D           C   A/B
z   0  0  0  0  1  1  1  0  1  0   1   0   0   0
```

Label $A$ & $B$ — Label $D$

Label $C$

We now can check transitions to states $A$ and $B$ by using the sequence 010. The fact that $S(13) = A$ can be verified by

| $t$ | 13 | 14 | 15 |
|---|---|---|---|
| $x$ | 0 | 1 | 0 |
|   | $A$ |   | $B$ |
| $z$ | 0 | 0 | 0 |

We also know that $S(15) = B$, since from $t = 0$ and $t = 2$ we can conclude that the input sequence 01 takes the machine from $A$ to $B$. The transition from $B$ to $A$ can be verified by

| $t$ | 15 | 16 | 17 | 18 |
|---|---|---|---|---|
| $x$ | 0 | 0 | 1 | 0 |
|   | $B$ | $A$ |   |   |
| $z$ | 0 | 0 | 0 | 0 |

Since the machine goes from $B$ to $A$ with input 0, $S(3) = A$ and $A$ responds to 10 with 01. Thus, by its response to 10, $S(14) = B$ or $C$. If $S(14) = C$, $S(16) = C$, because $S(12) = C$ and 10 takes the machine back to $C$. But $S(16)$ is known to be $A$. Therefore $S(14) = B$. The information obtained so far is displayed in the following flow table:

|   | 0 | 1 |
|---|---|---|
| $A$ | $B, 0$ | , 0 |
| $B$ | $A, 0$ | $B, 0$ |
| $C$ | , 1 | $A, 0$ |
| $D$ | , 1 | $C/D, 0$ |

The partial checking sequence and the states that can be labeled are shown below:

| $t$ | 0 | 1 | 2 | 3 | 4 | 5 | 6 | 7 | 8 | 9 | 10 | 11 | 12 | 13 | 14 | 15 | 16 | 17 | 18 | 19 |
|---|---|---|---|---|---|---|---|---|---|---|---|---|---|---|---|---|---|---|---|---|
| $x$ | 0 | 1 | 0 | 1 | 0 | 0 | 0 | 1 | 0 | 1 | 0 | 1 | 1 | 0 | 1 | 0 | 0 | 1 | 0 |   |
|   | $A$ | $B$ | $B$ | $A$ |   |   | $D$ |   |   |   |   |   | $C$ | $A$ | $B$ | $B$ | $A$ | $B$ | $B$ | $A$ |
| $z$ | 0 | 0 | 0 | 0 | 1 | 1 | 1 | 0 | 1 | 0 | 1 | 0 | 0 | 0 | 0 | 0 | 0 | 0 | 0 |   |

$S(4) = C$ or $D$, i.e., $N(A, 1) = C$ or $D$. Adding the sequence

# MACHINE IDENTIFICATION

|   | 19 | 20 | 21 |
|---|---|---|---|
|   | 1 | 1 | 0 |
| A |   |   |   |
|   | 0 | 0 | 1 |

establishes that $N(A, 1) = D$. Now, $S(7) = S(20) = D$. Therefore, $S(9) = S(22)$. But $S(9) = A$ or $D$ by its response to 10. $S(9)$ and $S(22)$ can be identified by applying a 0 at $t = 22$ and noting that the response is 1 establishing that $S(9) = S(22) = D$. Since $S(9) = D$, $S(11)$ is also $D$ because we can conclude from $S(7)$ and $S(9)$ that the input sequence 10 when applied to the machine in state $D$ returns it to state $D$. From $S(11)$ and $S(12)$, $N(D, 1) = C$. Therefore, $S(8) = C$. From $S(8)$ and $S(9)$, $N(C, 0) = D$. The only remaining entry to be verified is $N(D, 0)$. But we can determine that $S(4) = D$, and $N(D, 0) = C$ or $D$ from the 1 response to the 0 input in $S(4)$. But for either of these possibilities $S(6) = D$ and since $S(7) = D$, $N(D, 0) = D$.

|   | 21 | 22 |
|---|---|---|
|   | 0 | 0 |
| D |   |   |
|   | 1 | 1 |

Thus the checking experiment is complete. The length of the experiment is only 23 compared to 62 with Hsieh's method and 152 with Hennie's method (Hennie, 1964).

At the present time, no *algorithms* exist for obtaining *efficient* checking experiments for completely general machines. It is hoped that further research in this area will lead to systematic procedures for deriving checking experiments which compare favorably with those obtained by path sensitizing, or Seshu's procedure, at least for relatively small circuits.

## *Checking Sequences Under Restricted Fault Assumptions*

From our discussion of the methods of deriving tests for sequential machines, it is clear that the machine-identification approach leads to longer test sequences than the circuit-testing approach, although the former is capable of detecting a much larger class of faults. However, the derivation of tests is simpler with the machine-identification approach. In this section, we shall discuss the derivation of checking sequences under slightly more restricted assumptions regarding the realization of the machine and the type of faults. We shall see that these restrictions often lead to shorter checking sequences which are fairly easy to derive.

We shall assume that the state logic (SL) and the output logic (OL) are physically disjoint and that only one of them may be faulty at any time. It is also assumed that the fault does not cause the number of states to increase. The normal machine is assumed to have a synchronizing sequence. This can be in the form of a resetting signal.

Let us consider a sequence $T = \pi_1 \pi_2$, where $\pi_1$ verifies the output logic, assuming the state logic is correct, and $\pi_1 \pi_2$ verifies the state logic assuming that the output logic is correct. Let $\pi_1 = X_1 X_2$, where $X_1$ is a synchronizing sequence that takes the normal machine to the initial state $S_0$ and $X_2$ is an input sequence that takes the normal machine through all transitions. If the machine responds correctly to $\pi_1$, we can conclude that the output logic is correct. For, if the state logic is correct, all input combinations would have been applied to the output logic by the application of $\pi_1$ and any fault in it would have produced an incorrect response to $\pi_1$. On the other hand, if the state logic is faulty, the output logic cannot also be faulty (by our assumption that SL and OL cannot both be faulty). $\pi_2$ is constructed to verify all transitions under the assumption that OL is correct (i.e., all output entries in the flow table of the machine under test are known).

It is not necessary for $\pi_1$ and $\pi_2$ to be separate. In fact, if $\pi_2$ checks every transition under the assumption that the OL is correct and the machine responds correctly to $\pi_2$ then the machine is machine $M$ under the assumption that both SL and OL don't fail. Thus it is only necessary to design a checking experiment which checks all transitions assuming correct OL. This enables us to shorten the sequence. For instance, a checking sequence of length 21 can be derived for the machine of Example 3.11 under these restricted fault assumptions. The savings may be more dramatic for machines which have very long checking sequences as the following example from Hennie (1964) suggests.

**Example 3.12**

|   | 0 | 1 |
|---|---|---|
| A | A, 0 | B, 0 |
| B | A, 0 | C, 0 |
| C | A, 0 | D, 0 |
| D | A, 1 | D, 0 |

# MACHINE IDENTIFICATION

Note that the flow table has no distinguishing sequence and that a set of three characterizing sequences is required to identify all states. Therefore, Hennie's method using locating sequences will lead to a very long checking experiment. The machine has two simple I/O sequences: (0/1) for state $D$ and (1/0) (1/0) (0/0) for state $A$. Hsieh's method will therefore yield a shorter experiment. However, the simple I/O sequence (0/1) will have to be verified by displaying three other states which produce the I/O sequence (0/0) before the simple I/O sequence can be used for checking transitions. Under the restricted fault assumption, we start by assuming that the output entries are known. Therefore there is no need to verify the simple I/O sequence (0/1). We can use this and the known outputs to verify that the input sequence 110 can be used to identify state $A$.

We assume that the machine is initially in state $D$ (reached by applying the synchronizing sequence 111). Applying the input sequence 00 verifies that the initial state is $D$ and that $N(D, 0) \neq D$. Since the states $A$, $B$ and $C$ are output equivalent, we arbitrarily label $N(D, 0) = A$. (If we had chosen $N(D, 0) = B$ or $C$, the resultant table would just have the states relabeled.) Now we observe that if all the entries in the 1 column of the table are verified, the only state that can respond to the input sequence 110 with the output sequence 000 is state $A$.

| 1 | 2 | 3 | 4 | 5 | 6 | 7 | 8 | 9 | 10 | 11 | 12 |
|---|---|---|---|---|---|---|---|---|----|----|----|
| 0 | 0 | 1 | 1 | 1 | 0 | 1 | 1 | 1 | 0  | 1  | 0  |
| $D$ | $A$ | | | | $D$ | $A$ | | | $D$ | $A$ | |
| 1 | 0 | 0 | 0 | 0 | 1 | 0 | 0 | 0 | 1 | 0 | 0 |

To determine $N(A, 1)$ we apply the sequence 1110 to take the machine to state $A$, followed by 1 and 110. Since $S(10) = D$, we can conclude that $N(A, 1) \neq A$; otherwise we would have $S(8) = S(9) = S(10) = A$ (contradiction). To show that $N(A, 1) \neq D$, we add the sequence 10. Clearly, $S(11) = A$, and $S(12) \neq D$, since it responds to input 0 with output 0. Since $B$ and $C$ are output equivalent, we can label $S(8) = S(12) = B$ and $N(A, 1) = B$.

To determine $N(B, 1)$ we observe that $N(B, 1) \neq A$ or $B$, since this would imply $S(10) = B$. In order to establish that $N(B, 1) \neq D$, we take the machine to state $B$ again at $t = 18$ and apply the input sequence 10 as shown below:

```
12  13  14  15  16  17  18  19
 0   1   1   1   0   1   1   0
 B           D   A   B
 0   0   0   0   1   0   0   0
```

We label $S(9) = S(19) = C$ and conclude that $N(C, 1) = D$. The only entry yet to be checked in the 1 column is $N(D, 1)$. We observe that this can be done by inserting a 1 input when the machine is in state $D$ at $t = 10$, as shown below:

```
1 2 3 4 5 6 7 8 9 10 11 12 13 14 15 16 17 18 19 20
0 0 1 1 1 0 1 1 1  1  0  1  0  1  1  1  0  1  1  0
D A       D A B C    D  A  B           D  A  B  C
1 0 0 0 0 1 0 0 0  0  1  0  0  0  0  0  1  0  0  0
```

We should confirm that all transitions checked by the original sequence are still checked by this sequence. Using the same arguments as before, we can label the states as shown above. Since $S(11)$ is known to be state $D$, $S(10)$ cannot be $A$, $B$ or $C$. Therefore, $S(10) = D$ and $N(D, 1) = D$ leading to the following partial table.

|   | 0    | 1    |
|---|------|------|
| A | , 0  | B, 0 |
| B | , 0  | C, 0 |
| C | , 0  | D, 0 |
| D | A, 1 | D, 0 |

It is also clear from this partial table that the response to the input sequence 110 will uniquely identify state $A$.

The remaining three transitions can be checked using the input sequence 110 to identify state $A$ as shown below:

```
20 21 22 23 24 25 26 27 28 29 30 31 32
    0  1  1  0  0  1  1  0  1  0  1  1  0
 C  A  B  C  A  A  B  C  A  B  A
 0  0  0  0  0  0  0  0  0  0  0  0  0
```

Since the 0 input takes the machine to state $A$ from states $A$, $B$ and $C$, and the input sequence 110 applied to state $A$ also takes the machine

MACHINE IDENTIFICATION

to state $A$, we can shorten the checking experiment by inserting the sequence 110 to check $S(3)$, $S(14)$ and $S(21)$. Thus the following sequence of length 29 is a checking sequence for the machine under the restricted fault assumption:

| $t$ | 1 | 2 | 3 | 4 | 5 | 6 | 7 | 8 | 9 | 10 | 11 | 12 | 13 | 14 | 15 |
|---|---|---|---|---|---|---|---|---|---|---|---|---|---|---|---|
| Input | 0 | 0 | 1 | 1 | 0 | 1 | 1 | 1 | 0 | 1 | 1 | 1 | 1 | 0 | 1 |
| Output | 1 | 0 | 0 | 0 | 0 | 0 | 0 | 0 | 1 | 0 | 0 | 0 | 0 | 1 | 0 |

| | 16 | 17 | 17 | 18 | 20 | 21 | 22 | 23 | 24 | 25 | 26 | 27 | 28 | 29 |
|---|---|---|---|---|---|---|---|---|---|---|---|---|---|---|
| | 0 | 1 | 1 | 0 | 1 | 1 | 1 | 0 | 1 | 1 | 0 | 1 | 1 | 0 |
| | 0 | 0 | 0 | 0 | 0 | 0 | 0 | 1 | 0 | 0 | 0 | 0 | 0 | 0 |

The above checking experiment is considerably shorter than one derived using Hennie's algorithm. However, we have resorted to the use of *ad hoc* methods in deriving the experiment of length 29. Instead, we could have used Hsieh's method. The restricted fault assumption makes it unnecessary to verify the simple I/O sequence (0/1), and leads to shorter checking sequences than without these restrictions on the realization and the class of faults.

*Asynchronous Sequential Circuits*

The methods of deriving checking experiments discussed above may be extended to asynchronous circuits. However, because of the presence of certain difficulties peculiar to such circuits, it becomes necessary to impose additional constraints on the behavior of the normal and faulty machines. One of the main difficulties associated with asynchronous circuits is the possibility of critical races. Even if the normal circuit is race-free, the fault may cause critical races and consequently the behavior of the faulty machine may not be deterministic. Another difficulty is that repetitions of the same input cannot be allowed because the machine is designed to respond to input changes only. Thus it may be impossible to apply the same distinguishing sequence when the machine is stable under different inputs. The common assumption of single-input changes further complicates the derivation of checking experiments for asynchronous machines.

The following assumptions make the derivation of checking experiments for asynchronous circuits a simple extension of the synchronous case:

**1.** The flow table of the normal machine is strongly-connected, and reduced.

**2.** The faulty flow table has no cycles of states in any column and has no critical races.

**3.** The number of stable states in any column of the flow table does not increase as a result of the fault.

If multiple-input changes are allowed, the derivation of checking sequences under the above assumptions, proceeds as in the synchronous case, with the exception that distinguishing (or characterizing sequences) are derived for the set of stable states in each column. The checking experiment should display the responses of all the stable states in each column to the distinguishing sequence (or the set of characterizing sequences) for that column and also verify all the transitions in the table. If only single-input changes are permitted, then the normal flow table must be reduced under the single-input change restriction. (i.e., the table should not contain any pair of states which cannot be distinguished by some input sequence satisfying the single-input change restriction.) In this case, it is only possible to distinguish the normal circuit from any circuit (with no more stable states in any column) which is not equivalent to it under the single-input change restriction. The following example will demonstrate the generation of checking sequences in this case.

**Example 3.13**

|   | $I_1$ | $I_2$ | $I_3$ | $I_4$ |
|---|---|---|---|---|
| 1 | ①,0 | 3 | ①,0 | 2 |
| 2 | 1 | ②,1 | 1 | ②,0 |
| 3 | ③,1 | ③,0 | 1 | 4 |
| 4 | 3 | 2 | ④,0 | ④,1 |

In the above flow table, let us assume that only transitions between adjacent columns are permitted ($I_1$ and $I_4$ are considered adjacent). For the stable states in columns $I_1$, $I_2$ and $I_4$, the null input sequence is a distinguishing sequence (i.e., the states have different outputs and can be distinguished without applying any additional input). The input $I_4$ is a distinguishing sequence for the stable states in column $I_3$. The following sequence displays two distinct states in each column of the flow table.

# MACHINE IDENTIFICATION

| $t$ | 1 | 2 | 3 | 4 | 5 | 6 | 7 | 8 | 9 | 10 | 11 | 12 |
|---|---|---|---|---|---|---|---|---|---|---|---|---|
| Input | $I_1$ | $I_2$ | $I_1$ | $I_4$ | $I_3$ | $I_4$ | $I_3$ | $I_2$ | $I_1$ | $I_4$ | $I_3$ | $I_4$ |
| State | 1 | 3 | 3' | 4 | 4' | 4 | 4' | 2 | 1 | 2' | 1' | 2' |
| Output | 0 | 0 | 1 | 1 | 0 | 1 | 0 | 1 | 0 | 0 | 0 | 0 |

The states that are identified are labeled above. Note that the labels contain some primes. This is necessitated by the fact that the responses to the distinguishing sequence allow us only to label two distinct states in each column. However, we do not know whether a stable state in one column is the same as a stable state in another column, because they are identified by different distinguishing sequences. Using the information obtained from the sequence of length 12 given above, we can construct the following *primitive* (containing exactly one stable entry per row) flow table.

|    | $I_1$ | $I_2$ | $I_3$ | $I_4$ |
|----|-------|-------|-------|-------|
| 1  | ①, 0  | 3     | —     | 2'    |
| 2  | 1     | ②, 1  |       | —     |
| 3  | 3'    | ③, 0  |       | —     |
| 4  | —     |       | 4'    | ④, 1  |
| 1' | —     |       | ①, 0  | 2'    |
| 2' | —     |       | 1'    | ②, 0  |
| 3' | ③, 1  |       | —     | 4     |
| 4' | —     | 2     | ④, 0  | 4     |

The primitive flow table contains "don't cares" (indicated by dashes) because the single-input change restriction makes it impossible for the machine to be in these total states. The remaining transitions in the primitive flow table can be verified by adding the following sequence to the sequence already derived:

| $t$ | 13 | 14 | 15 | 16 | 17 | 18 | 19 | 20 | 21 | 22 | 23 | 24 | 25 | 26 | 27 | 28 |
|---|---|---|---|---|---|---|---|---|---|---|---|---|---|---|---|---|
| Input: | $I_1$ | $I_2$ | $I_3$ | $I_4$ | $I_3$ | $I_2$ | $I_1$ | $I_4$ | $I_1$ | $I_2$ | $I_1$ | $I_4$ | $I_3$ | $I_2$ | $I_3$ | $I_4$ |
| State: | 1 | 3 | 1' | 2' | 1' | 3 | 3' | 4 | 3' | 3 | 3' | 4 | 4' | 2 | 1' | 2' |
| Output: | 0 | 0 | 0 | 0 | 0 | 0 | 1 | 1 | 1 | 0 | 1 | 1 | 0 | 1 | 0 | 0 |

If input transitions are allowed between any pair of columns, the unspecified entries in the primitive flow table will have to be determined by a similar procedure. Ashkinazy (1969) has shown that for any asynchronous machine $M$ there exists a synchronous machine $M'$ such that a checking sequence for $M'$ is also a checking sequence for $M$ under the single-input change assumption. Thus the procedures derived for synchronous machines are also applicable to asynchronous machines.

## SUMMARY

In this chapter, we have presented several methods for deriving test sequences for sequential machines. These methods differ in the assumptions used, the computational complexity and the length of sequences derived. We shall now examine the validity of the assumptions and the conditions under which the different methods are likely to be useful.

One assumption which was particularly useful in deriving checking experiments was that the number of states of the machine does not increase due to the fault. Though this assumption is valid for a synchronous machine with exactly $2^k$ states for integral values of $k$, it is unrealistic when the number of states is not an integral power of 2. In the latter case, the assumption that the number of states in the faulty machine is less than twice that in the normal machine is justifiable. However, the experiments which are valid under this assumption tend to be very long. When the number of states is not an integral power of 2, the assumption that the number of states does not increase may be valid, if the circuit is designed such that the states that cannot be reached in the normal machine have a unique output combination associated with them. If there is no shared logic between the outputs and the state variables and only a single logical fault can occur, then this assumption becomes valid.

The assumption that the number of states does not increase due to any fault becomes even more questionable in asynchronous sequential circuits where in general, more than $[\log_2 n]$* state variables are necessary to realize an $n$-state machine. However, if the circuit is designed so that the states which are not stable in any column have a special output associated with them, then we can reasonably assume that the number of stable states in any column does not increase, provided that there is at most one fault and no shared logic between the outputs and the state variables.

All of the procedures for deriving tests for sequential circuits presented in this chapter have some undesirable properties, especially when used for

*$[\log_2 n]$ is the smallest integer that is greater than or equal to $\log_2 n$.

large circuits. The method of Poage and McCluskey is not computationally feasible except for circuits with only a few states. Extensions of the path-sensitizing method and the D-algorithm require a great amount of computation if a large number of faults is to be considered. The Sequential Analyzer may not find tests for some detectable faults. Also the need to simulate all faults makes a large number of passes through the simulation program necessary. Checking experiments which do not take the actual circuitry into account tend to be unnecessarily long, if all the faults that are detected by the experiments cannot actually occur in the circuit under test. In addition, they require the flow table of the normal machine. This may not be available for large circuits. The usefulness of checking experiments could increase dramatically for a technology in which detection of more complex logical faults than single stuck-type faults was required, especially if algorithms for generating more efficient checking sequences can be developed.

At the present time, the most potentially effective procedure seems to be to start with a pseudo-random input sequence or a sequence that "exercises" the circuit (i.e., causes the machine to perform all or most of its known functions). Usually the circuit designer can provide such a sequence. An example of such a sequence might be an input sequence which takes the good machine through all its transitions. The faults that are detected by this sequence can be determined by simulation (see Chapter 5). Hopefully, a sequence that detects a sizable majority of the faults can be designed in this manner. Tests for the remaining faults can then be derived using the extension of the D-algorithm or the path-sensitizing method.

## REFERENCES

Ashkinazy, A., "Fault Detection Experiments in Asynchronous Sequential Machines," *Proc. Eleventh Annual Symposium on Switching and Automata Theory*, 1970.

Gill A., *Introduction to the Theory of Finite State Machines*, McGraw-Hill, New York, 1962.

Harrison, M. A., "On Asymptotic Estimates in Switching and Automata Theory", *JACM*, vol. 13, pp. 151–157, 1966.

Hartmanis, J. and Stearns, R. E., *Algebraic Structure Theory of Sequential Machines*, Prentice-Hall Inc., Englewood Cliffs, New Jersey, 1966.

Hennie F. C., "Fault-Detecting Experiments for Sequential Circuits," *Proc. Fifth Annual Symposium on Switching Circuit Theory and Logical Design*, 95–110, 1964.

Hsieh, E. P., "Optimal Checking Experiments for Sequential Machines," *Ph.D. Dissertation*, Department of Electrical Engineering, Columbia University, 1969.

Moore, E. F., "Gedanken-experiments on Sequential Machines," *Automata Studies*, Princeton University Press, Princeton, New Jersey, 129-153, 1956.

Poage, J. F. and McCluskey, E. J., "Derivation of Optimum Test Sequences for Sequential Machines," *Proc. Fifth Annual Symposium on Switching Circuit Theory and Logical Design*, 121–132, 1964.

Seshu, S. and Freeman, D. N., "The Diagnosis of Asynchronous Sequential Switching Systems," *IRE Trans. on Elec. Computers* EC-11, 459–465, 1962.

## PROBLEMS

1. For the sequential circuit shown below, find a minimal length test sequence which detects the following single faults.
   a) $\alpha$ s-a-0
   b) $\beta$ s-a-1
   Assume initial state $A = 00$.

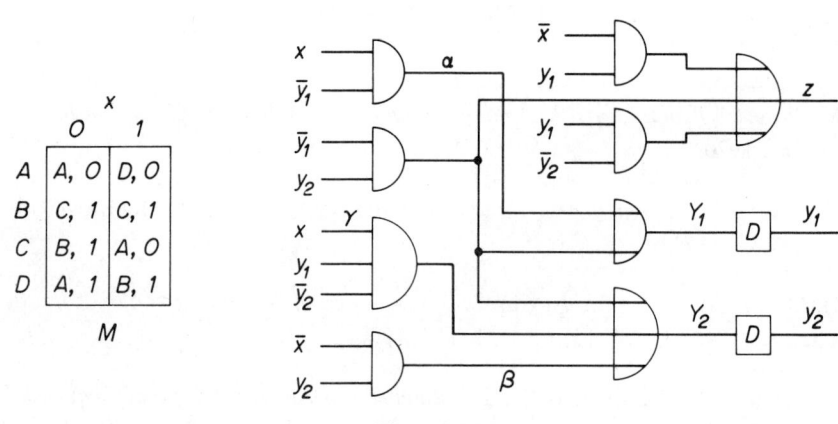

|   | x=0  | x=1  |
|---|------|------|
| A | A, 0 | D, 0 |
| B | C, 1 | C, 1 |
| C | B, 1 | A, 0 |
| D | A, 1 | B, 1 |

M

**Figure 3.10**

2. For the circuit of Fig. 3.10 find a test sequence for the fault $\gamma$ s-a-0 using the extended path-sensitizing procedure. Assume initial state $A = 00$.

3. For the flow table $M$ of Problem 1 find a checking sequence
   a) using Hennie's procedure
   b) using Hsieh's procedure.

4. For the following flow table derive a checking sequence using the nesting procedure and other *ad hoc* methods discussed in this chapter. Assume initial state $A$.

|   | 0    | 1    |
|---|------|------|
| A | C, 0 | D, 0 |
| B | B, 0 | D, 0 |
| C | D, 1 | A, 1 |
| D | C, 0 | B, 1 |

5. a) Prove Theorem 3.3
   b) Prove that every valid homing sequence contains a simple I/O sequence as a subsequence.

6. Using the restricted fault assumption derive a checking sequence for the following flow table.

|   | 0    | 1    |
|---|------|------|
| A | B, 0 | D, 0 |
| B | A, 0 | B, 0 |
| C | D, 1 | A, 0 |
| D | D, 1 | C, 0 |

7. Derive a checking sequence for the flow table of Example 3.12 under the restricted fault assumption, using Hsieh's method.

8. Derive a checking sequence for the asynchronous machine below using the assumptions on asynchronous checking sequences specified in this chapter and also the single-input change restriction.

|   | $x_1 x_2$ | | | |
|---|---|---|---|---|
|   | 00 | 01 | 11 | 10 |
| 1 | ①,0 | 2,0 | 4,1 | ①,0 |
| 2 | 3,1 | ②,0 | ②,0 | 3,1 |
| 3 | ③,1 | ③,0 | 4,1 | ③,1 |
| 4 | 1,0 | ④,1 | ④,1 | 3,1 |

9. Use the following procedure to derive a test sequence for the realization of the table of Problem 6, shown in Fig. 3.11.

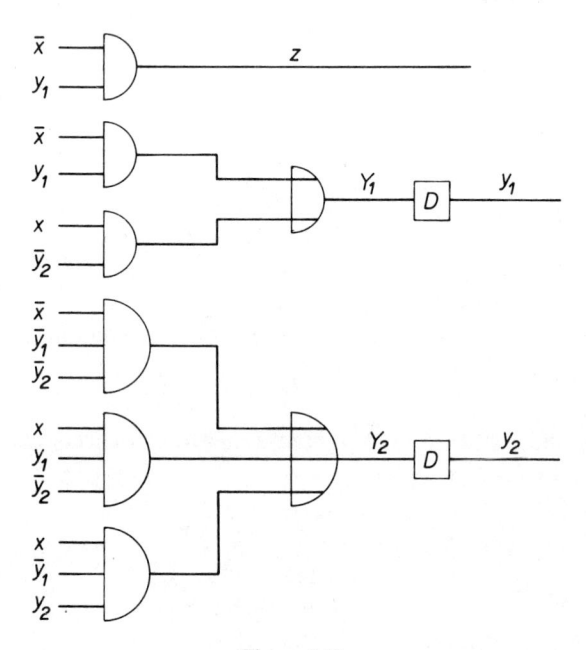

Figure 3.11

Derive a homing sequence to pass the normal machine into a known state, followed by an input sequence which passes the normal machine through all transitions. Determine what faults are detected by this sequence. Using the D-algorithm extend this sequence so as to detect all previously undetected faults.

10. Prove or disprove the following statement:
A reduced strongly connected sequential circuit realized with delays

as memory elements as in Fig. 1.5 will contain undetectable s-a-0 and s-a-1 faults if and only if the combinational part of the circuit is redundant.

11. Repeat Problem 10 for sequential circuit realizations with S-R flip-flops as memory elements.

CHAPTER 4

# ITERATIVE LOGIC ARRAYS

With the development of integrated circuits, the problem of minimizing the number of elements in a circuit has become less important than that of attaining structural simplicity and building a circuit from a standard set of subcircuits. This has resulted in the investigation of how to realize combinational circuits and sequential circuits through iterative arrays of combinational logic (Minnick, 1967; Arnold et al, 1970). Hopefully, such circuits will have the property of being easier to test, due to their geometrical regularity, than comparably sized noniterative circuits. In this chapter, we examine some of the problems associated with testing one- and two-dimensional arrays of combinational logic.

Tammaru (1968) has envisaged the use of arrays that can be tested easily as a step in the fabrication of large scale integrated logic structures. During fabrication, the cells in the array may be connected in a uniform manner using temporary metallization. The uniform array may be tested using a small number of tests. If all cells of the array are found to be good, the temporary metallization (or part of it) may be removed by etching and additional interconnections made by further metallization to obtain the desired logic. If the uniform array contains faulty cells which are locatable, these faulty cells may be avoided during the interconnections made by the final metallization.

Arrays are to be tested by applying test inputs to their accessible input terminals and observing the outputs on accessible output terminals. The accessible inputs and outputs are usually associated with the boundaries of the array. In addition, some input and output terminals of individual cells may also be accessible in some arrays. An array is said to be *testable* if it is possible to detect any faulty cells in the array. Of course any array may be completely tested for all detectable faults by applying all possible combinations of inputs. This is impractical due to the large number of tests that may be necessary. However, if an array is testable under the single-fault assumption, efficient tests can be derived for it. Thus, determination of the testability of an array is useful in deciding on the sufficiency of single-fault analysis in test generation.

The problem of testing iterative arrays has been studied under two different sets of assumptions. In the first set (Kautz, 1967), it is assumed that all possible cell inputs must be applied to each cell in order to test it completely and that the fault in a cell may affect the cell outputs in any arbitrary way. We shall refer to these as the *general-fault assumptions*. They are similar to those used in deriving checking sequences for sequential machines. A more restricted and possibly more realistic set of assumptions is that a cell can be tested completely by applying a specified subset of the set of all cell inputs and that each fault will affect the cell outputs in a particular known manner. Under these *restricted-fault assumptions*, the conditions for testability of arrays and locatability of faulty cells are less stringent (though more difficult to state) than with the general-fault assumptions. We shall study the problem under the restricted-fault assumptions (Menon and Friedman, 1971) and show how the results under the general-fault assumptions (Kautz, 1967) can be obtained from these.

We assume that the cells in the array are identical and that the size of the array is arbitrarily large, but finite. The results that are derived in this chapter are valid for any array composed of these cells, independent of the size of the array.* The array can have at most one fault at any given time and a complete set of tests for detecting all faults in any one cell, when operated by itself, is known. For any fault and any test that detects it, the outputs of the normal and faulty cells are known. Inter-cell connections are assumed to be fault-free since faults in the connections can be represented by equivalent faults in appropriate cells.

It is simple to show that the following conditions are necessary and sufficient for a cellular array to be testable:

**1.** It should be possible to apply to the input terminals of any cell,

---

*Hennie (1961) has denoted the class of all arrays with identical cell structure but arbitrary size as an *iterative system*. The term *iterative array* (with arbitrary size implied) is used in the same sense in this chapter.

a complete set of tests for detecting all faults in the cell, independent of the position of the cell in the array.

2. For each such test, it should be possible to propagate the effect of the fault to an observable output.

Note that these conditions correspond to the generation of the desired signal value at the location of a fault in a combinational circuit and the sensitization of a path to an observable output.

## ONE-DIMENSIONAL ARRAYS

We first consider one-dimensional arrays of combinational cells, where the signal flow is left to right. The notation to be used is shown in Fig. 4.1. A typical cell receives the input $x$ from its left hand neighbor and an

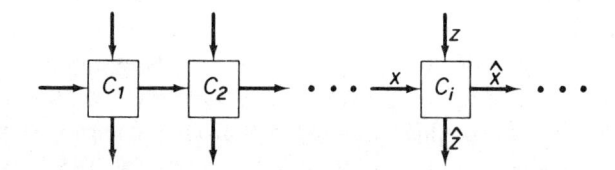

Figure 4.1. A typical cell in a one-dimensional array.

external input $z$. It generates an external output $\hat{z}$ and transmits an output $\hat{x}$ to its right hand neighbor. The controllable inputs consist of the $x$ input to the first (leftmost) cell and the $z$ inputs to all cells in the array. All $\hat{z}$ outputs and the $\hat{x}$ output of the last cell are observable. We assume that the $z$ input to cell $c_i$ is independent of the $z$ input to cell $c_j$ for $i \neq j$. We shall use subscripts to refer to specific inputs or outputs where necessary. The behavior of a cell can be described by a flow table, which has a row for each $x$ input (also referred to as state) and a column for each $z$ input. The entries in the table consist of pairs of cell outputs $(\hat{x}, \hat{z})$ for each combination $(x, z)$ of cell inputs. The entries in row $x_i$, column $z_j$ will be represented functionally as $\hat{x}(x_i, z_j), \hat{z}(x_i, z_j)$. Note that the variables are not necessarily binary and may represent combinations of binary variables.

*Testability*

In order for a fault to be detectable, it is necessary to be able to propagate the effect of the fault to some observable output (viz., the $\hat{z}$ output of some cell in the array or the $\hat{x}$ output of the last cell in the array).

# ONE-DIMENSIONAL ARRAYS

Two states $x_i$ and $x_j$ are defined as being *ultimately distinguishable* if there exists at least one combination of $z$ inputs to the array which causes some observable output to be different when $x_i$ and $x_j$ are applied to the first cell of an array of arbitrary size.

All pairs of ultimately-distinguishable states of a flow table can be found by constructing a pair-graph as follows: The nodes of the graph consist of all pairs of states. There is a directed edge from a node $(x_i, x_j)$ to a node $(x_m, x_n)$ if and only if there is some $z_k$ such that $\hat{x}(x_i, z_k) = x_m$ and $\hat{x}(x_j, z_k) = x_n$ or $\hat{x}(x_i, z_k) = x_n$ and $\hat{x}(x_j, z_k) = x_m$. Note that $m$ and $n$ need not be distinct from $i$ and $j$, but $i \neq j$ and $m \neq n$; that is, the pair-graph may contain nodes with self-loops. Any pair of states $(x_i, x_j)$ for which there exists some $z_k$ such that $\hat{z}(x_i, z_k) \neq \hat{z}(x_j, z_k)$ is ultimately distinguishable by definition. Any node which is in a closed loop (or has a self-loop) represents a pair of ultimately-distinguishable states. These states can be distinguished by observing the $\hat{x}$ output of the last cell of the array in response to the sequence of $z$ inputs defined by the loop and repeated as necessary, since the array is finite. If there is a directed path from some node in the pair-graph to a node representing an ultimately-distinguishable pair of states (determined by either of the conditions), then the first node and all the nodes along the path represent ultimately-distinguishable pairs of states. The entire pair-graph need not be constructed to determine if a particular pair of states is ultimately distinguishable. It is sufficient to construct only that part of the pair-graph which can be reached from the pair of states under consideration. The procedure can be terminated as soon as one node in the subgraph is found to represent an ultimately-distinguishable pair of states.

**Lemma 4.1:** *A test, $t_i$, for detecting a fault $f_i$ in an individual cell detects the same fault $f_i$ when the cell is part of a one-dimensional array if and only if the $\hat{z}$ output of the normal and faulty cells for $t_i$ are different or the $\hat{x}$ outputs of the normal and faulty cells for $t_i$ are ultimately distinguishable.* $t_i$ *is said to be* usable *for detecting the fault* $f_i$.

**Proof:** If the $\hat{z}$ outputs of the normal and faulty cells are different, obviously, the fault is detectable at this output. If the $\hat{x}$ outputs of the normal and faulty cells are ultimately distinguishable, there exists a combination of $z$ inputs which, when applied to the cells to the right of the cell being tested, causes some observable output to be different if the fault is present. In order to prove that one of these conditions is necessary, assume that for a fault $f_i$, and a test $t_i$, the $\hat{z}$ outputs of the normal and faulty cells are equal and the

$\hat{x}$ outputs are not ultimately distinguishable. Then when the cell is part of an array and $t_i$ is applied to that cell with fault $f_i$ all $\hat{z}$ outputs of the array are correct as is the rightmost border $\hat{x}$ output and the fault is not detected.

Thus a usable test is one for which the effect of the fault can be propagated to an observable output. In order for an array to be testable, it is also necessary to be able to apply a usable test to a cell for every fault in it, independent of the position of the cell in the array.

For any set $A$ of $x$ inputs (states) applicable to a cell, we denote the set of all obtainable $\hat{x}$ outputs by $N(A)$.

$$N(A) = \{x_i | x_i = \hat{x}(x_j, z_k), x_j \in A, z_k \in Z\}$$

where $Z$ is the set of $z$ inputs that may be applied to any cell. Also, $N^0(A) = A$ and $N^{k+1}(A) = N(N^k(A))$.

**Lemma 4.2:** *If* X *is the set of all* x *inputs (i.e., the set of labels of all rows of the flow table),* $N^k(X) \supseteq N^{k+1}(X)$ *for all* k $= 0, 1, 2, \ldots$.

**Proof:** For any two sets of $x$ inputs $A$ and $B$ such that $X \supseteq A \supseteq B$, it is clear from the definition of $N(A)$ and $N(B)$ that $N(A) \supseteq N(B)$. It also follows that $X \supseteq N(X)$. Therefore $N(X) \supseteq N(N(X)) = N^2(X)$. Lemma 4.2 follows by repeating the argument.

**Lemma 4.3:** *If* $N^{k+1}(X) = N^k(X)$ *for some* k, *then* $N^m(X) = N^k(X)$ *for all* m $>$ k.

**Proof:** Let the lemma be true for some $m > k$. $N^{m+1}(X) = N(N^m(X)) = N(N^k(X)) = N^{k+1}(X) = N^k(X)$; that is, the lemma is true for $m + 1$. Since $N^{k+1}(X) = N^k(X)$, the lemma is true for all $m > k$.

The following theorem gives the necessary and sufficient conditions for a one-dimensional array to be testable.

**Theorem 4.1:** *If all* x *inputs are applicable to the first cell of the array, a one dimensional array is testable for a given set of possible faults if and only if both of the following conditions are satisfied:* (1) *There is a usable test for detecting every possible fault in a cell.* (2) $N^{k+1}(X) = N^k(X) \supseteq T$ *for some integer* k, *where* T *is the set of* x *inputs contained in a complete set of usable tests for detecting all possible faults in a cell.*

# ONE-DIMENSIONAL ARRAYS

**Proof:** The necessity of the first condition follows from the fact that if there is no usable test for detecting a particular fault, the effects of that fault cannot be made to propagate to an observable output. The first condition is also sufficient to guarantee that if a usable test can be applied to a cell for every fault in a cell, the effect of the fault can be made to propagate to an observable output by a suitable choice of the $z$ inputs of the succeeding cells. From Lemmas 4.2 and 4.3, it follows that the second condition is necessary and sufficient to ensure that all $x$ inputs for a complete set of usable tests can be applied to any cell, independent of its location within the array. Thus the two conditions together satisfy the necessary and sufficient conditions for testability given earlier, as applied to one-dimensional arrays of arbitrary size.

Under the general-fault assumptions, $T = X$. All tests will be applicable to any cell in the array if and only if $N(X) = X$. Also, all pairs of states should be ultimately distinguishable. Thus, no two rows of the flow table can be identical. A one-dimensional array is testable under these assumptions if and only if every state appears in the flow table and no two rows of the flow table are alike. However, this is not necessary under the restricted-fault assumptions, as the following examples demonstrate.

**Example 4.1:** The flow table, realization and pair-graph of a cell of combinational logic are given in Fig. 4.2. The $x$-input states are coded using two variables, $x_1$ and $x_2$ as shown to the right of the flow table. The cells have no $\hat{z}$ output and the only observable output of the array is the $\hat{x}$ output of the last cell. State 2 does not appear in the table and therefore a one-dimensional array is not testable if all input combinations are required for testing any cell. If we restrict the faults that can occur in a cell to single inputs and outputs of gates being stuck at 0 or 1, we see that four tests $(x_1, x_2, z) = (0, 1, 0)$, $(1, 1, 0)$, $(0, 1, 1)$ and $(0, 0, 1)$ are sufficient for testing each cell. From the pair-graph we also see that all pairs of states are ultimately distinguishable because they lead to the loop containing $(0, 1)$ and $(1, 3)$. Thus any change in the $\hat{x}$ output of a cell can be made observable at the output of the last cell, and all tests are usable. Therefore $T = (00, 01, 11) = (0, 1, 3)$, the $x$ inputs of the aforementioned set of four tests for a cell. From the flow table, $N(X) = (0, 1, 3) = N^2(X) = T$. Thus all tests required for testing a cell are usable and by Lemma 4.3 can be applied independent of the position of the cell. Therefore any one-

|   | z |   | $x_1\ x_2$ |
|---|---|---|---|
|   | 0 | 1 |   |
| 0 | 0 | 1 | 0 0 |
| 1 | 0 | 3 | 0 1 |
| 2 | 1 | 1 | 1 0 |
| 3 | 1 | 3 | 1 1 |

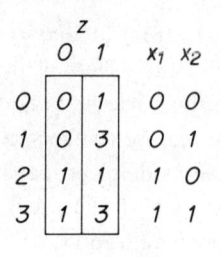

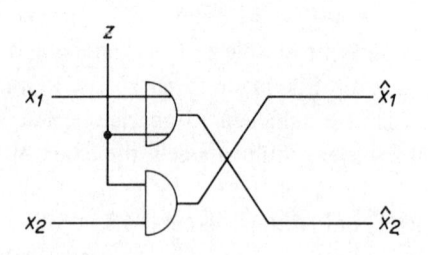

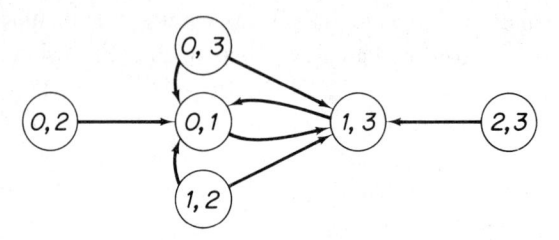

**Figure 4.2**

dimensional array of arbitrary size consisting of these cells is testable for the given set of faults.

**Example 4.2:** A one-dimensional array of cells whose flow table and pair-graph are shown in Fig. 4.3 is testable even though two rows of the flow table are identical.

|   | z |   | $x_1 x_2$ |
|---|---|---|---|
|   | 0 | 1 |   |
| 0 | 0 | 2 | 0 0 |
| 1 | 0 | 3 | 0 1 |
| 2 | 0 | 3 | 1 0 |
| 3 | 2 | 1 | 1 1 |

$\hat{x}_1 = \bar{x}_1 z + \bar{x}_2 z + x_1 x_2 \bar{z}$

$\hat{x}_2 = x_1 z + x_2 z.$

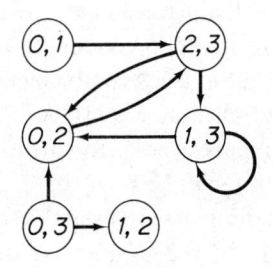

**Figure 4.3**

# ONE-DIMENSIONAL ARRAYS

If the logic in each cell is realized in a two-level sum-of-products form with no shared logic, a single fault at any input or the output of any gate in the realization will affect only $\hat{x}_1$ or $\hat{x}_2$, never both. From the pair-graph, it is clear that the only pair which is not ultimately distinguishable is the pair (1, 2). Since no fault can cause a 01 output to change to 10 or vice-versa, all tests for single faults in a cell are usable. Also

$$N(X) = (0, 1, 2, 3) = X,$$

that is, all inputs can be applied to any cell. Thus any arbitrary one-dimensional array of these cells is testable.

In the preceding discussion, we assumed that there were no restrictions on the $x$ inputs that may be applied to the first cell of an array. If the applicable inputs are restricted to a subset $X'$ of the set $X$ of all $x$ inputs, Theorem 4.1 must be modified so that a complete set of usable tests is applicable to every cell in the array. In this case, it may be necessary to apply different test sets to different cells.

In order for a complete set of tests to be applicable to the first cell, it is necessary that $X' \supseteq T$. Three different cases should be considered, depending upon the set $N(X')$.

1. If $X' \supseteq N(X')$, Theorem 4.1 is applicable as stated.
2. If $N(X') \supseteq X'$, $X' \supseteq T$ is clearly sufficient to ensure that all tests contained in $T$ can be applied to any cell in the array.
3. If $X'$ and $N(X')$ are not comparable, (i.e., $X' \not\supseteq N(X')$ and $N(X') \not\supseteq X'$), the following procedure is used to determine whether a complete set of usable tests can be applied to every cell in the array. We compute $N^i(X')$ for $i = 1, 2, 3, \ldots, k$, until $N^j(X') = N^k(X')$ for some $j$ and $k > j$. Since the flow table has a finite number of states, this condition will be satisfied for finite values of $j$ and $k$. It is clear from the definition of $N(X')$ that all $x$ inputs applicable to any cell will be contained in some $N^i(X')$, $i < k$. If $T_i$, $i = 1, 2, \ldots, m$ are the $x$ inputs of sets of usable tests for all faults in a cell, then $N^i(X') \supseteq T_p$ for $i = 1, 2, \ldots, k-1$ and any $p$, $1 \leq p \leq m$, is necessary and sufficient for the array to be testable using the $x$ inputs contained in $X'$.

**Example 4.3:** Consider the flow table of Fig. 4.3. Let us assume that each cell can be tested completely by either the test set $T_1 = (0, 1, 2)$

or $T_2 = (0, 2, 3)$. Let the $x$ inputs applicable to the leftmost cell of the array be restricted to (0, 1, 2).

$$X' = (0, 1, 2)$$

$$N(X') = (0, 2, 3)$$

$$N^2(X') = N^3(X') = (0, 1, 2, 3).$$

An array of such cells is testable with this restriction on the left boundary inputs. The first two cells are tested by the test sets $T_1$ and $T_2$ respectively and all other cells are tested by either test set.

*Derivation of Tests*

So far, we have only discussed the problem of determining if a given one-dimensional array is testable. We will now consider the derivation of efficient sets of tests from the flow table of a cell for the class of arrays constructed with this basic cell.

In order to test a cell $C_i$ in a one-dimensional array for a fault $\alpha$, the inputs to the cell should be set to values corresponding to a test for $\alpha$ and the $z$ inputs of the succeeding cells may have to be set to certain values to ensure propagation of the effect of the fault to an observable output. If the cell satisfies the conditions for testability discussed earlier, $x$ inputs to the leftmost cell and $z$ inputs to all cells in the array can simultaneously be set to satisfy both of the above conditions so as to test for any fault in any cell of the array. However, more efficient sets of tests can be found if faults in several cells in the array can be tested simultaneously. Tests should be chosen so that the conditions for propagation of the effect of a fault through a cell also test for some fault in the cell itself.

A graph similar to the pair-graph used to determine ultimately-distinguishable pairs of states is useful in deriving efficient tests. We shall refer to such a graph as a *testing graph*. We first consider the case where the cells do not have $\hat{z}$ outputs and then modify our procedure to the general case.

The construction of the testing graph of a given circuit and a given set of faults begins by deriving the complete set of tests and assigning a node of the graph to the $x$ input of each test. If $(x_i, z_i)$ is a test for a fault (or a set of faults) $\alpha$, and the normal and faulty $\hat{x}$ outputs of the cell with this test applied are $x_j$ and $x_k$ respectively, we represent this in the testing graph by

ONE-DIMENSIONAL ARRAYS

a directed edge labeled $z_i(\alpha)$ from the node $x_i$ to a node labeled with the ordered pair $(x_j, x_k)$. This procedure is repeated for all tests in the test set. For every node $(x_i, x_j)$ in the graph we draw an edge labeled $z_i$ to a node $(x_k, x_s)$, if and only if $\hat{x}(x_i, z_i) = x_k$, $\hat{x}(x_j, z_i) = x_s$ and $x_k \neq x_s$. Fault labels may be added to these edges as follows: If there is an edge labeled $z_i(\alpha)$ from a node $x_i$ to a node $(x_j, x_k)$, then the fault label $\alpha$ may be added to any edge labeled $z_i$ from a node $(x_i, x_q)$ to the node $(x_j, x_k)$ for any $x_q$. The validity of this operation follows from the fact that while applying an input $z_i$ to propagate an $x_i \longrightarrow x_q$ change through a cell, we are also applying the test $(x_i, z_i)$ for the fault $\alpha$ to it (if the cells to its left are fault free). Since the normal and faulty outputs for this test and fault are $(x_j, x_k)$ and $x_j = \hat{x}(x_i, z_i)$, $x_k = \hat{x}(x_q, z_i)$, the conditions for propagation through the next cell are the same. We are therefore justified in adding the fault label $\alpha$ to the edge from $(x_i, x_q)$ to $(x_j, x_k)$.

When the construction of the testing graph is complete, the following property of the graph can be used for deriving efficient sets of tests for testing an array of arbitrary size: If the graph contains a loop with $n$ nodes, all cells in the array can be tested for faults associated with the edge labels of the loop by exactly $n$ tests, independent of the number of cells in the array. If the array has $p$ cells and there is a connected chain of $k$ nodes leading to a loop in the graph, $p + k - 1$ tests are sufficient to test all cells in the array for faults contained in the edge labels of the chain. An efficient set of fault-detection tests can be obtained by finding loops in the testing graph such that the edge labels cover the largest number of faults and the total number of nodes in the loops is minimum.

**Example 4.4:** The circuit of Fig. 4.2 and its flow table are repeated in Fig. 4.4 with the interconnections suitably labeled. The faults to be detected and the tests for detecting them are listed in Table 4.1, where the subscripts of the wire labels indicate whether the fault causes

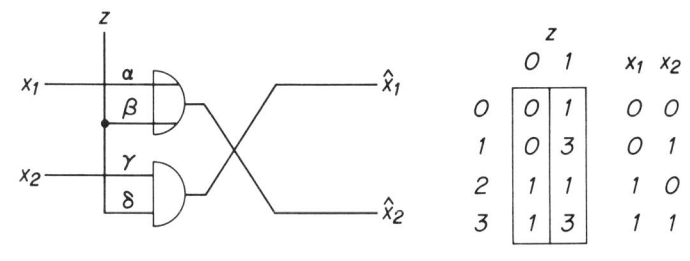

|   | z=0 | z=1 |   | $x_1 x_2$ |
|---|---|---|---|---|
| 0 | 0 | 1 |   | 0 0 |
| 1 | 0 | 3 |   | 0 1 |
| 2 | 1 | 1 |   | 1 0 |
| 3 | 1 | 3 |   | 1 1 |

Figure 4.4

the wire to be stuck at 0 or 1. The outputs of the normal and faulty cell for each test are also given.

| Fault | Test $x_1$ $x_2$ $z$ | Normal $\hat{x}_1$ $\hat{x}_2$ | Faulty $\hat{x}_1$ $\hat{x}_2$ |
|---|---|---|---|
| $\alpha_0$ | 1 0 0 | 0 1 | 0 0 |
|  | 1 1 0 | 0 1 | 0 0 |
| $\beta_0$ | 0 0 1 | 0 1 | 0 0 |
|  | 0 1 1 | 1 1 | 1 0 |
| $\gamma_0, \delta_0$ | 0 1 1 | 1 1 | 0 1 |
|  | 1 1 1 | 1 1 | 0 1 |
| $\alpha_1, \beta_1$ | 0 0 0 | 0 0 | 0 1 |
|  | 0 1 0 | 0 0 | 0 1 |
| $\gamma_1$ | 0 0 1 | 0 1 | 1 1 |
|  | 1 0 1 | 0 1 | 1 1 |
| $\delta_1$ | 0 1 0 | 0 0 | 1 0 |
|  | 1 1 0 | 0 1 | 1 1 |

**Table 4.1**

In the pair-graph of Fig. 4.5, fault labels added according to the rule discussed above are underlined. Since only edges emanating from nodes with single state labels are initially labeled with faults, note that all fault labels on edges from nodes labeled with pairs of states, and

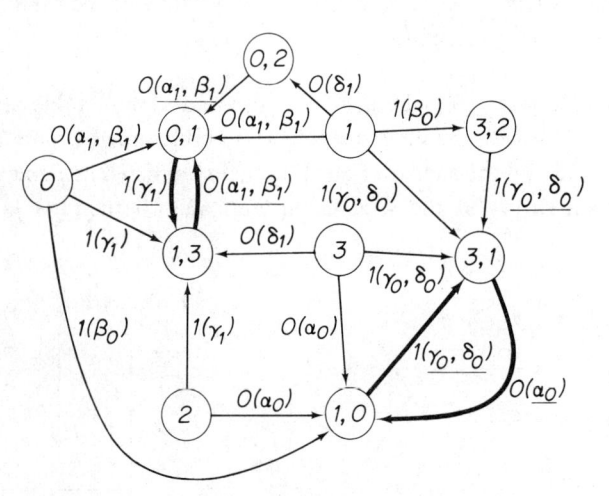

**Figure 4.5**

# ONE-DIMENSIONAL ARRAYS

only these, will be underlined. The pair-graph contains two loops with two nodes each (shown in heavy lines), whose labels cover all faults except $\beta_0$ and $\delta_1$. Thus four tests are sufficient for testing for all faults except these two. If the array has $p$ cells, $2p$ tests are necessary for testing for $\beta_0$ and $\delta_1$ in all cells. A $p$-cell array can be tested for all faults considered by $(2p + 4)$ tests, which in this case can be shown to be optimum. The four tests which test all cells simultaneously for some fault in the list are:

$$x^{(1)} \quad z^{(1)} \quad z^{(2)} \quad z^{(3)} \quad z^{(4)} \ldots$$

$$\begin{array}{cc} x_1 & x_2 \end{array}$$

$$\left.\begin{array}{cccccc} 0 & 0 & 1 & 0 & 1 & 0 \ldots \\ 0 & 1 & 0 & 1 & 0 & 1 \ldots \end{array}\right\} \text{Loop } (0, 1) \xrightarrow{1} (1, 3) \xrightarrow{0} (0, 1)$$

$$\left.\begin{array}{cccccc} 0 & 1 & 1 & 0 & 1 & 0 \ldots \\ 1 & 1 & 0 & 1 & 0 & 1 \ldots \end{array}\right\} \text{Loop } (1, 0) \xrightarrow{1} (3, 1) \xrightarrow{0} (1, 0)$$

Here, the superscripts refer to the positions of the cells in the array.

When the cells in the array have $\hat{z}$ outputs, the testing graph can be modified to take advantage of them. If for a test $(x_i, z_i)$ for a fault $\alpha$, the $\hat{z}$ outputs of the normal and faulty cells are different, there is no need to propagate the effects of the fault to the next cell. However, we would like to apply some test to the succeeding cells at the same time. If $\hat{x}(x_i, z_i) = x_j$, a directed edge labeled $z_i(\alpha)$ is drawn from the node $x_i$ to the node $x_j$ in the testing graph, indicating that any test $(x_j, z_k)$ may be applied simultaneously to the next cell. From every node in the graph labeled with a single state $x_i$, a directed edge labeled $z_j$ to a node $x_k$ is added if and only if $\hat{x}(x_i, z_j) = x_k$. If the graph contains a node labeled $(x_i, x_j)$, and $\hat{z}(x_i, z_k) \neq \hat{z}(x_j, z_k)$ and $\hat{x}(x_i, z_k) = x_m$, then an edge labeled $z_k$ is drawn from $(x_i, x_j)$ to $x_m$. This is because an $x_i \rightarrow x_j$ (where $x_i$ is the $\hat{x}$ output of a fault-free cell) change need not be propagated any further, and we may apply any test $(x_m, z_n)$ to the next cell.

Fault labels can be added to edges as in the case of iterative arrays without $\hat{z}$-outputs. Furthermore, if the graph contains an edge labeled $z_i(\alpha)$ from a node $x_i$ to a node $x_j$, this implies that the test $(x_i, z_i)$ detects the fault $\alpha$ by producing an incorrect $\hat{z}$ output and that the normal $\hat{x}$ output of the cell is $x_j$. Therefore, using an argument similar to the case without $\hat{z}$ outputs, the fault $\alpha$ may be added to the label of any edge labeled $z_i$ from $(x_i, x_k)$ to $(x_j, x_s)$, $x_i$ to $(x_j, x_s)$ or $(x_i, x_k)$ to $x_j$. Efficient test sets can be obtained as before, by selecting tests contained in loops, whenever possible.

## Example 4.5

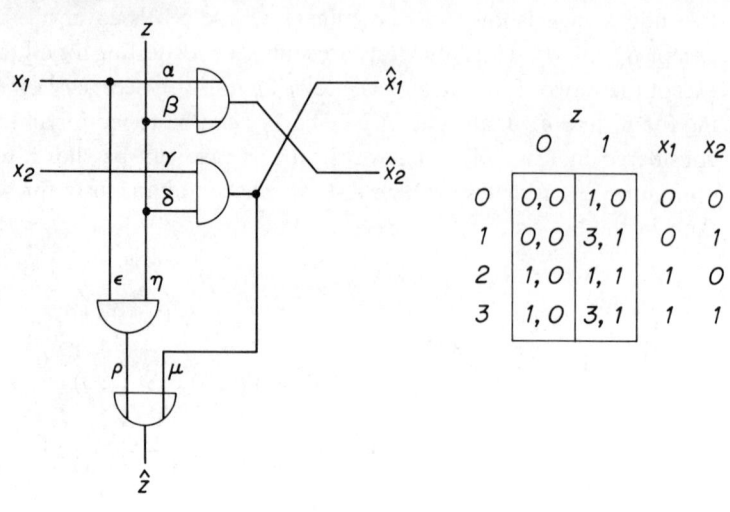

**Figure 4.6**

Figure 4.6 shows the circuit and flow table of a cell similar to that in Fig. 4.4 with an output $\hat{z} = x_1 z + x_2 z$ added. Considering the same set of faults as in Example 4.4, the complete set of tests is shown in Table 4.2, together with the normal and faulty cell outputs. The testing graph of Fig. 4.7 is constructed from Table 4.2. Fault labels which have been added have been underlined. From the graph

| Fault | Test $x_1\ x_2\ z\ \ (x,z)$ | Outputs Normal $\hat{x}_1\ \hat{x}_2\ \hat{z}\ \ (\hat{x},\hat{z})$ | Outputs Faulty $\hat{x}_1\ \hat{x}_2\ \hat{z}\ \ (\hat{x},\hat{z})$ | Detected at |
|---|---|---|---|---|
| $\alpha_0$ | 1 0 0 (2,0) | 0 1 0 (1,0) | 0 0 0 (0,0) | $\hat{x}$ |
|  | 1 1 0 (3,0) | 0 1 0 (1,0) | 0 0 0 (0,0) | $\hat{x}$ |
| $\beta_0$ | 0 0 1 (0,1) | 0 1 0 (1,0) | 0 0 0 (0,0) | $\hat{x}$ |
|  | 0 1 1 (1,1) | 1 1 1 (3,1) | 1 0 1 (2,1) | $\hat{x}$ |
| $\gamma_0, \delta_0$ | 0 1 1 (1,1) | 1 1 1 (3,1) | 0 1 0 (1,0) | $\hat{x}$ and $\hat{z}$ |
|  | 1 1 1 (3,1) | 1 1 1 (3,1) | 0 1 1 (1,1) | $\hat{x}$ |
| $\alpha_1, \beta_1$ | 0 0 0 (0,0) | 0 0 0 (0,0) | 0 1 0 (1,0) | $\hat{x}$ |
|  | 0 1 0 (1,0) | 0 0 0 (0,0) | 0 1 0 (1,0) | $\hat{x}$ |
| $\gamma_1$ | 0 0 1 (0,1) | 0 1 0 (1,0) | 1 1 1 (3,1) | $\hat{x}$ and $\hat{z}$ |
|  | 1 0 1 (2,1) | 0 1 1 (1,1) | 1 1 1 (3,1) | $\hat{x}$ |
| $\delta_1$ | 0 1 0 (1,0) | 0 0 0 (0,0) | 1 0 1 (2,1) | $\hat{x}$ and $\hat{z}$ |
|  | 1 1 0 (3,0) | 0 1 0 (1,0) | 1 1 1 (3,1) | $\hat{x}$ and $\hat{z}$ |

**Table 4.2**

# ONE-DIMENSIONAL ARRAYS

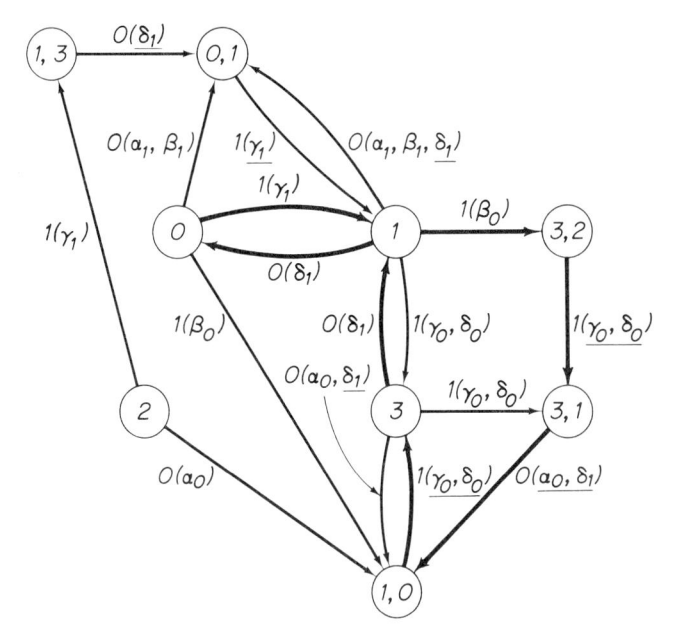

**Figure 4.7**

we see that the two loops $(1) \xrightarrow{0} (0, 1) \xrightarrow{1} (1)$, and $(1) \xrightarrow{1} (3, 2) \xrightarrow{1} (3, 1) \xrightarrow{0} (1, 0) \xrightarrow{1} (3) \xrightarrow{0} (1)$ cover all faults of the given set. Therefore, an array of arbitrary size can be tested for the given set of faults by the following eight tests:

```
x(1)    z(1) z(2) z(3) z(4) z(5) z(6) z(7) z(8) z(9) z(10)
x1 x2
0  1  0   1   0   1   0   1   0   1   0   1 ...  ⎫ Loop
0  0  1   0   1   0   1   0   1   0   1   0 ...  ⎬ (1) —0→ (0, 1)
                                                  ⎭  —1→ (1)
0  1  1   1   0   1   0   1   1   0   1   0 ...  ⎫ Loop
1  1  1   0   1   0   1   1   0   1   0   1 ...  ⎪ (1) —1→ (3, 2)
1  1  0   1   0   1   1   0   1   0   1   1 ...  ⎬ —1→ (3, 1) —0→
0  1  1   0   1   1   0   1   0   1   1   0 ...  ⎪ (1, 0) —1→ (3)
1  1  0   1   1   0   1   0   1   1   0   1 ...  ⎭ —1→ (1).
```

*Bounds on the Number of Tests*

It is possible to derive some bounds on the number of tests required for a one-dimensional array. Let $M$ and $N$ be the number of columns and rows respectively in the flow table describing the basic cell. In the worst case, $MN$

tests are necessary to test each cell, individually. For each test applied to a cell, there are $(N-1)$ possible incorrect $\hat{x}$ outputs, each of which may require a different combination of $z$ inputs on the cells to its right in order to propagate the effect to the right-hand boundary. Thus the number of tests required to test each cell in the array except the rightmost is $MN(N-1)$. The rightmost cell in the array requires only $MN$ tests because all its outputs are observable. Therefore, assuming that no overlapping of tests is possible, an upper bound on the number of tests required to completely test a one-dimensional array of $p$ cells is:

$$(p-1)MN(N-1) + MN < pMN^2$$

If no column of the flow table of a cell contains two or more identical entries, it follows that any change in the $x$ input of the cell will produce a change in the $\hat{x}$ or $\hat{z}$ output of the cell, independent of what the $z$ input is. This implies that any change in a cell output will become observable sooner or later and no special assignment of $z$ inputs is necessary for propagation. This reduces the upper bound on the number of tests to $pMN$. Further, if each $x$ state appears in the table exactly $M$ times, then the array can be tested with $MN$ tests, independent of $p$, since it is possible to overlap tests (Kautz, 1967).

*Location of Faults*

If the cells have $\hat{z}$ outputs a fault can be located to within one cell position of the faulty cell under the general-fault assumptions, if a complete set of tests can be applied to every cell in the array, and every pair of states in a basic cell have different $\hat{z}$ outputs in some column (Kautz, 1967). If $\hat{z}(x_i, z_k) \neq \hat{z}(x_j, z_k)$ and a fault in the $p^{th}$ cell causes its $\hat{x}$ output to be $x_j$ instead of $x_i$, then the $(p+1)^{st}$ cell can be made to produce an incorrect $\hat{z}$ output by applying $z_k$ to it. However, the same incorrect output can also be produced if the $p^{th}$ cell is normal and the $(p+1)^{st}$ cell is faulty. Thus the condition is sufficient for locating the fault to within one cell position of the faulty cell. Under the restricted-fault assumptions, better fault location may be possible, sometimes even in the absence of $\hat{z}$ outputs.

Let $t_i = (x_i, z_i)$ be a test for detecting a fault $f_i$ in a single cell. An input combination $m(t_i, f_i) = (x_m, z_m)$ is defined to be a *masking input* for the test $t_i$ and fault $f_i$ if the outputs of the normal and faulty cells with the masking input applied are the same as the output of the normal cell with the

ONE-DIMENSIONAL ARRAYS

test applied. That is,

$$\hat{x}_{f_i}(x_m, z_m) = \hat{x}(x_m, z_m) = \hat{x}(x_i, z_i),$$

where $\hat{x}_{f_i}$ is the $\hat{x}$ output of a cell containing the fault $f_i$.

A usable test $t_i$ for detecting a fault $f_i$ is defined to be *usable for locating* $f_i$ if there exists a masking input $m(t_i, f_i)$. Note that a particular test may be usable for locating more than one fault and that there may be more than one masking input associated with a test.

***Theorem 4.2:*** *The faulty cell in a one-dimensional array can be located if there exist a set of tests* T *and a corresponding set of masking inputs* M *such that for every allowable fault* $f_i$, *there is a test* $t_i \in$ T *which detects* $f_i$ *and a masking input* $m(t_i, f_i) \in$ M, *and* $N^k(X) = N^{k+1}(X) \supseteq T \cup M$, *for some k.*

**Proof:** $N^k(X) = N^{k+1}(X) \supseteq T \cup M$ implies that a set of usable tests for locating all faults and their masking inputs can be applied to any cell in the array. We show the sufficiency of the two conditions by demonstrating how the faulty cell can be located.

Let us assume that the application of a test $t_i$ indicated that there is a faulty cell in the array and that one of the faults which could have produced the observed response is $f_i$ in the first cell. We now change the cell inputs to the first cell *only* to a masking input $m(t_i, f_i)$ which, by definition, guarantees the $\hat{x}$ output of the first cell to be correct if the fault is $f_i$ or if it is normal. If the observed output is now correct, this implies that the $\hat{x}$ output of the first cell changed, because the inputs to the second cell onwards are kept unchanged when the masking inputs were applied to the first cell. Hence the first cell must be faulty. If the observed output with the masking inputs applied to the first cell is incorrect, then the fault $f_i$ is not present in the first cell.

If the observed incorrect output could have been produced by any other faults in the first cell, it will be necessary to apply the respective masking inputs for each of these faults. We can conclude that the first cell is faulty if the correct output is observed for at least one masking input. If all masking inputs produce incorrect outputs, the fault is not in the first cell, because the appropriate masking input insures a correct $\hat{x}$ output from the first cell and the single-fault assumption guarantees correct operation of the rest of the array. Note that we may not be able to determine which fault is present in the first cell even if we can establish that it is faulty.

If the first cell is not faulty, the second cell can be checked in a similar manner by applying masking inputs to it and keeping the $z$ inputs to the succeeding cells unchanged. Since the first cell has been proven to be fault free, masking inputs can be applied to the second cell. The same procedure is repeated for all succeeding cells until the faulty cell is located. This procedure does not require the cells to have $\hat{z}$ outputs.

**Example 4.6:** The flow table and a realization of the exclusive-OR function are shown in Fig. 4.8.

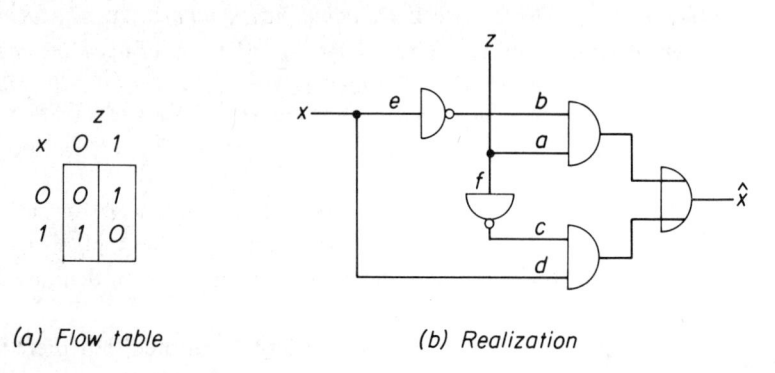

(a) Flow table

(b) Realization

**Figure 4.8**

| Fault | | Test | | Mask | |
|---|---|---|---|---|---|
| Wire | Stuck at | $x$ | $z$ | $x$ | $z$ |
| $a$ | 0 | 0 | 1 | 1 | 0 |
| $b$ | 0 | 0 | 1 | 1 | 0 |
| $c$ | 0 | 1 | 0 | 0 | 1 |
| $d$ | 0 | 1 | 0 | 0 | 1 |
| $e$ | 0 | 1 | 1 | 0 | 0 |
| $f$ | 0 | 1 | 1 | 0 | 0 |
| $a$ | 1 | 0 | 0 | 1 | 1 |
| $b$ | 1 | 1 | 1 | 0 | 0 |
| $c$ | 1 | 1 | 1 | 0 | 0 |
| $d$ | 1 | 0 | 0 | 1 | 1 |
| $e$ | 1 | 0 | 1 | 1 | 0 |
| $f$ | 1 | 1 | 0 | 0 | 1 |

**Table 4.3**

If the set of faults is restricted to s-a-0 and s-a-1 at gate inputs (except the inputs to the OR gate), the set of tests and masks shown in Table 4.3 are obtained.

# ONE-DIMENSIONAL ARRAYS

$$X = \{0, 1\}$$

$$T = M = X = N^k(X) \quad \text{for all } k.$$

The faulty cell in the array can therefore be located by observing the output of the last cell. If the output (or any input) of the OR gate in any cell may also be stuck at zero or one, the faulty cell cannot be located using the method given in the proof of Theorem 4.2, because there are no masking inputs for these faults.

Since masking inputs may not exist for all possible faults in a cell, it is useful to extend the above results to permit fault location to blocks of two or more cells, when location of the faulty cell itself is impossible. Let us denote the $\hat{x}$ output of a block of $p$ cells with input $x_i$ applied to the leftmost cell and $z$ inputs $z_{j1}, z_{j2}, \ldots, z_{jp}$ by $\hat{x}^p(x_i, \mathbf{z}_j)$.

$$\hat{x}^p(x_i, \mathbf{z}_j) = \hat{x}(\hat{x}(\ldots (\hat{x}(x_i, z_{j1}), z_{j2}) \ldots), z_{jp})$$

where $\mathbf{z}_j = z_{j1}, z_{j2}, \ldots, z_{jp}$. Let $t_i = (x_i, z_{i1})$ be a test for detecting a fault $f_i$ in a cell and let $z_{i2}, z_{i3}, \ldots, z_{ip}$ be the inputs to the following $p - 1$ cells so that the effect of the fault is propagated to the $\hat{x}$ output of the $p^{\text{th}}$ cell. An input combination $m(t_i, f_i) = (x_m, \mathbf{z}_m)$, where $\mathbf{z}_m = z_{m1}, z_{m2}, \ldots, z_{mp}$ is said to be a *masking input of degree* p for the test $t_i$ and fault $f_i$ if the $\hat{x}$ outputs of the normal and faulty $p$-cell block with $(x_m, \mathbf{z}_m)$ applied are the same as the output of the normal $p$-cell block with $(x_i, \mathbf{z}_i)$ applied. That is,

$$\hat{x}^p_{f_i}(x_m, \mathbf{z}_m) = \hat{x}^p(x_m, \mathbf{z}_m) = \hat{x}^p(x_i, \mathbf{z}_i),$$

where the subscript $f_i$ denotes the presence of the fault $f_i$ and $\mathbf{z}_i = z_{i1}, z_{i2}, \ldots, z_{ip}$. The masking input defined earlier may be considered to be a masking input of degree 1.

All faults in a one-dimensional array can be located to a block of $p$ cells if for every fault there exists a usable test and a masking input of degree $p$ that can be applied to every cell in the array. The procedure for locating the faulty block of $p$ cells is similar to that outlined in the proof of Theorem 4.2. Under the general fault assumptions, fault location to a $p$-cell block is possible in a one-dimensional array without $\hat{z}$ outputs, if the array is testable and for every pair of states $(x_i, x_j)$ there exist input combinations $\mathbf{z}_k = z_{k1}, z_{k2}, \ldots z_{k, p-1}$ and $\mathbf{z}_m = z_{m1}, z_{m2}, \ldots, z_{m, p-1}$ such that

$$\hat{x}^{p-1}(x_i, \mathbf{z}_m) = \hat{x}^{p-1}(x_j, \mathbf{z}_m) = \hat{x}^{p-1}(x_i, \mathbf{z}_k) \neq \hat{x}^{p-1}(x_j, \mathbf{z}_k).$$

The masking input concept can be further generalized to give necessary and sufficient conditions for fault location. The following theorem gives necessary and sufficient conditions for locating a fault in a one-dimensional array without $\hat{z}$ outputs, to a two-cell block. These conditions may be generalized for fault location to $p$-cell blocks, $p > 2$.

**Theorem 4.3:** *A fault which causes a cell to realize a function $\hat{x}'(x, z)$ instead of $\hat{x}(x, z)$ can be located to a two-cell block if and only if the fault is detectable and there exist two input combinations $(x_1, z_1, z_2)$ and $(x'_1, z'_1, z'_2)$ such that*
(1) $\hat{x}(\hat{x}'(x_1, z_1), z_2) = x_k$
    $\hat{x}(\hat{x}'(x'_1, z'_1), z'_2) = x'_k \neq x_k$
(2) $x_k$ *and* $x'_k$ *are ultimately distinguishable.*
(3) $\hat{x}(\hat{x}(x_1, z_1), z_2) = \hat{x}(\hat{x}(x'_1, z'_1), z'_2) = x_m.$

**Proof:** Consider a block of three cells and let the first cell be faulty, realizing $\hat{x}'$ instead of $\hat{x}$. This fault will be indistinguishable from some fault in the third cell which causes it to realize $\hat{x}''$ instead of $\hat{x}$, if and only if

$$\hat{x}''(\hat{x}(\hat{x}(x_1, z_1), z_2), z_3) = \hat{x}(\hat{x}(\hat{x}'(x_1, z_1), z_2), z_3)$$

for all $x_1, z_1, z_2, z_3$. Let $z_p$ be an input to the third cell that will cause a $x_k \rightarrow x'_k$ change in its $x$ input to propagate to the right-hand boundary. Thus $\hat{x}(x_k, z_p) \neq \hat{x}(x'_k, z_p)$. If the first cell realizes $\hat{x}'$ instead of $\hat{x}$, application of $(x_1, z_1, z_2, z_p)$ will produce an output that is different from the output produced by $(x'_1, z'_1, z'_2, z_p)$. If the first cell is not faulty but the third cell realizes $\hat{x}''$ instead of $\hat{x}$, $\hat{x}''(\hat{x}(\hat{x}(x_1, z_1), z_2), z_3) = \hat{x}''(\hat{x}(\hat{x}(x'_1, z'_1), z'_2), z_3)$ for all $z_3$ and the output at the right-hand boundary will be the same, proving the sufficiency of the conditions of Theorem 4.3.

To prove the necessity of these conditions, we show how $x''$ can be defined so as to make the faults in the first and third cells indistinguishable if any condition is not satisfied. If condition (3) is not satisfied for some pair of input combinations, i.e., $x(x(x_1, z_1), z_2) = x_m$ and $x(x(x'_1, z'_1), z'_2) = x'_m \neq x_m$, we define $x''(x_m, z_j) = x(x_k, z_j)$ and $x''(x'_m, z_j) = x(x'_k, z_j)$ for all $z_j$, whether or not conditions (1) and (2) are satisfied. Satisfaction of condition (2) implies satisfaction of condition (1). If condition (2) is not satisfied, but condition (3) is, we define $x''(x_m, z_j) = x(x_k, z_j)$ or $x(x'_k, z_j)$ for all $z_j$. With $x''$ defined in this way, the two faults are indistinguishable and the fault is not locatable to a two-cell block.

Satisfaction of the conditions of Theorem 4.3 for all faulty $\hat{x}$ functions

## TWO-DIMENSIONAL ARRAYS

is necessary and sufficient for locating a faulty two-cell block in the absence of $\hat{z}$ outputs, under the general fault assumptions. Theorem 4.3 also leads to the following simpler sufficient conditions for fault location to a two-cell block, under the general fault assumptions: All states appear as next-state entries in the flow table and for every pair of states $(x_i, x_j)$ there exist inputs $z_k, z'_k$ and $z_m, z'_m$ such that

$$\hat{x}(x_i, z_k) = \hat{x}(x_i, z'_k); \hat{x}(x_j, z_k) \neq \hat{x}(x_j, z'_k) \quad \text{and}$$

$$\hat{x}(x_i, z_m) \neq \hat{x}(x_i, z'_m); \hat{x}(x_j, z_m) = \hat{x}(x_j, z'_m).$$

## TWO-DIMENSIONAL ARRAYS

We shall restrict our attention to two-dimensional arrays with signal flow from left to right and top to bottom. The notation to be used is similar to that in the one-dimensional case and is shown in Fig. 4.9. A cell in the array will be identified by a pair of coordinates specifying its location. Thus, $C_{ij}$ refers to the cell in the $i^{\text{th}}$ row and $j^{\text{th}}$ column.

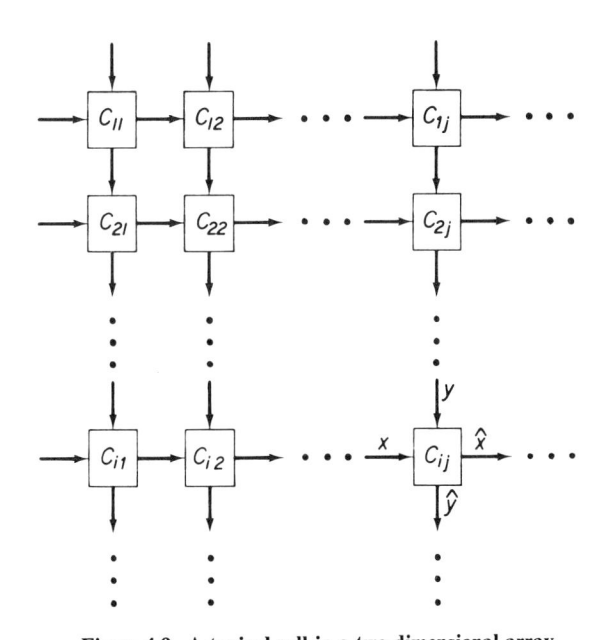

Figure 4.9. A typical cell in a two-dimensional array.

## Application of Cell Inputs

As discussed earlier, a complete set of tests for detecting all faults in a cell should be applied to each cell independent of its position in the array. The problem of determining the inputs applicable to an arbitrary cell in the array is a difficult one and may even be undecidable in the general case.

Kautz (1967) has pointed out the similarity between the problem of determining whether all cell inputs are applicable to every cell in the array and the "domino problem," which can be stated as follows: Given a set of square dominos, identified by the colors on the four edges, can the infinite plane be covered with dominoes of the given types (preserving their orientation) so that facing edges of all dominoes agree in color? Wang (1963) has shown that the general domino problem is undecidable; i.e., there are no finite algorithms to determine whether such a covering exists. The correspondence between an iterative array and a plane covered with dominoes is established by treating the $x$ and $y$ inputs and $\hat{x}$ and $\hat{y}$ outputs as the colors on the four edges of a square domino. The problem of determining whether all input states are applicable is different from the domino problem in two respects. First, the former requires that each domino type be usable in any arbitrary position of a quadrant of the infinite plane. The second difference is that in the iterative array problem, all possible combinations of $x$ and $y$ inputs (colors on the top and left edges) are known to occur in the set of domino types (assuming that all cell input combinations are allowable; i.e., the flow table is completely specified). It is not known whether these differences make the problem decidable.

Despite the uncertainty of this question, the testability of many classes of arrays is decidable. Since there are no known algorithms for determining the set of inputs applicable to all cells in a two-dimensional array, *supersets** and *subsets* of this set are often useful in determining whether an array is testable. The derivation of subsets of applicable inputs, which we shall now discuss, provides us a means for constructing tests for certain arrays.

A *tessellation* of an array is defined as a specification of cell states which are compatible with one another along cell interfaces for the entire array.

In a *diagonal tessellation*, the cells along a diagonal of the array are all

---

*If $S_1$, $S_2$ and $S$ are sets such that $S_1 \supseteq S \supseteq S_2$, we shall refer to $S_1$ as a superset of $S$ and $S_2$ as a subset of $S$.

## TWO-DIMENSIONAL ARRAYS

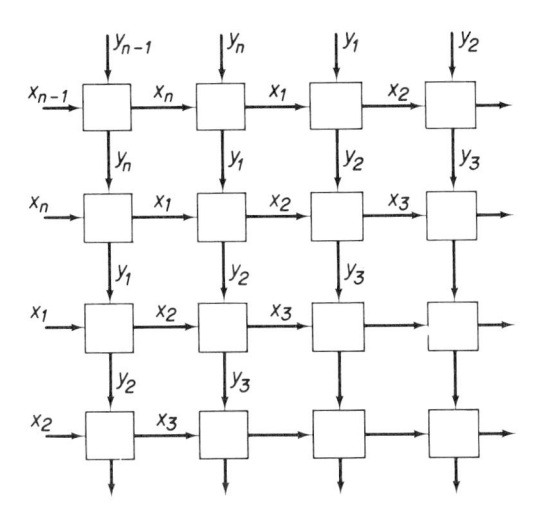

Figure 4.10. Example of a +45° diagonal tessellation.

in the same state, and the states of all adjacent diagonals are compatible. In Fig. 4.10, all cells on a +45° diagonal have identical inputs. Such a tessellation is referred to as a +45° tessellation. In order to satisfy the compatibility of adjacent diagonals, we require:

$$x_2 = \hat{x}(x_1, y_1); \; y_2 = \hat{y}(x_1, y_1); \; x_3 = \hat{x}(x_2, y_2); \; y_3 = \hat{y}(x_2, y_2); \; \ldots .$$

All cell input states contained in a +45° diagonal tessellation can be applied to all cells in an array. The input states for such tessellations can be determined from a successor graph constructed as follows: There is a node in the graph for every cell input state $(x_i, y_j)$. A directed edge is drawn from node $(x_i, y_j)$ to node $(x_k, y_m)$ if and only if $x_k = \hat{x}(x_i, y_j)$ and $y_m = \hat{y}(x_i, y_j)$. An input state $(x_i, y_j)$ can be in a +45° diagonal tessellation if and only if it is contained in a loop (or a self-loop) in the successor graph. If a loop contains $n$ nodes, all input states contained in the loop can be applied to all cells in the array by applying each of the $n$ states to the (1, 1) cell (top left hand corner) and applying the succeeding states in the loop to successive diagonals until the entire array is covered.

Cell-input states which are not applicable by +45° diagonal tessellations of cells can sometimes be applicable in similar tessellations of blocks of two or more cells. For instance, two cells where the $\hat{x}$ output of the first cell is connected to the x input of the second cell may be treated as a block. In fact, any sub-array of cells may be treated as a block, but the analysis becomes more tedious as the size of the sub-array increases.

## Example 4.7

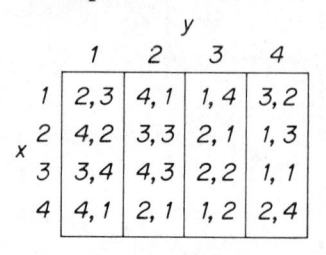

|   | y |   |   |   |
|---|---|---|---|---|
|   | 1 | 2 | 3 | 4 |
| 1 | 2,3 | 4,1 | 1,4 | 3,2 |
| x 2 | 4,2 | 3,3 | 2,1 | 1,3 |
| 3 | 3,4 | 4,3 | 2,2 | 1,1 |
| 4 | 4,1 | 2,1 | 1,2 | 2,4 |

(a) Flow table

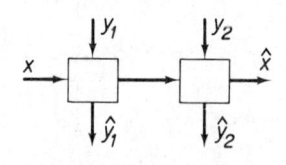

(b) Successor graph

(c) A two-cell block

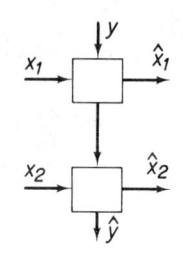

(d) Another two-cell block

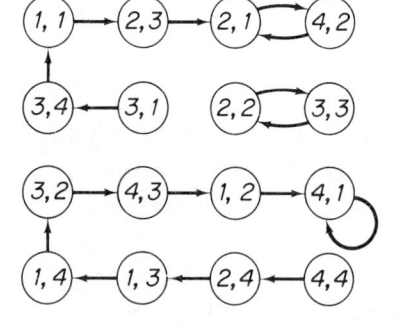

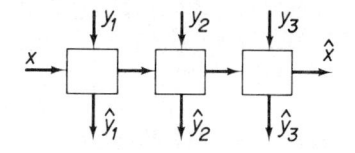

(e) A three-cell block

**Figure 4.11**

From the successor graph of Fig. 4.11(b), we see that the following input states are applicable, using $+45°$ diagonal tessellations: (2, 1), (4, 2); (4, 1); (2, 2), (3, 3). The successor graph of two-cell blocks shown in Fig. 4.11(c) has the following three loops:

$$(1, 12) \rightarrow (3, 33) \rightarrow (2, 21) \rightarrow (3, 34) \rightarrow (1, 23) \rightarrow (1, 12)$$

$$(2, 11) \rightarrow (4, 21) \rightarrow (4, 12) \rightarrow (2, 11)$$

$$(2, 23) \rightarrow (2, 32) \rightarrow (3, 13) \rightarrow (2, 42) \rightarrow (4, 31) \rightarrow (2, 23)$$

From these loops, we see that the additional applicable cell-input states are: (1, 1), (1, 2), (2, 3), (2, 4), (3, 1), (4, 3). By examining the intercell connections within blocks, we find that no additional cell-

TWO-DIMENSIONAL ARRAYS 129

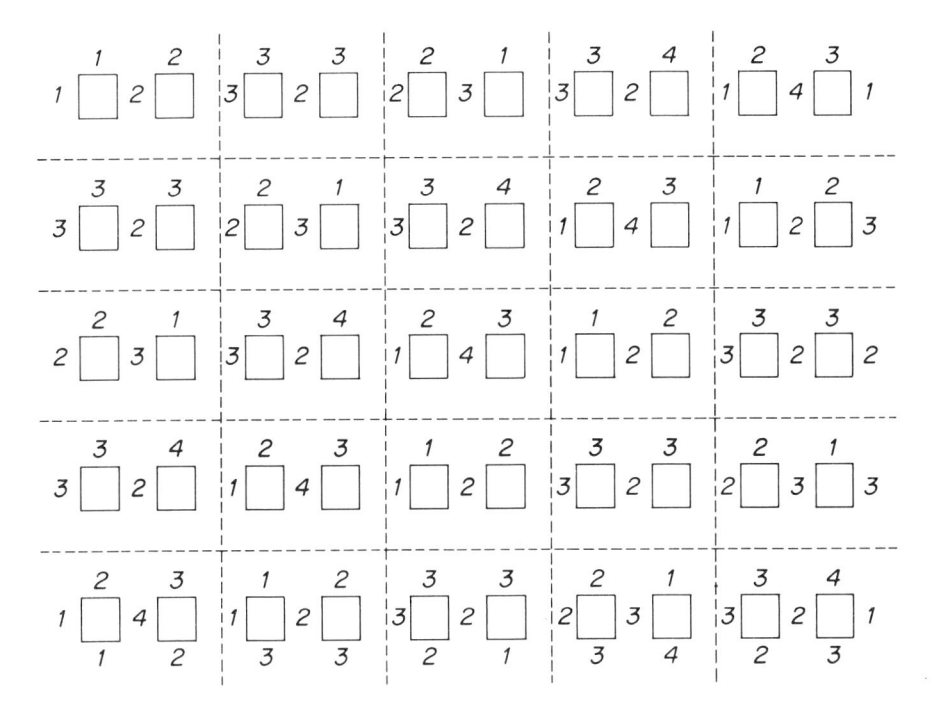

*(f) Example of a diagonal tessellation
Two-cell blocks*

**Figure 4.11** (continued)

input states are applicable using these loops. It can also be verified that the two-cell block of Fig. 4.11(d) does not yield any additional applicable inputs. The remaining five input states can be shown to be applicable by considering the three-cell block of Fig. 4.11(e), whose successor graph has the following loops (in addition to others not listed):

$$(1, 113) \rightarrow (1, 322) \rightarrow (2, 411) \rightarrow (4, 332) \rightarrow (4, 241) \rightarrow (2, 133)$$
$$(1, 224) \rightarrow (1, 113)$$

$$(1, 341) \rightarrow (3, 424) \rightarrow (2, 114) \rightarrow (2, 214) \rightarrow (1, 341)$$

$$(1, 314) \rightarrow (1, 433) \rightarrow (2, 221) \rightarrow (4, 331) \rightarrow (2, 243) \rightarrow (1, 314)$$

Note that the applicability of the cell-input states (4, 4) and (3, 2) can be determined only by examining intercell connections, as the loops are specified above. A diagonal tessellation of two-cell blocks, corresponding to the loop $(1, 12) \rightarrow (3, 33) \rightarrow (2, 21) \rightarrow (3, 34) \rightarrow (1, 23)$ › $(1, 12)$ is shown in Fig. 4.11(f).

The procedure described above gives us a subset of the set of applicable cell inputs and also a method of constructing larger subsets. In Example 4.7, it was not necessary to consider blocks containing more than three cells, because all inputs were found to be applicable by considering blocks containing up to three cells. This may not be true in general and we have no method of determining when to terminate the procedure. Thus the procedure may not yield the complete set of applicable cell inputs. However, the procedure may be terminated when the set of applicable cell inputs contains a complete set of tests whose effects can be made to propagate to an observable output.

The procedure discussed above did not take into account any constraints which may be imposed on the inputs to the boundary cells. Diagonal tessellations satisfying the constraints can be obtained by including in the successor graph only those cell inputs which satisfy the constraints.

Another type of diagonal tessellation which can be obtained is one in which cells along any $-45°$ diagonal have the same inputs and all adjacent diagonals are compatible as shown in Fig. 4.12. In Fig. 4.12 we require:

$$x_2 = \hat{x}(x_1, y_1); \; y_1 = \hat{y}(x_2, y_2); \; x_3 = \hat{x}(x_2, y_2); \; y_2 = \hat{y}(x_3, y_3); \ldots$$

A graphical procedure similar to the one discussed earlier can be used for obtaining $-45°$ diagonal tessellations. The nodes in the graph consist of

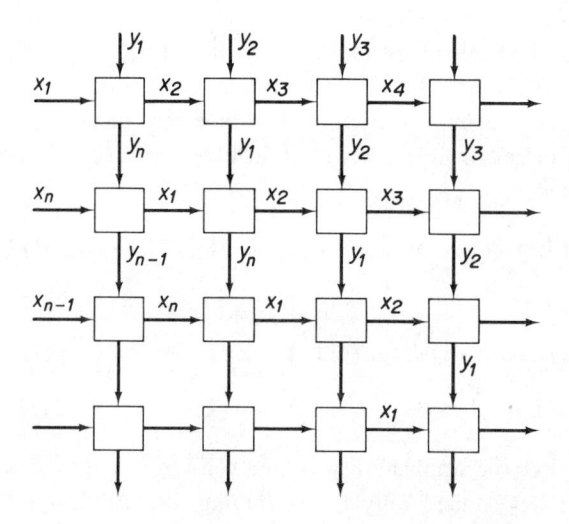

Figure 4.12 Example of a $-45°$ diagonal tessellation.

# TWO-DIMENSIONAL ARRAYS

cell-input states. A directed edge is drawn from the node $(x_i, y_j)$ to the node $(x_k, y_m)$ if and only if $x_k = \hat{x}(x_i, y_j)$ and $y_j = \hat{y}(x_k, y_m)$. Unlike the successor graph discussed earlier, it is now possible to have more than one edge emanating from any node. $-45°$ diagonal tessellations can be formed using the nodes contained in any closed loop (or self-loop) of the graph. The procedure can be extended to blocks containing two or more cells in an obvious manner. In Example 4.8, we obtain $-45°$ diagonal tessellations for the cell of Example 4.7.

**Example 4.8**

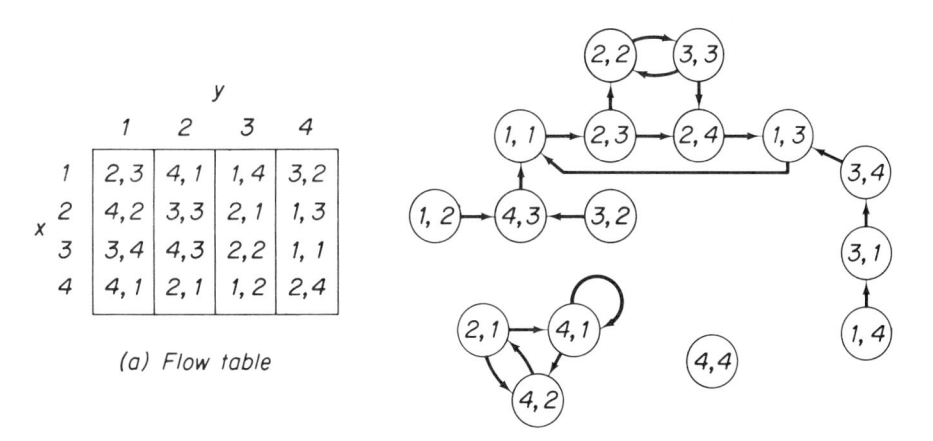

|   | y |   |   |   |
|---|---|---|---|---|
|   | 1 | 2 | 3 | 4 |
| 1 | 2,3 | 4,1 | 1,4 | 3,2 |
| 2 | 4,2 | 3,3 | 2,1 | 1,3 |
| 3 | 3,4 | 4,3 | 2,2 | 1,1 |
| 4 | 4,1 | 2,1 | 1,2 | 2,4 |

x

*(a) Flow table*

*(b) Graph for −45° tessellations*

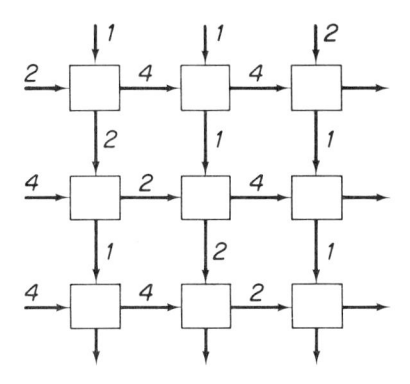

*(c) A −45° diagonal tessellation*

**Figure 4.13**

From the graph of Fig. 4.13(b), we see that the following nine of the sixteen input states are applicable using two $-45°$ diagonal tessellations: (1, 1), (2, 3), (2, 2), (3, 3), (2, 4), (1, 3) and (2, 1), (4, 1), (4, 2). The diagonal tessellation corresponding to the loops (2, 1) $\rightarrow$ (4, 1) $\rightarrow$ (4, 2) $\rightarrow$ (2, 1) is shown in Fig. 4.13(c).

Since the procedures discussed above do not enable us to determine the complete set of cell inputs applicable to any cell in a two-dimensional array, a superset of the set of applicable cell inputs is desirable. This will allow us to assert that some arrays are not testable. All cell inputs are applicable to any cell in a two-dimensional array only if, for every possible state $(x_k, y_m)$, the $x$-state $x_k$ occurs in the flow table as an $\hat{x}$ entry in a column $y_i$, and the $y$-state $y_m$ occurs as a $\hat{y}$ entry in a row $x_j$, such that $(x_j, y_i)$ also occurs as an entry (Kautz, 1967). The algorithm given below for a superset of the applicable cell inputs follows from the above result.

Let us assume that all $x$ inputs are applicable to cells along the left-hand boundary and that all $y$ inputs are applicable to cells on the top boundary. Let these sets of $x$ and $y$ inputs be denoted by $X$ and $Y$ respectively. Let $S_{11}$ be the set of all inputs applicable to $C_{11}$, i.e.,

$$S_{11} = \{(x_i, y_j) | x_i \in X; y_j \in Y\}.$$

$S_{kk}$ is defined recursively as follows:

$$S_{kk} = \{(x_i, y_j) | x_i = \hat{x}[x_p, \hat{y}(x_m, y_n)]; y_j = \hat{y}[\hat{x}(x_m, y_n), y_q] \text{ for } \\ x_p \in X, y_q \in Y, (x_m, y_n) \in S_{k-1,k-1}\}.$$

With reference to Fig. 4.14, if $S_{k-1,k-1}$ is the set of inputs applicable to cell $C_{k-1,k-1}$, $S_{kk}$ is the set of inputs applicable to cell $C_{kk}$, assuming that all $x \in X$ and all $y \in Y$ are applicable to cells $C_{k,k-1}$ and $C_{k-1,k}$ respectively.

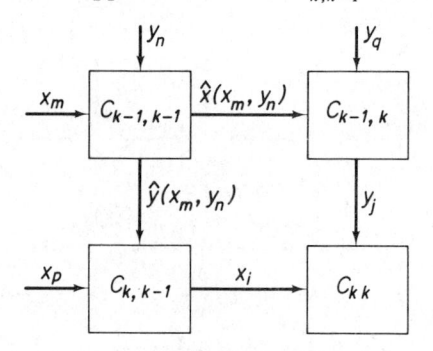

**Figure 4.14**

Since the last two assumptions may not be true, $S_{kk}$ is not the set of all cell inputs applicable to cell $C_{kk}$, but contains it.

It follows from the definition of $S_{kk}$ that $S_{kk} \supseteq S_{k+1,k+1}$ and that if $S_{kk} = S_{k+1,k+1}$, then $S_{mm} = S_{kk}$ for all $m > k$. Since the number of elements in $S_{11}$ is equal to the total number, $N$ of input combinations applicable to a cell, the procedure will terminate in at most $N$ steps, yielding a superset of the applicable cell inputs. If this set is equal to the largest set obtainable by tessellations, it is the complete set of applicable cell inputs. Also, if the superset does not contain a set of cell inputs for testing all faults in a single cell, an arbitrary two-dimensional array of these cells will be untestable.

The superset obtained by the procedure described above can be improved by suitably restricting inputs to the cells $C_{k,k-1}$ and $C_{k-1,k}$ respectively. Let $X_{ij}$ and $Y_{ij}$ represent the $x$ and $y$ inputs respectively, applicable to the cell $C_{ij}$. Clearly, $X_{i+1,j} \subseteq X_{ij} \subseteq X$ and $Y_{i,j+1} \subseteq Y_{ij} \subseteq Y$, where $X$ and $Y$ are sets of all $x$ and $y$ inputs. The recursive definition of $S_{kk}$ may then be modified as follows:

$$S_{kk} = \{(x_i, y_j) \mid x_i = \hat{x}[x_p, \hat{y}(x_m, y_n)]; y_j = \hat{y}[\hat{x}(x_m, y_n), y_q] \text{ for } $$
$$x_p \in X_{k-1,k-1}; y_q \in Y_{k-1,k-1}; (x_m, y_n) \in S_{k-1,k-1}\}.$$

Further improvement of the superset may also be obtained by considering blocks of cells as in the case of diagonal tessellations discussed earlier.

*Propagation of Faults*

In order for an array to be testable, it is necessary to propagate the effect of every fault to some observable cell output. The following theorem gives sufficient conditions for the effect of a fault to propagate to an observable output in a $+45°$ diagonal tessellation.

**Theorem 4.4:** *In a $+45°$ tessellation of cells corresponding to an isolated closed loop in the successor graph, the change of any cell output will result in the change of at least one observable output.*

**Proof:** In an isolated loop, there is only one edge which enters any node. This implies that a particular cell output state can be produced by exactly one cell-input state. Thus the inputs to the cells on the lower and righthand boundaries are uniquely determined for the observable outputs to be correct. These then uniquely define additional cell inputs. Continuing the procedure, the complete diagonal tessellation is obtained. The observable outputs cannot be the same for any other tessellation and the theorem follows.

If no two entries in the flow table are alike, the successor graph will consist of disjoint loops only. All cell inputs are applicable by $+45°$ tessellations in which any change of cell output will propagate to some observable output.

Theorem 4.4 is also applicable to $+45°$ tessellations of blocks, but only with respect to the inputs and outputs of blocks and not the intercell leads within a block. Clearly, the change of state of an intercell lead will cause some change in the observable outputs if and only if it causes the outputs of the block to change. Note that Theorem 4.4 is concerned with propagation without changing the inputs to the array from those corresponding to the diagonal tessellation.

**Example 4.9**

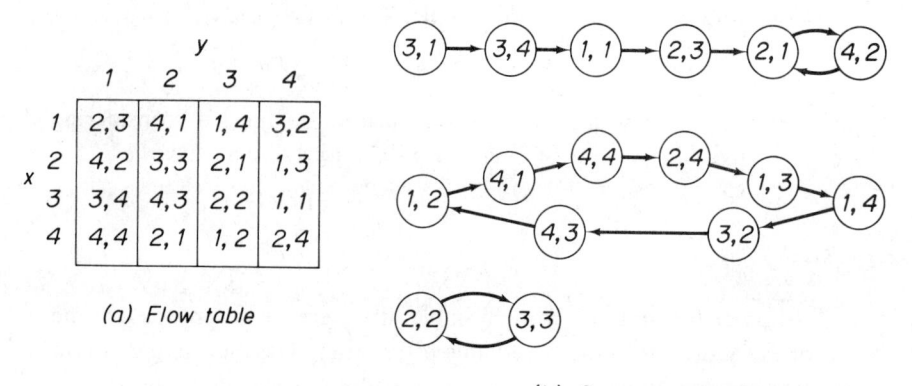

|   | 1 | 2 | 3 | 4 |
|---|---|---|---|---|
| 1 | 2,3 | 4,1 | 1,4 | 3,2 |
| 2 | 4,2 | 3,3 | 2,1 | 1,3 |
| 3 | 3,4 | 4,3 | 2,2 | 1,1 |
| 4 | 4,4 | 2,1 | 1,2 | 2,4 |

(a) Flow table

(b) Successor graph

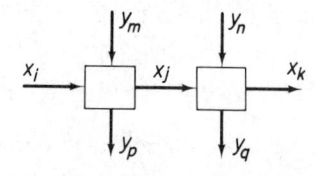

(c) Two-cell block

Figure 4.15

# TWO-DIMENSIONAL ARRAYS

The successor graph of Fig. 4.15(b) has two isolated loops yielding the following two $+45°$ diagonal tessellations in which the effect of any fault will propagate to some observable output.

(1, 2), (4, 1), (4, 4), (2, 4), (1, 3), (1, 4), (3, 2), (4, 3),

(2, 2), (3, 3).

Using two-cell blocks of Fig. 4.15(c), the successor graph has two isolated loops:

(1, 14) → (1, 33) → (1, 44) → (1, 21) → (4, 14) → (2, 44) → (3, 32)

→ (3, 23) → (1, 32) → (4, 41) → (4, 42) → (3, 43) → (1, 14)

(1, 24) → (2, 14) → (2, 24) → (1, 31) → (2, 43) → (1, 34) → (3, 42)

→ (4, 11) → (4, 44) → (1, 43) → (2, 22) → (4, 33) → (1, 24)

The additional input states (1, 1), (3, 4) and (2, 1) contained in blocks (1, 14), (1, 44) and (4, 41) now become applicable. We determine whether a change in an intercell lead will be masked, by referring to Fig. 4.15(c). It is clear that the only change in the intercell lead that will be masked, if any, is the change from $x_j$ to $x_f$ such that $\hat{x}(x_f, y_n) = \hat{x}(x_j, y_n) = x_k$ and $\hat{y}(x_f, y_n) = \hat{y}(x_j, y_n) = y_q$. For example, in the block with input (1, 14), $y_n = 4$, $(x_k, y_q) = (1, 3)$. No change in the intercell lead will be masked because there is only one (1, 3) entry in column 4. Since no two entries in any column of the flow table of the example are identical, no change in the intercell lead of any two-cell block of the type shown in Fig. 4.15(c) will be masked.

In Example 4.9, it can be verified that any change in a diagonal tessellation with states (2, 1) and (4, 2) will propagate to some output even though the loop containing these states has a branch. This is because the only change that will be masked is one in which the inputs of a cell change from (4, 2) to (2, 3). Any attempt to make this change, keeping the outputs unchanged leads to some inconsistency, indicating that the only tessellation that will produce the correct outputs is the diagonal tessellation itself. However, no general nonexhaustive algorithm to perform such analysis has been discovered.

Kautz (1967) has obtained sufficient conditions for the propagation of a fault by ensuring propagation in the $x$ or $y$ direction. These are: (1) In each column of the flow table, no two $\hat{x}$ entries are alike, or (2) in each row of the flow table, no two $\hat{y}$ entries are alike. When a specific test is applied to a cell with a specific fault, the normal and faulty outputs of the cell are usually known. It is therefore sufficient to determine if this particular change, but not necessarily all changes, can be propagated to observable outputs. This corresponds to the concept of *ultimate distinguishability* discussed earlier for one-dimensional arrays. The following procedure determines whether a single change in an $x$ state or a $y$ state in a tessellation will propagate along the $x$ or $y$ direction to a boundary of the array, without changing any of the inputs to the array. It does not give us any information regarding their propagation along other paths.

To determine $x$ changes that will propagate in the $x$ direction for a given tessellation, we construct a pair-graph whose nodes are pairs of cell input states $(x_i, y_j/x_k, y_j)$ where $(x_i, y_j)$ is an input state appearing in the tessellation and the change $x_i \longrightarrow x_k$ is caused by a fault. A directed edge is drawn from this node to the node $(x_m, y_n/x_p, y_n)$ if and only if $(x_m, y_n)$ is the input state of the right-hand neighbor as specified by the tessellation, $x_p = \hat{x}(x_k, y_j)$ and $x_p \neq x_m$. The pair-graph contains a node for every pair of input states, such that the first is contained in the tessellation and the second is obtained by a change in the $x$ input of the first which can result from a fault. Thus, if the tessellation contains $m$ input combinations and the flow table has $n$ rows, there will be $m(n-1)$ nodes in the pair-graph. By our construction, there will be at most one edge emanating from each node. Clearly, an $x$ change will propagate along the $x$ direction, assuming that the inputs to the array are not changed, if and only if the node representing the change is in a closed loop or leads to a closed loop of the pair-graph. It must be noted that propagation along the $x$ direction may be possible even if this condition is not satisfied, if the inputs to the cells on the top boundary are changed from the values specified by the tessellation. A similar graph can be constructed to determine propagation of a $y$ change in the $y$ direction.

If the $y$ inputs of the cells to the right of the faulty cell are unknown, a sufficient condition for propagation of an $x_i \longrightarrow x_j$ change in the $x$ direction can be stated as follows: In each column of the flow table, no two $\hat{x}$ entries are alike in rows corresponding to $x$ states reachable from $x_i$ and $x_j$ respectively by any sequence of $y$ inputs. A similar condition is obtained for propagation of a $y$ change along the $y$ direction. Allowing all $x$ and $y$ changes, these conditions become that no two rows have identical $\hat{x}$ entries in any column and no two columns have identical $\hat{y}$ entries in any row (Kautz, 1967).

# TWO-DIMENSIONAL ARRAYS

**Example 4.10:** The flow table of Fig. 4.13(a) is repeated in Fig. 4.16(a). For the −45° diagonal tessellation corresponding to the loop (1, 1) → (2, 3) → (2, 2) → (3, 3) → (2, 4) → (1, 3) → (1, 1) of Fig. 4.13(b) and propagation along the $x$ direction, the pair-graph of Fig. 4.16(b) is obtained. From the pair-graph, we see that all $x$ changes except the following will propagate indefinitely along the $x$ direction:

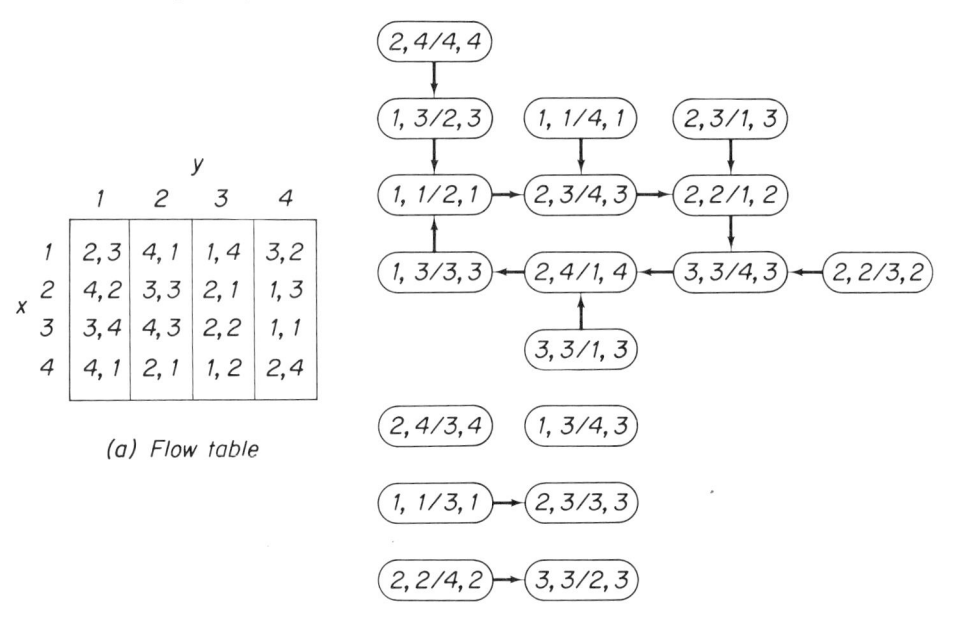

(1, 1) → (3, 1); (2, 3) → (3, 3); (2, 2) → (4, 2); (3, 3) → (2, 3);

(2, 4) → (3, 4); (1, 3) → (4, 3).

|   | 1 | 2 | 3 | 4 |
|---|---|---|---|---|
| 1 | 2,3 | 4,1 | 1,4 | 3,2 |
| 2 | 4,2 | 3,3 | 2,1 | 1,3 |
| 3 | 3,4 | 4,3 | 2,2 | 1,1 |
| 4 | 4,1 | 2,1 | 1,2 | 2,4 |

(a) Flow table

(b) Pair-graph for propagation in x direction

**Figure 4.16**

Under the general-fault assumptions, sufficient conditions for propagation of a fault in two-dimensional iterative arrays can be conveniently expressed in terms of information losslessness, a concept originally applied to sequential machines.

A sequential machine is defined to be *information-lossless* (Huffman, 1959) if the output sequence and the initial and final states uniquely determine the input sequence.

A two-dimensional array of cells is defined as *x-information-lossless* (*x*-IL), if for any column of cells in the array, the $y$ input to the first cell, the $\hat{y}$ output of the last cell and the $\hat{x}$ outputs of all cells in that column uniquely determine the $x$ inputs to all cells of the column.

The similarity between $x$-information losslessness of an array and information losslessness of a sequential machine becomes clear, if we treat the spatial sequences of $x$ inputs and $\hat{x}$ outputs as the input and output sequences (timewise) of a sequential machine whose states are represented by the $y$'s in the array. By considering rows of cells, *y-information losslessness* of an array may be defined in a similar way.

**Lemma 4.4:** *Any change of an* x *variable (or a* y *variable) in a two-dimensional array will propagate to an observable output if the array is* x-*IL (or* y-*IL)*.

**Proof:** If the array is $x$-IL, the $y$ input to the first cell, the $\hat{y}$ output of the last cell and the $\hat{x}$ outputs of all cells of the last (rightmost) column uniquely determine the $x$ inputs to that column. Since these are the $\hat{x}$ outputs of the next to last column, the $x$ inputs to this column can also be determined uniquely. Repeating this procedure, the signals on all $x$ leads in the array are determined uniquely for any given set of array outputs and $y$ inputs. Therefore, a change in any $x$ lead of the array will cause a change in an observable output. The $y$-IL case can be proved by considering rows of cells.

**Theorem 4.5:** *A change of signal on any interconnection in a two-dimensional array will propagate to an observable output if* (1) *the array is* x-*IL and no row of the flow table contains two or more identical entries, or* (2) *the array is* y-*IL and no column contains two or more identical entries.*

**Proof:** If the array is $x$-IL any $x$ change will propagate to some output (by Lemma 4.4). If no row contains two or more identical entries, any $y$ change will propagate in the $y$ direction or cause an $x$ change, which will propagate to some output. The proof of the second part is similar.

An array is $x$-IL if the sequential machine represented by its flow table, treating $x$ and $\hat{x}$ as input and output and $y$ and $\hat{y}$ as present and next states, is information-lossless. Similarly, if we treat $y$ and $\hat{y}$ as input and output and $x$ and $\hat{x}$ as present and next states, and the sequential machine represented by the flow table under this interpretation is IL, then the array is $y$-IL.

In order to determine whether a given flow table is information-lossless, we construct a test table (Huffman, 1959) whose rows are states and whose columns are outputs. Each entry indicates the sets of possible next states, referred to as a *p-set*, for the given output and present state. For every *p*-set appearing in the test table as an entry, we add a row labeled with that *p*-set, provided that such a row does not already exist. Entries in these rows are the set of possible next states for the present *p*-set and each output. The procedure is continued until no further *p*-sets are added to the test table.

**Example 4.11**

$x$

| | 0 | 1 |
|---|---|---|
| 1 | 1, 1 | 3, 1 |
| 2 | 5, 0 | 2, 1 |
| 3 | 4, 0 | 1, 0 |
| 4 | 3, 0 | 2, 0 |
| 5 | 2, 1 | 1, 0 |

Flow table

$z$

| | 0 | 1 |
|---|---|---|
| 1 | – | 13 |
| 2 | 5 | 2 |
| 3 | 14 | – |
| 4 | 23 | – |
| 5 | 1 | 2 |
| 13 | 14 | 13 |
| 14 | 23 | 13 |
| 23 | 145 | 2 |
| 145 | 123 | 123 |
| 123 | 145 | 123 |

Test table

A flow table and its test table (taken from Huffman, 1959) are shown above. Row 1 of the test table contains the *p*-set 13 in column 1, indicating that if the present state is 1 and the output is 1, the next state can be 1 or 3. An output of 0 is impossible if the present state is 1. The first row in the second section of the table indicates that if the present state is 1 or 3, the next state will be 1 or 4 if the output is 0 and 1 or 3 if the output is 1.

***Theorem 4.6:*** *A sequential machine represented by a flow table is information-lossless if and only if no state has two or more identical entries and no two states with the same* (s, z) *entry (next state and output) are in the same* p-*set of the test table.*

**Proof:** Necessity: Assume entry $(s_i, z_j)$ appears in states $s_a$ and $s_b$ which are in the same *p*-set. Since $s_a$ and $s_b$ are in the same *p*-set there is an initial state $s_0$ and two input sequences $X_0$, $X_1$ which lead to states $s_a$ and $s_b$ respectively with the same output sequence $Z$. Therefore, initial state $s_0$, final state $s_i$ and output sequence $Zz_j$ does not uniquely determine the input sequence and hence the flow table is not information lossless.

Sufficiency: For any output sequence, given the initial state and final state we can list the possible set of states for each output in the output sequence. Each of these corresponds to a $p$-set. We are given the last $(s, z)$ entry and the last $p$-set. By the assumption of the theorem this determines the next to last state and hence the last input. This procedure is repeated until the entire input sequence is determined. In the previous example, states 2 and 5 and 3 and 5 have repeated pairs but do not occur in any $p$-set. Hence the machine is information lossless. If a machine has no repeated $(s, z)$ entries then it is trivially lossless.

**Example 4.12:** Consider the flow table and the test tables for determining if it is $x$-IL or $y$-IL as shown below:

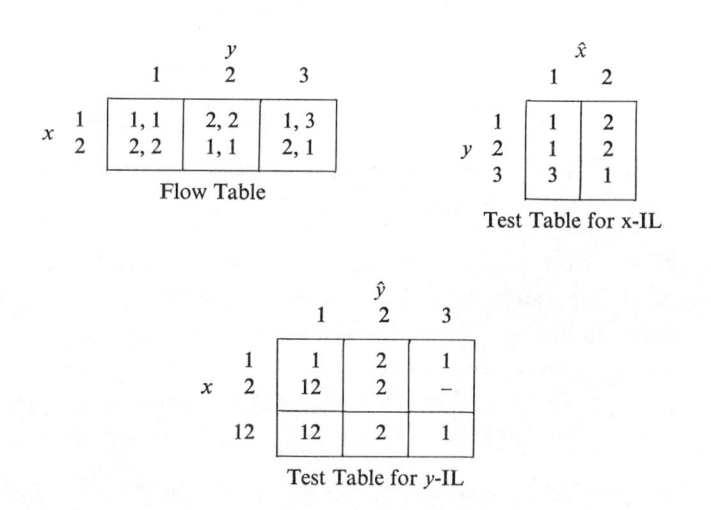

Flow Table

|   | $y$=1 | $y$=2 | $y$=3 |
|---|---|---|---|
| $x$=1 | 1, 1 | 2, 2 | 1, 3 |
| $x$=2 | 2, 2 | 1, 1 | 2, 1 |

Test Table for x-IL

|   | $\hat{x}$=1 | $\hat{x}$=2 |
|---|---|---|
| $y$=1 | 1 | 2 |
| $y$=2 | 1 | 2 |
| $y$=3 | 3 | 1 |

Test Table for y-IL

|   | $\hat{y}$=1 | $\hat{y}$=2 | $\hat{y}$=3 |
|---|---|---|---|
| $x$=1 | 1 | 2 | 1 |
| $x$=2 | 12 | 2 | – |
| 12 | 12 | 2 | 1 |

From the test tables, it is seen that the flow table is $x$-IL. It is not $y$-IL, because $x$-states 1 and 2, both of which have the entries (1, 1) and (2, 2), are contained in the $p$-set 12 of the test table. However, the effect of any fault will propagate to an output because the flow table is $x$-IL and no row contains identical entries.

# TWO-DIMENSIONAL ARRAYS

*Bounds on the Number of Tests*

We now consider some bounds on the number of tests required for detecting all faults in a two-dimensional array. If the flow table of a cell has $M$ columns and $N$ rows, under the general-fault assumption, it may produce any one of $MN-1$ faulty output pairs in response to a test. Each of these may necessitate different inputs on succeeding cells to propagate the effect of the fault to an observable boundary. Thus, testing a single cell may require $MN(MN-1)$ tests and $pqMN(MN-1)$ tests may be necessary to test a $p$ by $q$ array. This upper bound on the number of tests can be refined somewhat by taking into account the fact that the $\hat{x}$ outputs of the last column and the $\hat{y}$ outputs of the last row of cells are observable. The greatest lower bound on the number of tests required under the general fault assumption is $MN$, since that many tests may be required to test a single cell. The following theorems by Kautz (1967) state the conditions under which the lower bound can be attained.

**Theorem 4.7:** *If no two entries in the flow table of a cell are identical then any two-dimensional array of such cells can be tested with* $MN$ *tests.*

**Proof:** Since no two entries are alike, all $MN$ cell input combinations appear in the flow table exactly once. Thus all $MN$ states appear in loops of the successor graph defined earlier for $+45°$ tessellations and the loops are isolated. If a loop contains $K$ cell tests, these tests can be applied to all cells in the array by a $+45°$ diagonal tessellation containing them and $(K-1)$ shifts. Thus $MN$ array tests are sufficient for applying all $MN$ cell tests to all cells and by Theorem 4.4, the effect of any fault will propagate to some observable output.

**Theorem 4.8:** *A two-dimensional array whose basic-cell flow table has no two identical $\hat{x}$ entries in any column and no two identical $\hat{y}$ entries in any row can be tested with* $MN$ *tests.*

**Proof:** We show that all $MN$ cell input states are contained in $-45°$ diagonal tessellations by proving that all states are contained in loops of the graph for obtaining such tessellations. The graph will contain only disjoint loops if and only if there is exactly one edge entering each node and one edge leaving each node.

Let $\hat{x}(x_i, y_j) = x_m$. Since no row of the flow table has two identical $\hat{y}$ entries, every row must contain each $y_k$ as a $\hat{y}$ entry exactly once. Therefore, there must be some column, say $y_n$, such that $\hat{y}(x_m, y_n) = y_j$ and the node $(x_i, y_j)$ has exactly one edge emanating from it. This is true for all nodes.

Suppose that the graph contains an edge each from nodes $(x_i, y_j)$ and $(x_p, y_q)$ to $(x_m, y_n)$. Then, by the construction of the graph,

$$\hat{x}(x_i, y_j) = x_m; \quad \hat{y}(x_m, y_n) = y_j$$

$$\hat{x}(x_p, y_q) = x_m; \quad \hat{y}(x_m, y_n) = y_q$$

Therefore, $y_j = y_q$, and $\hat{x}(x_i, y_j) = \hat{x}(x_p, y_j) = x_m$; i.e., there are two identical $\hat{x}$ entries in the $y_j$ column—contradiction. Hence, there can be at most one edge entering a node.

Since there is exactly one edge emanating from each node, and there can be at most one edge entering any node, it follows that there is exactly one edge entering each node. Therefore, all input states are contained in loops of the graph and all cell input states are applicable by $-45°$ tessellations. As in Theorem 4.6, $MN$ tests are sufficient for applying all these cell inputs to all cells in the array. Since no two $\hat{x}$ entries are alike in any column, any $x$ change produced by a fault will propagate in the $x$ direction. Similarly the absence of identical $\hat{y}$ entries in any row guarantees the propagation of any $y$ change along the $y$ direction.

*Limitations of the Test-Derivation Procedures*

The procedures discussed so far allow us to determine tests which are applicable to all cells in a two-dimensional array and also cell-output changes which will propagate to observable outputs. These lead to sufficient conditions for the testability of two-dimensional arrays. Necessary and sufficient conditions for testability of two-dimensional arrays have yet to be found and this problem may be recursively unsolvable. The following is an example (Kautz, 1967) of an array that is testable. However the set of tests for this array cannot be derived by the previously discussed procedures.

**Example 4.13**

|   |   | $y$ |   |
|---|---|---|---|
|   |   | 0 | 1 |
| $x$ | 0 | 0, 0 | 0, 1 |
|   | 1 | 0, 1 | 1, 0 |

# TWO-DIMENSIONAL ARRAYS

The flow table of the basic cell which realizes $\hat{x} = xy$; $\hat{y} = x \oplus y$, is shown above. Arnold et al (1970) have shown how arrays of such cells, with minor modifications, can be used for realizing arbitrary combinational functions or sequential machines.

The flow table is $y$-IL and no column contains identical entries. Hence, the effect of any fault will propagate to the boundary. It is, therefore, sufficient to apply all cell input states to all cells in the array. It can be easily verified that the states (0, 0) and (0, 1) can be applied to all cells using the methods discussed earlier. But we have been unable to construct diagonal tessellations of blocks of cells which contain the remaining two cell input states. However, if all 1's are applied to the left-hand boundary, we obtain the pattern shown in Fig. 4.17.

For any 3 column array of such cells, (1, 1) and (1, 0) states can be applied to all cells by 8 tests. In general, if the array is $p$ cells wide, these two tests can be applied by $2^p$ tests. Two tests are necessary for

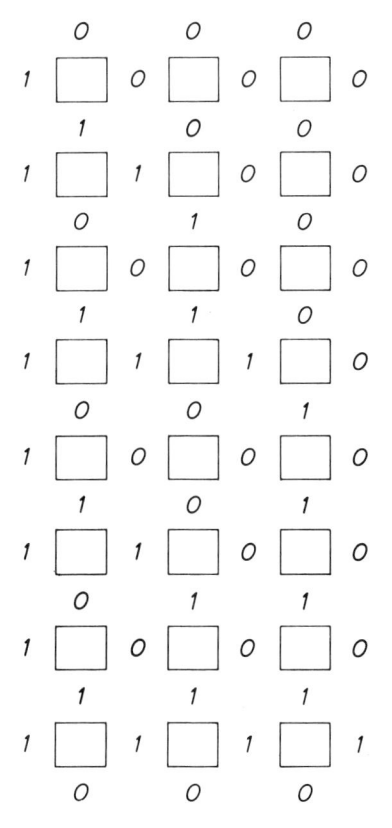

**Figure 4.17**

applying (0, 0) and (0, 1) to all cells, leading to the result that a *p*-column array is testable with $2^p + 2$ tests.

## ARRAYS OF SEQUENTIAL MACHINES

We now consider the problem of determining whether a one-dimensional array of identical sequential machines is testable (Breuer, 1968). The model and notation used are shown in Fig. 4.18.

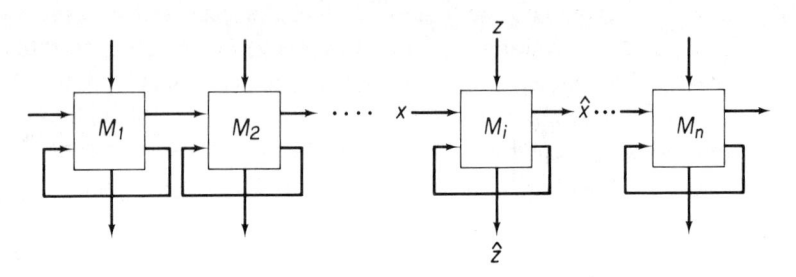

**Figure 4.18**

The main difference between the problem of testing such an array and an array of combinational cells is that the tests for each basic cell now consist of input sequences rather than input combinations. A fault in a cell may cause it to go to an incorrect internal state, but produce correct outputs. The effect of the fault may not become apparent at the $\hat{x}$ or $\hat{z}$ outputs of the cell itself until some later time. Additional sequences of inputs may then be necessary to propagate a change in $\hat{x}$ to an observable output.

In order to be able to apply all test sequences to all cells in the array, it is sufficient to be able to apply all input sequences to any cell in the array. It can be shown that the problem of determining whether any sequential machine can generate all output sequences is decidable (Breuer, 1968). However, the application of all input sequences may not be necessary for testing an individual cell.

A sequential machine is defined as *information lossless of finite order* (ILF) if there exists a positive integer, $r$, such that the initial state and a sequence of $r$ outputs uniquely determine the first input. The class of ILF machines is contained in the class of IL machines. Huffman (1959) and Even (1965) have given procedures for determining whether a strongly-connected machine is ILF.

A cell in a one-dimensional array of sequential machines is defined to be *x-ILF* if the initial state and an $\hat{x}$-output sequence of finite length are sufficient to determine the sequence of $z$ inputs. Similarly, it is *x/z-ILF* if the $z$ input sequence can be determined from a knowledge of the $\hat{x}$- and $\hat{z}$-output sequences of finite length.

Breuer (1968) has shown that any fault will propagate to an observable output if the cell is *x-* or *x/z*-ILF. This result is similar to the result presented in the preceding section for propagation of the effects of a fault in a two-dimensional array. The rows (or columns) of the two-dimensional array may be thought of as a sequential machine. The $x$ (or $y$) signals in the array may be considered as representing internal states. Since the two-dimensional arrays are finite, the final states of the equivalent array of sequential machines are known. Consequently, the weaker condition of information losslessness presented in the preceding section is sufficient for two-dimensional arrays of combinational cells.

## TREE STRUCTURES

Techniques similar to those discussed earlier in this chapter are useful for testing other uniform structures composed of identical modules. One such case is the tree-type circuit. These circuits have independent inputs and no intermodule reconvergent fan-out. Each module is assumed to contain combinational logic only and has one or more binary outputs. In the latter case, we can treat it as having a single output which may have more than two values.

In a tree circuit of the type under consideration, it can be seen that all input combinations are applicable to any module if and only if a module is capable of producing all output values. If at most one module can be faulty at any time, only one subset of the input variables to any module can be faulty. The effect of a fault can be made to propagate to the output under the general-fault assumption, if and only if, for every change in a single subset of the input variables to a module there exists a set of values for the other inputs to the module, which will cause its output to be different.

**Example 4.14:** Consider a tree-type structure composed of modules shown in Fig. 4.19, proposed by Arnold et al (1970). In a tree of such modules, $y_1$ and $y_2$ are connected to the outputs of modules in the preceding level, but $x$ is an external input. Clearly, the module is

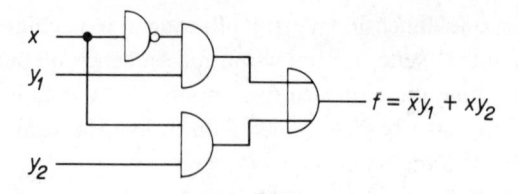

**Figure 4.19**

$$f = \bar{x}y_1 + xy_2$$

capable of producing the 0 output and the 1 output. Therefore, all input combinations are applicable to any module in the tree, provided that the $x$ inputs are independent and so are the $y$ inputs to the modules in the first level. The only changes caused by faults that have to be propagated through a module are changes in its $y$ inputs. Since any change in $y_1$ will cause the output to change if $x = 0$, and any change in $y_2$ will affect the output if $x = 1$, all faults can be made to propagate to the output and the tree is testable.

Four tests, $\bar{x}\bar{y}_1 y_2$, $\bar{x}y_1 \bar{y}_2$, $x\bar{y}_1 y_2$ and $xy_1\bar{y}_2$ are sufficient for detecting all s-a-0 and s-a-1 faults in a module. Since the $x$ inputs required for making the output of a module sensitive to a change in a $y$ input are different for the two $y$ inputs, only one path in the tree can be sensitized at any time. Thus $2^{n-1}$ combinations of $x$ inputs are necessary to sensitize all paths in an $n$-level circuit. Also, there are two tests for each cell for each value of its $x$ input. Thus at least $2 \times 2^{n-1} = 2^n$ tests are necessary for testing the entire tree. Since for each $x$ input, the two tests in the set produce opposite outputs from a module, all modules along a path can be tested simultaneously and $2^n$ tests are also sufficient for testing an $n$-level tree.

In the above discussion, we assumed that the $x$ inputs to all modules in the array were independent. Since only modules along one path are tested at any time, the preceding arguments remain valid if the $x$ inputs to all modules in one level of the tree are constrained to be the same.

Arnold et al (1970) have shown that any binary-input synchronous sequential machine can be realized using trees of these modules with a synchronous delay added to the output of each module. The $x$ inputs of all modules are connected together. However, because of the delay in each module, the application of an $x$-input sequence applied to such a circuit is equivalent to the application of independent $x$ inputs to each level of the combinational tree without delay. Thus, a sequential machine realized using an

$n$-level tree can be tested for all s-a-0 and s-a-1 faults in the tree by a sequence of length $2^n$.

Similar techniques can be applied to trees of other types of modules. For example, if a parity-check circuit is built as a tree of $n$-input parity check modules, $2^n$ tests are necessary and sufficient for testing each module. Each module has the property that any single input change will cause its output to change, and propagation conditions need not be considered. It can be shown (Friedman, 1966) that any tree-type structure without convergent fan-out of $n$-input parity check modules can be tested with $2^n$ tests, independent of the size of the tree.

## SUMMARY

Necessary and sufficient conditions for the detection and sufficient conditions for the location of any single faulty cell in a one-dimensional array of combinational cells were derived. A procedure for deriving efficient sets of fault-detection tests for such arrays was also presented. In the case of two-dimensional arrays, we were only able to obtain sufficient conditions for testability, and the general problem of testability may be undecidable. A method of deriving tests by means of tessellations was presented. Though this method is useful for deriving efficient tests for some arrays, there exist testable arrays for which tests cannot be derived using this method. The problems of testing one-dimensional arrays of sequential machines and tree structures were briefly discussed.

## REFERENCES

Arnold, T. F., Tan, C. J. and Newborn, M. M., "Iteratively Realized Sequential Circuits", *IEEE Trans. on Computers* C-19, 54–66, 1970.

Breuer, M. A., "Fault Detection in a Linear Cascade of Identical Machines", *Proc. 9th Annual Symposium on Switching and Automata Theory*, 235–243, 1968.

Even, S., "On Information Lossless Automata of Finite Order", *IEEE Trans. on Electronic Computers* EC-14, 561–569, 1965.

Friedman, A. D., "Deriving Near-Minimal Sets of Diagnostic Tests for Modularized Parity Check Circuit and Parallel Binary Adders", *Bell Telephone Laboratories Internal Memorandum* (unpublished), 1966.

Hennie, F. C., *Iterative Arrays of Logical Circuits*, M.I.T. Press and John Wiley & Sons, 1961.

Huffman, D. A., "Canonical Forms for Information Lossless Finite-State Logical Machines", *IRE Trans. on Circuit Theory* CT-6, 41-59, 1959. Also in *Sequential Machines: Selected Papers*, E. F. Moore, Ed., Addison-Wesley, Reading, Mass. 132–156, 1964.

Kautz, W. H., "Testing for Faults in Combinational Cellular Logic Arrays", *Proc. 8th Annual Symposium on Switching and Automata Theory*, 161–174, 1967.

Menon, P. R. and Friedman, A. D., "Fault Detection in Iterative Logic Arrays," *IEEE Trans. on Computers*, 524–535, 1971.

Minnick, R. C., "A Survey of Microcellular Research", *J. ACM* 14, 203–241, 1967.

Tammaru, E., "Efficient Testing of Combinational Logic Cells in Large-Scale Arrays", *Tech. Report No. 4601-1*, Stanford Electronics Laboratories, Stanford University, 1968.

Wang, H., "Dominoes and the AEA Case of the Decision Problem", *Proc. Symp. Mathematical Theory of Automata*, Polytechnic Institute of Brooklyn, 23–55, 1963.

## PROBLEMS

1. For a one-dimensional array whose basic cell is the circuit of Fig. 4.6, find a set of tests which detect the following faults: $\{\epsilon_0, \epsilon_1, \eta_0, \eta_1, \rho_0, \rho_1, \mu_0, \mu_1\}$.

2. Derive a minimal set of tests for detecting all single s-a-0 and s-a-1 faults in a one-dimensional array of cells of the type shown in Fig. 4.20.

3. a) For the circuit of Fig. 4.4, what is the largest set of faults permissible if every fault must be locatable to a single cell.
   b) Repeat (a) for the circuit of Fig. 4.6.

4. For each of the following basic cells it can be decided whether any

PROBLEMS 149

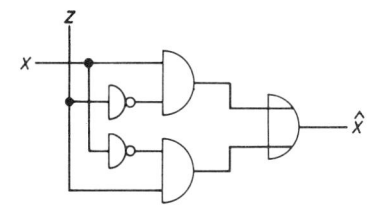

**Figure 4.20**

two-dimensional array composed of such cells is testable under the general fault assumptions using the techniques of this chapter. In each case determine whether the array is testable and specify a set of tests if possible.

a)

|   | 1    | 2    | 3    |
|---|------|------|------|
| 1 | 1, 2 | 3, 3 | 3, 2 |
| 2 | 2, 2 | 1, 3 | 2, 3 |
| 3 | 3, 2 | 2, 1 | 1, 1 |

b)

|   | 1    | 2    | 3    |
|---|------|------|------|
| 1 | 2, 3 | 1, 3 | 3, 3 |
| 2 | 2, 1 | 3, 1 | 1, 2 |
| 3 | 2, 2 | 3, 1 | 3, 2 |

5. Prove that the testability of the array shown in Fig. 4.21 is decidable.

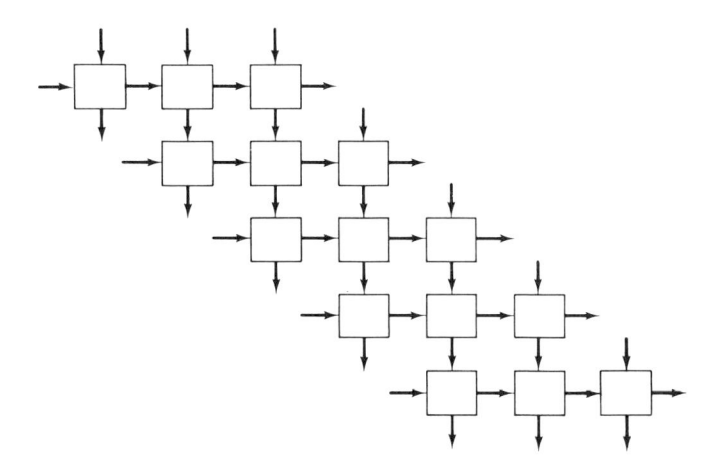

**Figure 4.21**

6. a) For a tree with no intercell reconvergent fan-out whose basic cell is shown below, show that any fault can be detected using only 4 tests.
   b) How many tests are required to locate a fault to within a cell?

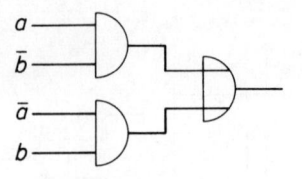

**Figure 4.22**

7\*.  Let $P_r$ be the set of all input combination pairs applicable to cell $C_{rr}$ of a two-dimensional array.

Prove or disprove the following conjecture. If $P_i = P_{i+n}$ then $P_j = P_{j+n}$ for all $j \geq i$. In particular, if $P_1 = P_2 = \mathbf{U}$ (the universal set) does $P_i = \mathbf{U}$ for all $i > 3$. (Note that if this conjecture were true the problem of determining the set of inputs applicable to all cells in the network would be decidable).

CHAPTER 5

# SIMULATION TECHNIQUES

Digital simulation is widely used for checking designs of digital circuits before actual fabrication. In this chapter, we discuss the application of simulation techniques to the derivation of fault-detection tests and the compilation of diagnostic dictionaries for digital circuits. We shall not be concerned with programming details but shall present only the principal features of two of the currently used simulation programs.

A simulation program usually computes the signals on different wires in a circuit for given initial states and inputs. Either synchronous or asynchronous operation may be assumed. In the synchronous case time is treated as a discrete variable and the signal values are of interest only at specified instants of time. In asynchronous operation the possibility of critical races must also be taken into account. For simplicity, the elements in a circuit are considered to be ideal and any delay associated with an element is considered to be a lumped delay at its output.

One application of simulation in testing is for the verification of tests which have already been derived. After simulating the normal circuit with the test applied, the circuit with the specified fault is simulated and the outputs of the two simulations are compared. This not only checks whether a particular fault is detected by a given test, but also determines the outputs and time at which the fault is detected. This information may then be used to construct a fault dictionary. Simulation is also useful for determining the set of faults detected by a given test. In this connection, we shall discuss a program which is not a simulator in the sense discussed in the preceding paragraph.

Let us assume that input changes occur at fixed instants of time and only the steady state values of signals are of interest, as in the case of synchronous operation. Under these conditions, the most straightforward method of simulation involves merely computing the output of each gate in the circuit, making use of its inputs and the type of gate. The simulation for any instant of time is complete when the outputs of all gates have been computed and are consistent with inputs and gate types. This procedure, though simple, is inefficient for the following two reasons. First, the number of times the output of a gate is to be computed depends upon the order in which the outputs of different gates are computed. For example, let the outputs of gates $A$ and $B$ be inputs to gate $C$. If the state of $C$ is computed before the states of both $A$ and $B$ have been determined, it may be necessary to recompute the state of $C$ after computing $A$ and $B$. Secondly, it may be unnecessary to compute the new states of some gates because their inputs are known to be unchanged for a particular change in circuit inputs. In our example, the state of $C$ need not be computed if neither $A$ nor $B$ changes state as a result of an input change.

The efficiency of simulation can be improved by organizing the circuit description in such a manner that no gate is simulated until all gates feeding it have been simulated. This can be done for circuits without feedback by arranging the gates according to levels, the level of a gate being the smallest integer greater than the levels of the gates feeding it. The circuit inputs (primary inputs) are assigned level 0. In circuits with feedback, feedback loops are assumed to have been opened before assigning levels. Thus, the level assigned to a gate in a loop is dependent on where the loop is broken.

Further improvements in the speed of simulation can be obtained by computing the states of only those gates for which one or more inputs have changed (Menon, 1965; Chang et al., 1970). This technique is known as *selective trace*. Its efficiency is usually improved by arranging the gates according to their levels. If the output of a gate (or a primary input) changes, the gates fed by it (its fan-out) are identified as needing simulation. Simulation of individual gates is performed in the order of their level numbers but only the gates whose inputs have changed are simulated. Feedback leads are identified and the simulation is repeated if a feedback wire has changed state. In synchronous circuits with multi-phase clocks, further reductions in simulation time may be possible by simulating only those parts of the circuit which can change state during the particular clock phase under consideration.

Simulation programs can be divided into two broad classes depending upon how the description of the circuit to be simulated is utilized. In one class called the *compiler-driven simulator*, the circuit description is treated as a source program in a high-level programming language. The preprocessor of the simulator, which is in effect a compiler for the language used for circuit description, generates the code for simulating each of the circuit elements. Simulation of the circuit is then accomplished by executing the program compiled by the preprocessor. This type of simulator is usually efficient for circuits of moderate size, say up to several hundred gates. One disadvantage of this type of simulator is that selective trace cannot be used. The *Sequential Analyzer* (Seshu and Freeman, 1962) is a compiler-driven simulator.

In the second class of simulator called the *table-driven simulator*, the circuit description is stored in the form of tables. The simulation program uses these tables as data. This method is useful for larger circuits because of the ability to use computer memory more efficiently. Although this may require more time for fetching data, the use of selective trace, which is now possible, more than compensates for it. Armstrong's program (Armstrong, 1968, 1971), which we shall discuss later in this chapter, is an example of a table-driven simulator.

Simulation is possible at different levels of detail. We shall be concerned primarily with *gate-level simulation* because it is the most useful for generating and verifying tests. Simulation can also be carried out on a *functional level*. Here, each part of a circuit, possibly containing many gates, is treated as a "black box" performing a specified input/output mapping. In simulating large circuits, it may be convenient to simulate some parts at the functional level and others at the gate level. Faults are assumed to be present only in the part which is simulated at the gate level. The effects of these faults on the entire system can be determined without a time-consuming gate-level simulation of the entire system.

Although functional simulation is quite simple conceptually, there is one major difficulty in its application. This is the lack of a satisfactory method of describing nontrivial subsystems for functional simulation. Until better methods of functional description are developed, functional simulation is likely to be restricted to relatively simple circuits such as shift registers and adders.

We shall now discuss the principal features of two specific simulation programs which are quite different in their approach.

## THE SEQUENTIAL ANALYZER

The Sequential Analyzer (Seshu and Freeman, 1962; Seshu, 1964, 1965; Chang et al., 1970) is a set of computer programs capable of simultaneously simulating a normal digital circuit and the effect of several different faults on it and also deriving fault-detection or diagnostic test sets for the circuit. Although several subsequent improved versions of the Sequential Analyzer exist, we shall use the original version (Seshu and Freeman, 1962) to demonstrate some of the techniques.

The Sequential Analyzer is a compiler-driven simulator applicable to asynchronous sequential circuits represented by the Huffman model (Huffman, 1954). The basic assumptions used are:

1. The class of possible failures is known, finite, and permanent.
2. Each failure transforms the given sequential circuit into another sequential circuit with the same number of memory elements.
3. It is possible to reset the feedback lines to a known initial state, even under failure conditions.

The asynchronous model of sequential circuits is used in order to develop a simulation program that is general enough to be applicable to different types of machines. For example, the programs can be readily modified for simulating and deriving tests for synchronous machines. In this case, the critical race analysis and the restrictions on input changes to be discussed later are no longer necessary. Another reason for using the asynchronous model is that under failure conditions, a normally synchronous machine may behave like an asynchronous machine.

The *logic organizer* is a preprocessor for the actual simulation program, and organizes the gates in the circuit according to levels, as discussed earlier. The inputs to the program consist of the circuit description and a list of feedback lines. The logic organizer temporarily disconnects these feedback lines and attempts to order the gates according to levels. It also checks for additional closed loops in the circuit and prints out the loops detected. If loops are detected, it is necessary to run the program again after specifying additional feedback lines where these loops may be broken.

After the gates in the circuit have been ordered according to levels by the logic organizer, the *logic compiler* generates the instructions for simulating each gate in the circuit. A physical fault in the circuit causes the sequential circuit to realize a machine which is different from the normal machine. The normal machine and a number of faulty machines (the number being determined by the word length of the computer on which the simulation program is run) are simulated simultaneously. This is done by modifying each gate output by *failure-injection words* which represent the effect of each fault on the output of the gate being simulated. The failure-injection words for given sets of faults are also generated by the logic compiler. For example, if the bits of a word represent the signals on the same wire for the different machines being simulated (i.e., in the presence of different faults), a s-a-1 fault on the wire in one of the failed machines can be simulated by ORing a failure-injection word containing a 1 in the corresponding bit position and 0's elsewhere. Similarly, the effect of a s-a-0 fault can be simulated by ANDing a failure-injection word containing a 0 in the appropriate position and 1's elsewhere.

The program generated by the logic compiler merely computes the signal values on all lines in the combinational-logic circuits of the normal and faulty machines. The effect of changes of the signals on the feedback lines is determined by the *Huffman Analysis Program* which is a subroutine of the Sequential Analyzer. This program compares the new values of the signals on the feedback lines with the old values for each of the machines being simulated. If they are equal for some machine, that machine is in a stable state. If they differ in exactly one variable, the value of the signal is updated and the simulation is repeated. If they differ in more than one variable, a race exists. In order to determine whether the race is critical, the behavior of the particular machine is simulated for all possible orders in which the feedback variables may change. If simulation indicates that two or more stable states can be reached, the race is critical and the simulation is terminated. The simulation is also terminated if instability in the form of logical oscillations or cyclic behavior is detected. Note that the simulation is terminated for all machines even though only one machine may exhibit these properties. Clearly, it is possible to continue simulation of the machines in which there are no critical races or oscillations. This feature has been included in later versions.

The Sequential Analyzer can be used in two ways. It can be used to determine the set of faults that are detected by a given test. It can also be incorporated in a test generation program. Here again, the function of the simulator is essentially to determine the usefulness of a heuristically-derived test.

The test generation procedure is essentially trial and error. Four different strategies are used for determining the next set of inputs to be applied. These are "best next or return to good input", "wander", "combinational" and "reset". An index of usefulness is maintained for each strategy and strategies are always reordered according to this index. Thus the strategy which has been proven to be the best is chosen first, followed by the second best and so on.

All the test sequences derived are required to satisfy the condition that only one input variable changes at a time. This is because of the assumption that the circuit is asynchronous. Before changing any input variable on a trial basis the current state of the circuit is saved. This permits returning to this state if the trial change is found to be useless. The state of the circuit is updated if the trial change is found to be useful according to the current criterion. We shall discuss criteria of usefulness later in this section.

The "next best or return to good input" strategy tries each of the next inputs, differing in only one bit from the present input, to determine if any of them is useful. The input with the largest gain according to the current criterion is used and all useful inputs are saved in a list of good inputs. If no useful input is found, an attempt is made to use an input from the list of good inputs. Since the good input tried may not be adjacent to the present input, all input sequences from the present input to the good input with only one variable changing at a time and no variable changing more than once are tried and the best sequence is chosen. The inputs in the list of good inputs may not be useful because the feedback lines may have changed state. If no useful input can be found, the next strategy is tried.

The "wander" strategy attempts to take a specified number of pseudo-random steps. After each step, all adjacent inputs are examined to see if any one of them is useful. The most useful input is used if such an input is found. Otherwise, another pseudo-random step is taken and the procedure is repeated until the specified number of steps has been taken.

In the "combinational" strategy, a test for a given fault is generated, treating the circuit as combinational. The test is then applied by using a sequence which would lead the good machine to the state of the derived test. The procedure is repeated for each of the faults being considered. Since the signals on the feedback wires are not controllable, the tests may not be useful. If any useful test is found it is used.

The "reset" strategy tries each of the allowed resets followed by a fixed number of steps to see if any useful information is obtainable. If no useful test is found by any of the methods, the program comes to an unsuccessful termination. Though the program is not guaranteed to derive a complete set of detection or diagnostic tests, a fairly large subset is usually generated. The Sequential Analyzer used in the test generation mode is rather inefficient because of the trial and error nature of the process.

The Sequential Analyzer can be used to obtain test sets for fault detection or diagnosis. The criterion of usefulness of a test depends upon whether detection or diagnosis is desired. For detection it is sufficient to distinguish the good machine from all the faulty machines, whereas the machine has to be identified for diagnosis. In terms of the diagnostic tree discussed in Chapter 2, for fault detection we are interested only in the branches of the tree containing the good machine. We extend the tree until one branch contains only the good machine. For diagnosis, each terminal branch should contain a single machine.

For fault detection, the number of faulty machines $n$ contained in the same subset as the good machine is used as a measure of usefulness, and the input which minimizes this is chosen. The criterion used for deriving diagnostic tests is that of information gain. As a result of the application of the input under consideration and all previous inputs in the sequence, let the set of machines be divided into $n$ subsets and let the probability that the machine belongs to the $j^{th}$ subset be $p_j$, and

$$\sum_{j=1}^{n} p_j = 1.$$

Then the information (in bits) (Shannon, 1948) obtained from the entire input sequence is given by

$$\mathscr{I} = -\sum_{j=1}^{n} p_j \log_2 p_j.$$

Since the entire input sequence except for the last input has already been chosen, the input yielding the highest value of $\mathscr{I}$ will lead to the largest information gain.

**Example 5.1:** This example demonstrates how the choice of the next input is dependent on the criterion of usefulness employed. Let $(I_1, I_2)$ be the set of inputs applicable to a machine $M_0$, and let $M_1$, $M_2$, $M_3$, $M_4$ and $M_5$ be faulty machines. From the initial state with the input $I_1$ applied, let the output of machines $M_0$ and $M_1$ be 0 and the output of the other machines be 1. Also, let the input of $I_2$ cause machines $M_0$, $M_1$ and $M_2$ to produce 0 outputs and the others to produce 1 outputs. For fault detection, the criteria of usefulness for the inputs $I_1$ and $I_2$ are $n_1 = 2$ and $n_2 = 3$ respectively. The input $I_1$ is chosen as the next input for fault detection. If the amounts of information after applying inputs $I_1$ and $I_2$ are represented by $\mathscr{I}_1$ and $\mathscr{I}_2$ respectively and the probabilities of the machine under test to be $M_i, i = 0, 1, \ldots, 5$ are equal, then

$$\mathscr{I}_1 = -\tfrac{2}{6} \log_2 \tfrac{2}{6} - \tfrac{4}{6} \log_2 \tfrac{4}{6} = 0.92 \text{ bit}$$

$$\mathscr{I}_2 = -\tfrac{3}{6} \log_2 \tfrac{3}{6} - \tfrac{3}{6} \log_2 \tfrac{3}{6} = 1 \text{ bit}$$

Thus, the input $I_2$ is preferable for diagnosis. Note that in the above computation of $\mathscr{I}_1$ and $\mathscr{I}_2$, we have assumed that the fault has not been detected; that is, we are interested in detection and diagnosis. If the fault has already been detected, we know *a priori* that the machine is not $M_0$. If the machine is equally likely to be any one of the five faulty machines,

$$\mathscr{I}_1 = -\tfrac{1}{5}\log_2 \tfrac{1}{5} - \tfrac{4}{5}\log_2 \tfrac{4}{5} = 0.720$$

$$\mathscr{I}_2 = -\tfrac{2}{4}\log_2 \tfrac{2}{5} - \tfrac{3}{5}\log_2 \tfrac{3}{5} = 0.972,$$

indicating that the application of $I_2$ will still result in the greater information gain.

## ARMSTRONG'S METHOD

Whereas the Sequential Analyzer determines the set of faults detected by a particular test by simulating all faulty machines with the test applied, Armstrong (1968, 1971) makes use of a procedure similar to path-sensitizing. For any given test, the normal machine is simulated and the results are used for determining the set of faults detected by it. Though the analysis involved in determining the fault set for a given test is likely to be more time consuming than a single pass through the Sequential Analyzer, this approach seems to be preferable when the number of faults to be considered is large. In such a case, many passes through the Sequential Analyzer may be necessary to simulate all the faulty machines. Though Armstrong's program was written for a specific large asynchronous multi-processor, the method seems to have general applicability.

The simulator is table-driven. The circuit description is contained in tables which are accessed by the program during execution. Simulation is at the gate level though several gates are sometimes treated as a single logical unit. Each gate or logical unit is referred to as a *node*. The simulation program updates its computation at successive fixed intervals of simulated time equal to the average delay per gate. The variation in delays is considered to be too small to affect the results of the simulation and no race analyses are undertaken. Feedback loops in the circuit are not identified and do not affect the program. This is because of the assumption of the fixed delay associated with every gate. The selective trace technique discussed earlier is used. Since the interval of simulation is equal to the average gate delay and all changes in

# ARMSTRONG'S METHOD

gate outputs are to be computed, it is not necessary to assign levels to gates. The output of any node is computed if and only if one or more of its input values changed during the preceding interval.

Whenever the output of a node is computed, the list of single faults which will cause the output of the node to be different from its normal value is also determined. This is called the fault list of the node. The fault list of a node is kept up-to-date by recomputing it whenever one or more inputs to the node change. Error symptoms consisting of signal values on monitored outputs in the presence of faults are determined from the fault lists of these outputs as shown in the following example.

**Example 5.2**

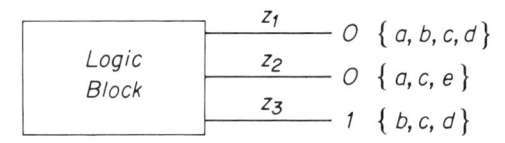

```
                  z₁
┌─────────┐ ──────── 0  {a, b, c, d}
│  Logic  │    z₂
│  Block  │ ──────── 0  {a, c, e}
│         │    z₃
└─────────┘ ──────── 1  {b, c, d}
```

**Figure 5.1**

| Faults | Error Symptoms |     |     |
|--------|:---:|:---:|:---:|
|        | $z_1$ | $z_2$ | $z_3$ |
| $a$    | 1 | 1 | 1 |
| $b, d$ | 1 | 0 | 0 |
| $c$    | 1 | 1 | 0 |
| $e$    | 0 | 1 | 1 |

**Table 5.1**

Figure 5.1 gives the normal outputs and the fault lists associated with the three output wires $z_1$, $z_2$ and $z_3$ of a circuit, when a particular test is applied. The error symptoms given in Table 5.1 are the actual values of the outputs under the different fault conditions and are obtained directly from the fault lists.

The fault list associated with each node is derived from the fault lists associated with the inputs of the node, the values of the inputs in the normal circuit and the type of the node. The following example demonstrates the derivation of the fault lists for a NOR gate.

**Example 5.3:** Let the fault lists associated with the inputs to the NOR gate of Fig. 5.2 for the values of signals shown be $A$, $B$, $C$, and $D$. We wish to compute the fault list $E$ associated with its output.

$A = \{a, b, c, d\}$ — 1
$B = \{a, b, e\}$ — 1
$C = \{b, c\}$ — 0
$D = \{e\}$ — 0

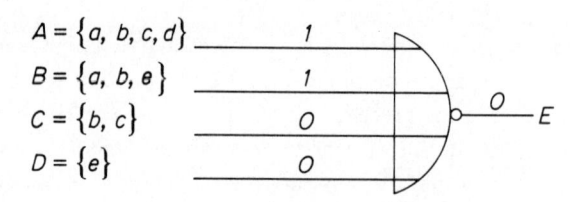

output 0 — $E$

**Figure 5.2**

In Fig. 5.2, note that several faults appear in more than one fault list. This indicates reconvergent fan-out. That is, the effect of these faults will propagate to the NOR gate under consideration along different paths, when the particular input combination is applied to the circuit.

In order for the effect of a fault to propagate through the NOR gate, the output must change to 1 and hence all its inputs must be 0. This is possible only for faults that are contained in both $A$ and $B$ but not $C$ or $D$. If the fault causing the output of the NOR gate to be s-a-1 is denoted by $f$, we have:

$$E = A \cap B \cap (\overline{C \cup D}) \cup \{f\}$$
$$= \{a, b, c, d\} \cap \{a, b, e\} \cap (\overline{\{b, c\} \cup \{e\}}) \cup \{f\}$$
$$= \{a, f\}.$$

In the example, if the normal inputs to the NOR gate are 0010 and the input fault lists are unchanged, the fault list of the output is:

$$E = (\bar{A} \cap \bar{B} \cap C \cap \bar{D}) \cup \{f\} = \{f\}$$

For the same fault lists at the inputs and the normal inputs of 0000,

$$E = A \cup B \cup C \cup D \cup \{g\}$$
$$= \{a, b, c, d, e, g\}$$

where $g$ represents the output of the NOR gate s-a-0.

Fault lists for other types of gates can be derived in a similar manner, as illustrated in the following example.

**Example 5.4:**

Figure 5.3 shows the normal signals with the test $\bar{x}_1 x_2 \bar{x}_3 \bar{x}_4$ applied. Denoting s-a-0 and s-a-1 faults by subscripts 0 and 1 respectively and

# ARMSTRONG'S METHOD

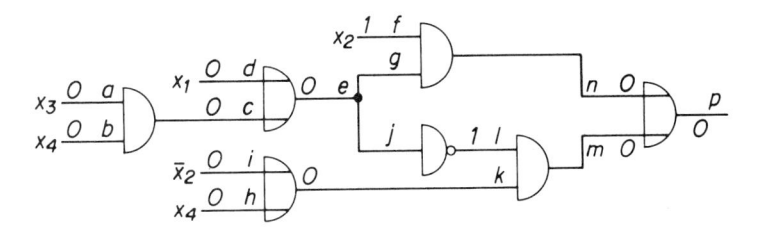

**Figure 5.3**

the fault list of each wire by the corresponding upper case letter, we obtain the following fault lists for the circuit:

$A = \{a_1\}$

$B = \{b_1\}$

$C = (A \cap B) \cup \{c_1\} = \{c_1\}$

$D = \{d_1\}$

$E = D \cup C \cup \{e_1\} = \{c_1, d_1, e_1\}$

$F = \{f_0\}$

$G = E \cup \{g_1\} = \{c_1, d_1, e_1, g_1\}$

$H = \{h_1\}$

$I = \{i_1\}$

$J = E \cup \{j_1\} = \{c_1, d_1, e_1, j_1\}$

$K = I \cup H \cup \{k_1\} = \{i_1, h_1, k_1\}$

$L = J \cup \{l_0\} = \{c_1, d_1, e_1, j_1, l_0\}$

$M = (K \cap \bar{L}) \cup \{m_1\} = \{i_1, h_1, k_1, m_1\}$

$N = (G \cap \bar{F}) \cup \{n_1\} = \{c_1, d_1, e_1, g_1, n_1\}$

$P = N \cup M \cup \{p_1\} = \{c_1, d_1, e_1, g_1, n_1, i_1, h_1, k_1, m_1, p_1\}$

As mentioned earlier, the program does not explicitly recognize feedback loops. No race analysis is performed and critical races in the normal or faulty circuit are not detected. (One exception is in the computation of the output fault lists of flip-flops.) If the normal circuit is unstable for some input combination, the simulated outputs of some nodes may oscillate, though the simulation program does not explicitly recognize this condition. Even if the normal circuit is stable, the presence of some fault may lead to instability. This will result in oscillations of the fault lists computed by the program. The program continues computing oscillating fault lists until they stabilize or the inputs are changed or until a specified time interval has elapsed after the logic values in the normal circuit have stabilized. In doing this as well as in computing fault lists for sequential circuits, care must be taken to be consistent when the effects of a fault feed back on that same wire as in the extension of the path-sensitizing technique of Chapter 3. In general, if at the time of computation the normal value of some wire $c$ is 0, the fault list for that wire cannot contain $c_0$ but must contain $c_1$ (and vice versa for $c = 1$). Thus if the fault list propagating to wire $c$, contains $c_0$ and $c$ is normally 0, $c_0$ is deleted and replaced by $c_1$, and, if the fault list propagating to $c$ contains $c_1$ this is left unchanged.

Flip-flops can usually be represented by circuits containing two or more gates and some feedback. For example, a set-reset (SR) flip-flop can be represented by a pair of cross-connected NOR gates as shown in Fig. 5.4.

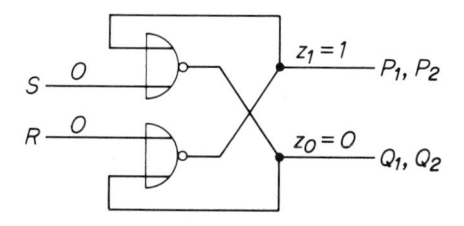

**Figure 5.4**

If races are ignored and the delays associated with the gates are equal to the other delays in the circuit, a flip-flop can be simulated by simulating the individual gates. The fault lists associated with the outputs of a flip-flop at any time will depend upon the fault lists associated with its inputs, and the outputs during the preceding interval of time. Let $S$ and $R$ be the input fault lists and $P_1$ and $Q_1$ the output fault lists associated with the outputs $z_1$ and $z_0$ respectively. Considering the individual NOR gates in the flip-flop and ignoring faults in the flip-flop itself, the output fault lists for the next interval of simulation with the inputs shown in Fig. 5.4 are:

$$P_2 = R \cup Q_1$$

$$Q_2 = P_1 \cap \bar{S}$$

The above equations indicate that $z_1 = 0$ (i.e., $z_1$ is faulty) whenever the reset signal or the past output $z_0$ is faulty. Similarly $z_0 = 1$ when the past output $z_1 = 0$ and the set signal is correct (0).

If we assume that the delays associated with the NOR gates of the flip-flop are small enough to enable the flip-flop to reach a stable state within

# ARMSTRONG'S METHOD

the interval of simulation and that the delays in the two gates are widely different, then a detailed analysis of the flip-flop with all combinations of faulty inputs and faulty past states is necessary. Table 5.2 shows all different fault-list intersections, and the new output fault lists, if any, in which each intersection should be contained, for the normal values of the past state and present inputs of the flip-flop, indicated in Fig. 5.4. In the table, intersections of sets are shown as products. Excluding the critical race condition $P_1 \bar{Q}_1 \bar{R} S$, we obtain the following fault lists:

$$P'_2 = R \cup (Q_1 \cap \bar{S})$$

$$Q'_2 = (R \cap \bar{S}) \cup (Q_1 \cap \bar{S})$$

$P_2$ and $Q_2$ were derived assuming synchronous operation while the derivation of $P'_2$ and $Q'_2$ assumed asynchronous operation. By iterating $P_2$ and $Q_2$ we would get the same results as $P'_2$ and $Q'_2$ except for "don't care" conditions and critical races which may lead to oscillations in $P_2$ and $Q_2$. These do not include the faults that may occur in the flip-flop itself, but take advantage of the impossible combinations listed in the table, to simplify the expressions.

| Intersection | Contained in | Remarks |
|---|---|---|
| $\bar{P}_1 \bar{Q}_1 \bar{R} \bar{S}$ | – | |
| $\bar{P}_1 \bar{Q}_1 \bar{R} S$ | – | |
| $\bar{P}_1 \bar{Q}_1 R \bar{S}$ | $P_2, Q_2$ | |
| $\bar{P}_1 \bar{Q}_1 R S$ | $P_2$ | Both outputs become 0 |
| $\bar{P}_1 Q_1 \bar{R} \bar{S}$ | x | Previous outputs $z_0 = z_1 = 1$ impossible |
| $\bar{P}_1 Q_1 \bar{R} S$ | x | —ditto— |
| $\bar{P}_1 Q_1 R \bar{S}$ | x | —ditto— |
| $\bar{P}_1 Q_1 R S$ | x | —ditto— |
| $P_1 \bar{Q}_1 \bar{R} \bar{S}$ | * | Both outputs are initially 0 implying both $R$ and $S$ were 1 during the preceding interval. The final state reached by the flip-flop may depend upon the order in which $R$ and $S$ change (critical race). |
| $P_1 \bar{Q}_1 \bar{R} S$ | – | |
| $P_1 \bar{Q}_1 R \bar{S}$ | $P_2, Q_2$ | |
| $P_1 \bar{Q}_1 R S$ | $P_2$ | Both outputs 0. |
| $P_1 Q_1 \bar{R} \bar{S}$ | $P_2, Q_2$ | |
| $P_1 Q_1 \bar{R} S$ | – | |
| $P_1 Q_1 R \bar{S}$ | $P_2, Q_2$ | |
| $P_1 Q_1 R S$ | $P_2$ | Both outputs 0. |

**Table 5.2**

A practical problem which may arise is that the initial states of some flip-flops and the values of some inputs are unknown. These unknown values may cause the outputs of some nodes to be unknown. The simulator computes the outputs of nodes with unknown inputs only if the remaining inputs to the node uniquely define its output. In order to derive the correct fault lists in the presence of unknown signals, it is necessary to consider all combinations of values for the unknown signals. Since this will result in significant increases in the simulation time, an approximate method is adopted. If the output of a gate is unknown, its output fault list is treated as indeterminate. If the output of a gate with some unknown inputs is known, the output fault list is generated in the manner discussed earlier, using the fault lists of only the known inputs, and the output fault list is flagged, indicating that these faults may not be detectable if the unknown inputs assume certain values. If either input of a flip-flop is unknown, both output fault lists are treated as indeterminate.

**Example 5.5:** The fault lists determined using the above approximate method may be incorrect sometimes. In Fig. 5.5, let the input $y$ to the $X = \{a, b, c\}$ OR gate be unknown and let the input $x$ have the value and

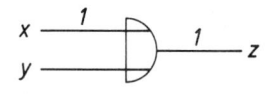

**Figure 5.5**

fault list shown. Ignoring the unknown input $y$, the output fault list (consisting of only those faults that propagate through the gate) is $Z = \{a, b, c\}$. If $y = 0$ and $Y = \{a, b\}$, then $Z = X \cap \bar{Y} = \{c\}$, whereas if $y = 1$ and $Y = \{a, b\}$, $Z = X \cap Y = \{a, b\}$. If there is no element in common between the fault lists $X$ and $Y$, the correct output fault list will be the same as that obtained by the approximate method or it will be empty. If $Y = \{d\}$, the correct values of $Z$ are $\{a, b, c\}$ and $\Phi$ for $y = 0$ and $y = 1$ respectively.

## SUMMARY

The main feature of the Sequential Analyzer is its ability to simulate a number of faulty machines simultaneously. The programs have been written for asynchronous sequential circuits but can be easily modified for simulating synchronous circuits. Although the program is capable of deriving tests for sequential circuits, it does this by a trial and error procedure and is rather slow. This feature of the Sequential Analyzer may therefore be useful only as a supplement to other test-derivation procedures.

The Sequential Analyzer we have discussed is a compiler-driven simulator. A table-driven version of the program may have certain advantages in simulating large circuits because selective trace can then be incorporated. However, the effectiveness of selective trace when many faulty machines are simulated simultaneously has not been established.

Armstrong's method has been programmed only for a specific system and direct comparisons of speed between this program and the Sequential Analyzer are difficult. The general principle of computing fault lists instead of simulating faulty circuits may have wide-spread application. It is likely to have a speed advantage over the Sequential Analyzer when the number of faults to be considered is large. A more general simulation program using Armstrong's technique but including some features of the Sequential Analyzer like race analysis and different delays in gates seems to be desirable. The method can probably be modified to generate tests in a manner similar to the Sequential Analyzer.

## REFERENCES

Armstrong, D. B., "A Logic Fault Simulator for the SENTINEL Data Processing System", Bell Telephone Laboratories Internal Memorandum, 1968.

Armstrong, D.B., "A Deductive Method for Simulating Faults in Logic Circuits", *IEEE Trans. on Computers*, 464–471, 1972.

Chang, H. Y., Manning, E. G. and Metze, G., *Fault Diagnosis in Digital Systems*, Wiley-Interscience, 1970.

Huffman, D. A., "The Synthesis of Sequential Switching Circuits", *J. Franklin Inst.*, 257, 161–190 and 275–303, 1954.

Menon, P. R., "A Simulation Program for Logic Networks", Bell Telephone Laboratories Internal Memorandum, 1965.

Seshu, S., "The Logic Organizer and Diagnosis Programs", Coordinated Science Laboratory, University of Illinois, Urbana, Report R-226, 1964.

Seshu, S., "On an Improved Diagnosis Program", *IEEE Trans. on Electronic Computers*, EC-14, 76–79, 1965.

Seshu, S. and Freeman, D. N., The Diagnosis of Asynchronous Sequential Switching Systems", *IRE Trans. on Electronic Computers* EC-11, 459–465, 1962.

Shannon, C. E., "A Mathematical Theory of Communication", *BSTJ*, vol. 27, 379–423, 623–656, 1948.

## PROBLEMS

1. For the circuit of Fig. 3.1 in the initial state 00, find the set of faults detected at the output by the input sequence 01101, using Armstrong's procedure.

2. For the circuit of Fig. 3.1 and the set of faults $\{a_0, a_1, d_0, d_1, e_0, e_1\}$ and initial state 00, using Seshu's procedure
   a) Find a test sequence which detects all faults.
   b) Find a test sequence which locates all faults. Assume synchronous operation.

3. a) For the circuit of Fig. 5.6 and the set of faults $\alpha$ s-a-1, $\beta$ s-a-1, $\gamma$ s-a-0, $\delta$ s-a-0 and initial state 00, use Seshu's procedure to find a test sequence which detects all detectable faults assuming asynchronous operation. Assume that only single-input changes are permitted.
   b) Can the fault $\delta$ s-a-0 be detected? Explain.

4. For the flip-flop of Fig. 5.4, find the output fault lists $P_2$, $Q_2$ as functions of fault lists $S$, $R$, $P_1$, $Q_1$ assuming asynchronous operation, with the set and reset inputs equal to 1 and 0 respectively and past outputs $z_0 = 0$ and $z_1 = 1$.

5. Assuming that the inputs $x_1$ and $x_2$ in Fig. 5.7 are unknown, determine the output fault list using Armstrong's approximate method. Compare this fault list with the fault lists for the different combinations of values of $x_1$ and $x_2$.

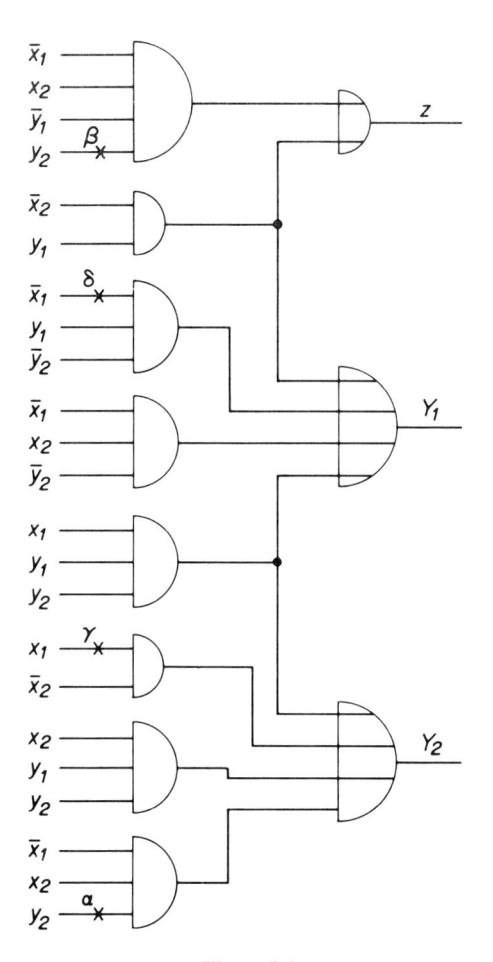

**Figure 5.6**

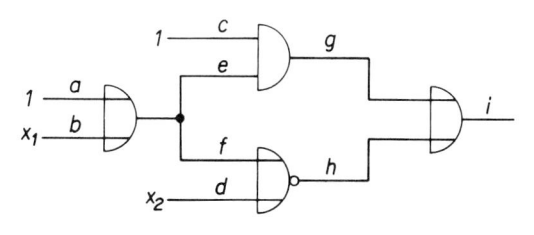

**Figure 5.7**

CHAPTER 6

# DESIGN TECHNIQUES

Our discussion so far has been restricted to the problem of deriving tests for given digital circuits. The design of the circuits under consideration was assumed to be complete and we had no control over it. However, the number of tests or the length of the test sequence required is dependent not only on the function realized but also on the particular realization. Thus, the ease of testing is one factor which should be taken into account during the design.

At present, there are no systematic techniques for designing digital circuits which are easy to test and maintain. In the first part of this chapter, we shall present a few of the techniques which may be useful in designing combinational and sequential circuits. Some aspects of system organization and their effect on testing are also considered.

In certain applications where repair is impossible, it may be necessary to design circuits so that they will not fail during their mission. When the mission is relatively short, the circuits can be designed so that they operate correctly provided that the number of faults does not exceed a specified number. This is accomplished by means of various fault-masking redundancy techniques, some of which are presented later in this chapter.

Finally, we examine two examples of self-checking systems, where reliable opeation is required over relatively long periods of time. Although these systems are also redundant, the redundancy is at the subsystem level. Individual circuits are irredundant and fault-detection and diagnostic

# DESIGN TO SIMPLIFY TESTING

tests are used for identifying the faulty subsystem and isolating it from the system. We also present a theoretical model of self-checking systems.

## DESIGN TO SIMPLIFY TESTING

Our primary consideration will be the design of circuits that can be tested by relatively few tests or short test sequences. The problem of making the test set simpler to derive will be a secondary consideration. The feasibility of the proposals made here will depend upon the circuit technology. We shall present a few methods (which are by no means exhaustive) for designing specific types of circuits that are relatively easy to test.

### Combinational Circuits with Small Test Sets

In deriving a test for a particular fault in a combinational circuit, we sensitize a path from the location of the fault to an output. A test for the fault will also detect faults along the sensitized path. It therefore seems likely that a multi-level realization of a function will require fewer tests than a two-level realization. In most cases, two-level circuits may be among the worst, as far as the size of the test set is concerned. This may not always be true because of the possibility of sensitizing several paths simultaneously in the two-level realizations of some functions. The following is an example of a function whose two-level realization requires a much larger test set than a multi-level realization.

> **Example 6.1:** Consider an $n$-input parity-check function. The map of the function has a checkerboard pattern of 0's and 1's and the two level sum-of-products realization of Fig. 6.1(a) will require $2^{n-1}$ minterms. The function can also be realized as a tree of two-input exclusive-OR's as shown in Fig. 6.1(b). All $2^n$ input combinations are necessary to test the two-level sum-of-products realization for all single s-a-1 and s-a-0 faults. On the other hand, it can be shown that the tree structure can be tested for the same set of faults by four tests, independent of $n$ (Problem 6, Chapter 4).

Since a tree of two-input exclusive-OR's is easily testable, the realization of a function where a parity-check function is factored out and realized by such a tree may be testable by fewer tests than the usual sum-of-products.

(a)

(b)

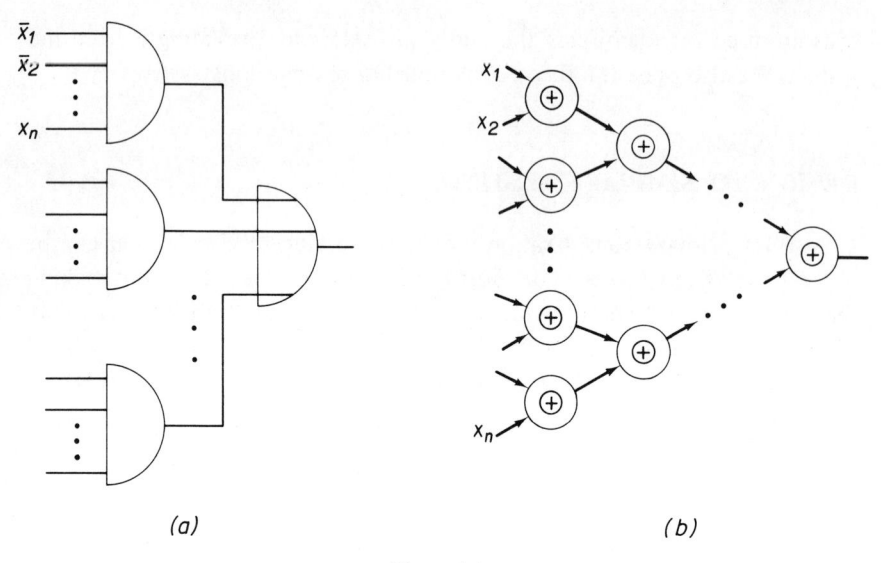

**Figure 6.1**

However, there are no known algorithms (short of enumeration) for obtaining such realizations. The factored realization given in the following example was obtained by enumeration.

**Example 6.2:** Consider the function $f = \bar{B}\bar{D} + \bar{A}\bar{C}\bar{D} + A\bar{B}\bar{C} + AC\bar{D} + \bar{A}BCD$. It can be verified that 12 tests are necessary to detect all faults in the minimal two-level sum-of-products realization of this

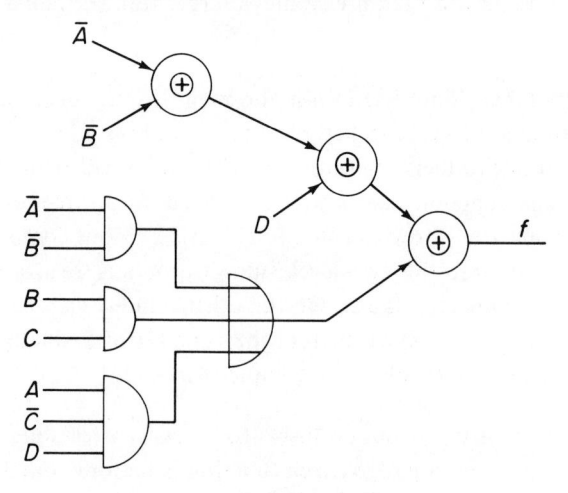

**Figure 6.2**

DESIGN TO SIMPLIFY TESTING 171

function. If the function is written as $f = \bar{A} \oplus \bar{B} \oplus D \oplus (\bar{A}\bar{B} + BC + A\bar{C}D)$ and realized as shown in Fig. 6.2, six tests are sufficient to detect all faults. The six tests are: $A\bar{B}\bar{C}\bar{D}$, $\bar{A}\bar{B}\bar{D}$, $ABCD$, $\bar{A}B\bar{C}D$, $A\bar{B}CD$ and $A\bar{C}D$. Another factored realization, $f = (\bar{D} + A\bar{C}) \oplus (\bar{A}B \oplus B\bar{C})$ can be shown to require only five tests (Problem 6, Chapter 2).

*Fault-Locatable Combinational Circuits*

Another important problem is that of designing circuits so that faults can be easily located. The fault is to be located as closely as possible, under the single-fault assumption. A certain amount of ambiguity about the location of a physical fault is inherent in all circuits. For example, it is impossible to distinguish between a s-a-1 fault at an input of an OR gate and a s-a-1 fault at its output. Since the input to one gate may be the output of another gate, our objective must be limited to locating the fault to within a pair of interconnections along a path.

In any circuit, a fault that cannot be located to within a pair of interconnections along a path is called *non-fault locatable (nfl)*.

**Example 6.3:** Consider the function $f_1 = \bar{A}\bar{B}\bar{C} + ABD + ACD$ realized as shown in Fig. 6.3. The faults $B$ s-a-1 on gate $G_1$ and $C$ s-a-1

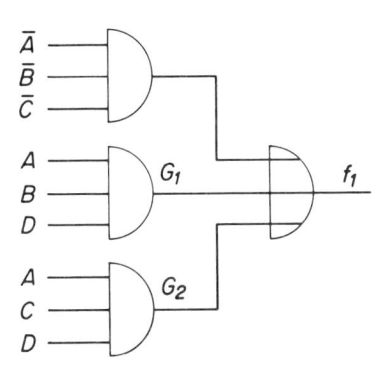

Figure 6.3

on gate $G_2$ are detected only by the test $A\bar{B}\bar{C}D$. These two faults are therefore indistinguishable and form what we shall call an *nfl pair*. The difficulty can be resolved by realizing $f_1$ in the factored form $\bar{A}\bar{B}\bar{C} + AD(B + C)$ as shown in Fig. 6.4. Here $B$ and $C$ are inputs to

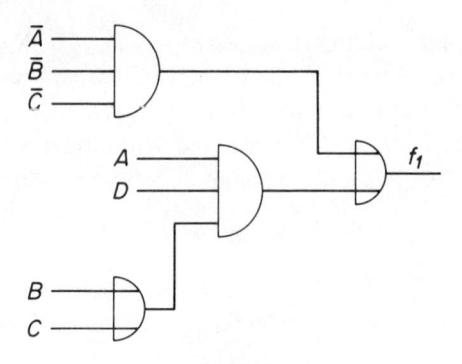

**Figure 6.4**

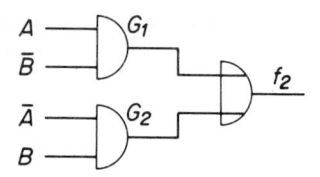

**Figure 6.5**

the same OR gate and the faults need not be distinguished. However, such simple factoring cannot always be done. Consider $f_2 = A\bar{B} + \bar{A}B$, whose realization is shown in Fig. 6.5. Here s-a-1 faults on $A$ of $G_1$ and $B$ of $G_2$ are indistinguishable, as are s-a-1 faults on $\bar{B}$ of $G_1$ and $\bar{A}$ of $G_2$. The more complex functions examined in the following examples demonstrate some of the problems which may arise in attempting to eliminate nfl fault pairs by the use of simple factorings.

**Example 6.4**

$$f_3 = \bar{A}\bar{D} + \bar{A}\bar{B}\bar{C} + ABD + ACD.$$

The only nfl pair consists of s-a-1 faults on the input leads $B$ and $C$ of the gates realizing the terms $ABD$ and $ACD$. Denoting the test sets for these faults by $T_B$ and $T_C$, we have $T_B = T_C = A\bar{B}\bar{C}D$. If we factor out $(B + C)$ as in Example 6.3, we get $f'_3 = \bar{A}\bar{D} + \bar{A}\bar{B}\bar{C} + AD(B + C)$ and the nfl pair $(B, C)$ has been eliminated. However in $f'_3$, the test set for $A$ s-a-1 is $T_A = \bar{A}D(B + C)$ and the faults $(\bar{D}, A)$ s-a-1 form an nfl pair since $T_{\bar{D}} = T_A$. On the other hand, there are two appearances of $A$ in $f_3$, one having the test $\bar{A}DB$ and the other $\bar{A}DC$. $\bar{D}$ s-a-1 is detectable by either of the two tests, and can be distinguished from a s-a-1 fault on either appearance of $A$ by applying both tests.

DESIGN TO SIMPLIFY TESTING 173

Thus in eliminating the nfl pair $(B, C)$ we have introduced the nfl pair $(A, \bar{D})$. Note that $f_3$ can be rewritten as

$$f_3 = \bar{A}(\bar{D} + \bar{B}\bar{C}) + AD(B + C)$$
$$= \bar{A}(\overline{D(B + C)}) + A(D(B + C)) = A \oplus \overline{D(B + C)}.$$

**Example 6.5**

$$f_4 = A\bar{C}\bar{D} + \bar{A}\bar{B}\bar{C} + \bar{A}CD + BC\bar{D}$$

For s-a-1 faults

$$T_A = \bar{A}BC\bar{D} = T_C \text{ for the literal } C \text{ in term } BC\bar{D}$$

$$T_D = \bar{A}\bar{B}CD = T_C \text{ for the literal } \bar{C} \text{ in term } \bar{A}\bar{B}\bar{C}$$

We can eliminate these nfl pairs if we can factor $f_4$ into a form in which both members of an nfl pair are connected to the same OR gate. The simple product-of-sums form of $f_4$ is such a factoring

$$f_4 = (A + C + \bar{B})(\bar{C} + D + B)(\bar{A} + \bar{D})$$

for this example and this realization contains no nfl pairs.

Example 6.6 demonstrates a function for which both the product-of-sums and sum-of-products forms have nfl pairs but which can be realized without any nfl pairs.

**Example 6.6**

$$f_5 = \bar{A}\bar{B}\bar{C} + ABD + ACD$$

$$T_B = T_C = A\bar{B}\bar{C}D \text{ for the s-a-1 faults}$$

The product-of-sums form is

$$f_5 = (A + \bar{B})(A + \bar{C})(\bar{A} + D)(\bar{A} + B + C)$$

$$T_B = T_C = \bar{A}\bar{B}\bar{C} \text{ for the s-a-0 faults.}$$

However, $f_5$ is equal to the previously considered function $f_1$ for which we have shown that the realization $\bar{A}\bar{B}\bar{C} + AD(B + C)$ has no nfl pairs.

A function is defined as *essentially nfl* if every possible irredundant realization of the function using AND's, OR's and NOT's has nfl faults. It can be shown by enumeration that all irredundant AND-OR-NOT realizations of the function $A\bar{B} + \bar{A}B$ contain nfl pairs. Therefore, this function is essentially nfl.

Since we have no systematic procedure for determining whether an arbitrary function is essentially nfl, it seems desirable to show how to realize an important class of functions by *totally fault-locatable* circuits (i.e., containing no nfl pairs). We then show how an arbitrary circuit can be made totally fault-locatable by converting it to a member of this class.

A combinational function $f(x_1, x_2, \ldots, x_n)$ is defined to be *unate* if its reduced sum-of-products form expression does not contain a term with $x_i$ and also a term with $\bar{x}_i$ (i.e., each variable appears complemented or uncomplemented, but not both). For example $f = ABC + \bar{A}BD$ is not unate whereas $f = ABC + B\bar{D}$ is unate.

**Theorem 6.1:** *No unate function is essentially nfl.*

**Proof:** Consider a unate function $f(x_1, x_2, \ldots, x_n)$. If no input appears in two terms, then a simple two-level AND-OR realization is totally fault locatable. Assume that $x_1$ appears in $k \geq 2$ terms. The function can be written as:

$$f = x_1(g_1(x_2, \ldots, x_n) + \cdots g_k(x_2, \ldots, x_n)) + f_1(x_2, \ldots, x_n).$$

Let $g_1(x_2, \ldots, x_n) + \cdots + g_k(x_2, \ldots, x_n) = G_1(x_2, \ldots, x_n)$. The function $f$ can be realized as shown in Fig. 6.6. Table 6.1 shows the complete set of tests for the different faults in this realization.

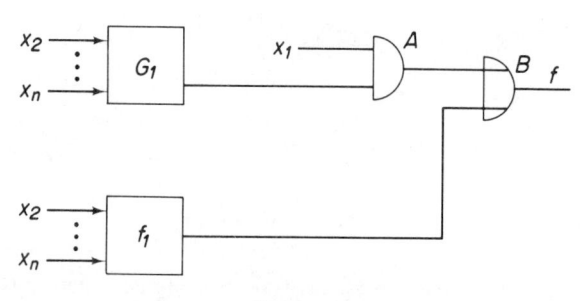

Figure 6.6

DESIGN TO SIMPLIFY TESTING 175

| Gate or Block | Type of Faults | Tests |
|---|---|---|
| $A$ | s-a-0 | $x_1 G_1 \bar{f}_1$ |
|  | s-a-1 | $\bar{x}_1 G_1 \bar{f}_1, x_1 \bar{G}_1 \bar{f}_1$ |
| $B$ | s-a-0 | $x_1 G_1 \bar{f}_1, (\bar{x}_1 + \bar{G}_1) f_1$ |
|  | s-a-1 | $(\bar{x}_1 + \bar{G}_1) \bar{f}_1$ |
| $G_1$ | s-a-0 | $x_1 T_{G_1}(x_2 \cdots x_n) \bar{f}_1$ |
|  | s-a-1 | where $T_{G_1}$ is an input combination which propagates the effect of the fault to the output of $G_1$ |
| $f_1$ | s-a-0 | $(\bar{x}_1 + \bar{G}_1) T_{f_1}(x_2 \cdots x_n)$ |
|  | s-a-1 | where $T_{f_1}$ is an input combination which propagates the effect of the fault to the output of $f_1$ |

Table 6.1

From Table 6.1, we see that faults in $f_1$ and $G_1$ are distinguishable, since faults in $f_1$ have tests with $x_1 = 0$ while faults in $G_1$ only have tests with $x_1 = 1$. We also note that a s-a-0 fault on the output of $G_1$ cannot be distinguished from a fault on the output of $A$ or input of $B$. However, this amount of ambiguity is inherent in all circuits. Similarly, we do not expect to distinguish between faults on the outputs of $f_1$ and $B$.

The only other faults which should be made distinguishable are those on gate $A$ and in $f_1$. These faults can be indistinguishable if and only if

$$\bar{x}_1 G_1 \bar{f}_1 = (\bar{x}_1 + \bar{G}_1) T_{f_1}(x_2, \ldots, x_n).$$

This implies that

$$\bar{G}_1 T_{f_1}(x_2, \ldots, x_n) = 0 \quad \text{and}$$

$$G_1 \bar{f}_1 = T_{f_1}(x_2, \ldots, x_n), \text{ for some fault in } f_1.$$

Since $G_1 \bar{f}_1 = T_{f_1}$ implies that $\bar{G}_1 T_{f_1} = 0$, we need consider only the former. Without loss of generality, we can assume that all the variables $x_1, x_2, \ldots, x_n$ appear uncomplemented in the function $f$. The functions $G_1$ and $f_1$ can then be expressed as sums-of-products containing only uncomplemented variables. Let $f_1$ contain a term $S_1 = x_2 x_3 \ldots x_r$, which satisfies the condition $G_1 \bar{f}_1 = T_{f_1}$. The tests $T_{f_1}$ for faults in the realization of this term are of the following form, assuming a sum-of-products realization of $f_1$:

$$\bar{x}_2 x_3 \cdots x_r \bar{x}_{r+1} \cdots \bar{x}_n$$

$$x_2 \bar{x}_3 \cdots x_r \bar{x}_{r+1} \cdots \bar{x}_n$$

$$x_2x_3 \cdots \bar{x}_r\bar{x}_{r+1} \cdots \bar{x}_n$$

$$x_2x_3 \cdots x_r\bar{x}_{r+1} \cdots \bar{x}_n$$

It can be shown that this set is sufficient for testing a realization of $f_1$ in the factored form. Since $G_1$ and $f_1$ both contain only uncomplemented literals, $T_{f_1} = G_1\bar{f}_1$ if and only if $G_1 = S_1 = x_2x_3 \ldots x_r$ or $G_1 = S_2$, where $S_2$ is obtained by deleting exactly one literal from $S_1$. However, if $G_1 = S_1$, $f$ will be redundant and the term $x_1S_1$ may be deleted from $f$. Thus the only case where the realization of Fig. 6.6 is nfl is when $G_1 = S_2$. Without loss of generality, let $S_2 = x_3x_4 \ldots x_r$. Now, the sum-of-products form of $f$ will contain terms of the form $x_1x_3 \ldots x_r$ and $x_2x_3 \ldots x_r$. In this case $f$ can be realized by factoring out $(x_1 + x_2)$ as shown in Fig. 6.7.

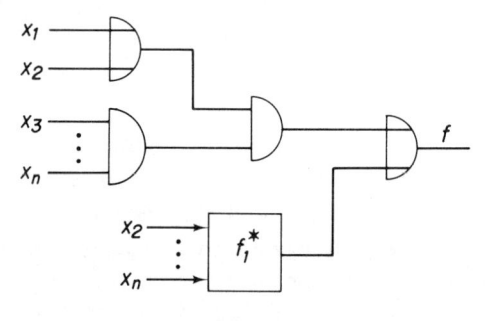

**Figure 6.7**

In order to complete the procedure, we apply the same factoring technique to $f_1$ (or $f_1^*$) and $G_1$ until further factorization is impossible. If $G_1 = S_{21} + \ldots + S_{2k}$ and $f_1$ has terms $x_pS_{21},\ldots, x_pS_{2k}$, such factorization may introduce the nfl pair $(x_1,x_p)$ which can be eliminated by combining the separate appearances of the factor $S_{21} + \ldots + S_{2k}$. By combining series of AND gates and series of OR gates, the resulting realization will have alternating AND and OR gates along any path and fault location is possible to within a pair of interconnections along a path. This realization is sufficient for total fault locatability.

**Example 6.7**

$$f = ABC + BCD + DEF$$
$$= A(BC) + (BC)D + DEF$$

Here $G_1 = BC$ and $f_1 = BCD + DEF$. Since $G_1$ is contained in a term of $f_1$, we should factor out $(A + D)$ to obtain the following totally

# DESIGN TO SIMPLIFY TESTING

fault locatable realization:

$$f = (A + D)BC + DEF$$

**Example 6.8**

$$f = ABC + BCD + AEF + GEF$$
$$= A(BC + EF) + BCD + GEF$$

Note that $G_1 = BC + EF$ has one term each contained in $BCD$ and $GEF$. It is not necessary to factor out $(A + D)$ or $(A + G)$ since $G_1$ is not a single term (see the Proof of Theorem 6.1). No further factorization is necessary since the terms in $G_1$ have no literal in common, nor do the terms in $f_1$. If $f = ABC + BCD + AEF + DEF$, it should be realized as $(A + D)(BE + EF)$.

**Example 6.9**

$$f = ABCD + ABEF + CDEF$$
$$= A(BCD + BEF) + CDEF$$
$$= A(B(CD + EF)) + CDEF$$
$$= AB(CD + EF) + CDEF$$

A totally fault-locatable realization of the function is shown in Fig. 6.8.

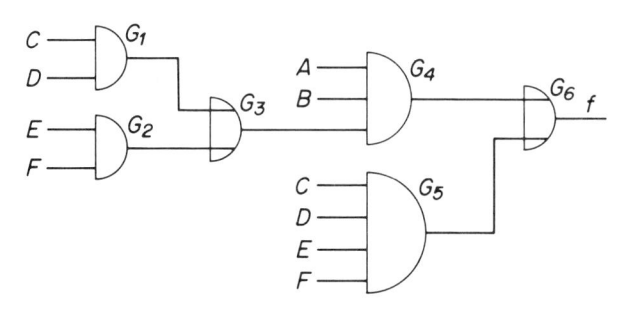

**Figure 6.8**

The preceding discussion leads to a method of obtaining a totally fault-locatable realization of any combinational function. If we allow every variable and its complement to be independent of each other while testing, any function of $n$ variables can be represented as a unate function of at most

2n variables and a totally fault-locatable realization using Theorem 6.1 can be obtained. For example, $f = A\bar{B} + \bar{A}B$ can be written as $f = AC + BD$, where $C = \bar{B}$ and $D = \bar{A}$ under operating conditions and $A$, $B$, $C$ and $D$ are independent under testing conditions. In this manner, we increase the number of tests that can be applied to the circuit. It is not surprising that the fault resolution is improved as a consequence.

*Sequential Circuits with Distinguishing Sequences*

It was shown in Chapter 3 that the design of checking experiments is considerably simplified if the machine has a distinguishing sequence. The checking experiments are also much shorter. A machine which contains* a given sequential machine and also possesses a distinguishing sequence can be obtained by adding outputs to the given machine. The following example demonstrates the simplification of the checking experiment resulting from the addition of a suitable output.

**Example 6.10:** The flow table shown below is the same as that in Example 3.10, but with an output added.

|   | 0 | 1 | $y_1$ | $y_2$ |
|---|---|---|---|---|
| A | B, 00 | D, 00 | 0 | 0 |
| B | A, 01 | B, 01 | 0 | 1 |
| C | D, 10 | A, 00 | 1 | 0 |
| D | D, 11 | C, 01 | 1 | 1 |

Clearly, the machine has a distinguishing sequence of length 1, viz., $x = 0$. It can be verified that the following is a checking sequence for the machine with the initial state $A$:

0010010011010.

Thus by adding a single output, the checking sequence is greatly shortened and compares favorably with the shortest sequence derived in Chapter 3. The reduction in the length of the checking sequence can be obtained without any added logic by using the state assignment

---

*A machine $M'$ contains $M$ if there is some subset $z'$ of the outputs of $M'$ such that the outputs of $M$ and the $z'$ outputs of $M'$ are identical for any input sequence and any initial state.

# DESIGN TO SIMPLIFY TESTING

shown to the right of the flow table. Note that the added output always has the same value as the state variable $y_2$, and simplified testing is possible merely by making $y_2$ observable. In general, an increase in the number of observation points will improve the testability of a circuit.

Particularly efficient checking experiments can be derived for flow tables which have distinguishing sequences consisting of repetitions of a single input. Hennie's method may be used to derive efficient checking sequences for such machines, as shown in the following example.

**Example 6.11**

|   | 0 | 1 |
|---|---|---|
| A | B, 0 | B, 0 |
| B | C, 0 | B, 1 |
| C | D, 1 | E, 0 |
| D | A, 1 | D, 0 |
| E | E, 1 | C, 1 |

The sequences 000 and 110 are both distinguishing sequences for this machine. Using the distinguishing sequence 000, the following checking sequence can be derived for the machine in the initial state $A$:

000000010001000100010001000.

This short sequence could be obtained only by overlapping the distinguishing sequences for different states in the first part of the experiment. However, this is not possible with the distinguishing sequence 110, and a much longer experiment will result if we attempt to derive a checking experiment using it.

Another type of machine for which relatively short checking experiments can be derived is the *definitely diagnosable* machine (Kohavi and Lavallee, 1967). A machine is said to be definitely diagnosable if for some finite $k$, every input sequence of length $k$ is a distinguishing sequence for the machine. The integer $k$ is referred to as the *order* of diagnosability.

Kohavi and Lavallee (1967) have presented a procedure for adding outputs to any given sequential machine to make it definitely diagnosable. The method is also applicable for obtaining a distinguishing sequence consisting of a sufficient number of repetitions of a single input symbol.

The procedure begins with the construction of the *testing graph of the machine*. This graph is similar to the pair-graph used in Chapter 4. The nodes of the graph correspond to unordered pairs of states of the machine. The graph may also contain terminal nodes corresponding to single states. A directed edge labeled $(x_p/z_q)$ is drawn from node $(i, j)$ to node $(k, l)$ if the output of the machine with input $x_p$ is $z_q$ for both states $i$ and $j$, and $k$ and $l$ are the next states. If the outputs are different for a particular input no edge is drawn in the graph. If the next state and output are the same for some input an edge is drawn to a terminal node labeled with the next state.

A machine is definitely diagnosable if and only if its testing graph has no loops or terminal nodes. In order to make a given machine definitely diagnosable, we merely define additional outputs to eliminate terminal nodes and open all loops. If the length of the longest path in the loop-free testing graph is $k$, the order of diagnosability of the augmented machine will be $k + 1$.

**Example 6.12:** Consider the flow table of Example 3.10, which is repeated below:

|   | 0    | 1    |
|---|------|------|
| A | B, 0 | D, 0 |
| B | A, 0 | B, 0 |
| C | D, 1 | A, 0 |
| D | D, 1 | C, 0 |

The testing graph of the machine is shown in Fig. 6.9. The graph has three loops and one terminal node. The assignment of an additional

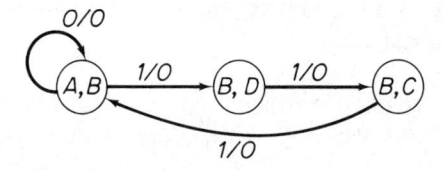

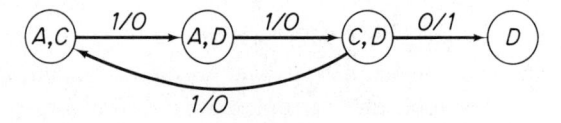

Figure 6.9

# DESIGN TO SIMPLIFY TESTING 181

output as shown below will open the loops and also eliminate the terminal node D.

|   | 0     | 1     |
|---|-------|-------|
| A | B, 00 | D, 00 |
| B | A, 01 | B, 01 |
| C | D, 10 | A, 01 |
| D | D, 11 | C, 0– |

The testing graph of the augmented machine is shown in Fig. 6.10. Note that only one or two of the edges indicated by broken lines

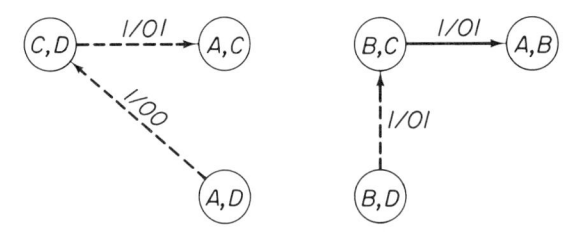

**Figure 6.10**

will be present, depending on the value assigned to the unspecified output. Assigning the value of 1 to this output makes the order of diagnosability equal to 3, whereas the order will be 2 if the value 0 is assigned.

Although any input sequence of length $k$ may be used as a distinguishing sequence in deriving a checking experiment for a definitely diagnosable machine of order $k$, present methods cannot use more than one distinguishing sequence effectively. For present techniques, it seems more desirable to design the machine so that it has a distinguishing sequence that is convenient to use, such as one containing repeated inputs. The length of such a distinguishing sequence may also be less than the order of diagnosability of the machine.

The procedure discussed above for obtaining a definitely diagnosable machine containing a given machine can be modified in an obvious way to obtain a machine which has a distinguishing sequence consisting of a certain repeated input. In this case, it is sufficient to eliminate terminal nodes and loops from a subgraph of the testing graph, whose edges have the input label which is to be repeated in the distinguishing sequence.

## Double-Rank and Multiple-Rank Circuits

A difficult problem in the development of diagnostic tests for asynchronous sequential circuits is the necessity to detect the presence of critical races and unstable conditions in the faulty machine. This is usually done by simulating the faulty machine, and a considerable part of the simulation time is taken up in tracing the signals through closed loops to determine the steady-state values of observable outputs, whenever race conditions occur (Seshu and Freeman, 1962). The generation of tests for comparably sized combinational circuits is much easier due to the absence of feedback. In synchronous circuits, the clock pulses prevent signals from flowing around loops and race analysis is not necessary except when faults in the clocking circuitry are to be considered.

A frequently suggested idea for simplifying the test generation problem for asynchronous sequential circuits is to introduce additional circuitry so as to logically open all feedback loops during testing, thus reducing the test generation problem to the combinational case. Double-rank and multiple-rank circuits (Hall, 1966; Friedman and Menon, 1969), which we shall now discuss, do not have closed loops and are relatively easy to test.

The model of a double-rank circuit is shown in Fig. 6.11. The external input to the circuit is $x$ and $g_1$ and $g_2$ are gating signals which alternately

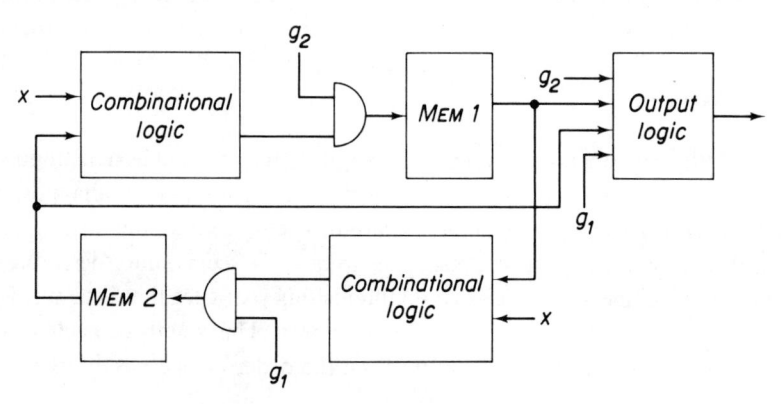

**Figure 6.11**

change through the sequence 0-1-0 and are never 1 simultaneously. When $g_1 = 1$, the outputs of the memory devices MEM 1 are used to change the state of the memory devices MEM 2 and when $g_2 = 1$, the reverse occurs. The memory devices may be banks of set-reset flip-flops. A sequential machine can be realized as a double-rank circuit for single-input changes or multiple-

# DESIGN TO SIMPLIFY TESTING 183

input changes and the gating signals $g_1$ and $g_2$ can be generated internally. Double-rank circuits with reduced dependence (Friedman and Menon, 1969) can be obtained by extending the procedures of Hartmanis and Stearns (1965).

Double-rank sequential circuits can be generalized to multiple-rank circuits for flow tables with more than two input columns in the following way. If the flow table has $m$ columns denoted by $I_1, \ldots, I_m$, define $m$ ranks by sets of state variables so that two states have the same coding in the $i^{th}$ rank variables if and only if the next state entries are identical in column $I_i$.

Then the state variable logic for an $i^{th}$ rank variable $y_j$ can be defined in the following manner:

$$Y_j = I_i y_j + \sum_{m \neq i} I_m f_m(\mathbf{y}^m) \quad \text{where } \mathbf{y}^m \text{ is the set of } m^{th} \text{ rank variables.}$$

If set-reset flip-flops are used as memory devices, the input equations to the flip-flop representing the state variable $y_j$ are:

$$S_{y_j} = \sum_{m \neq i} I_m f_m(\mathbf{y}^m)$$

$$R_{y_j} = \sum_{m \neq i} I_m \bar{f}_m(\mathbf{y}^m)$$

The variables in the $i^{th}$ rank remain unchanged when the input is $I_i$. Again, the inputs must be coded so that different parts of the circuit cannot respond to two input states $I_j$ and $I_k$, $j \neq k$ simultaneously. One method for accomplishing this is by encoding the input states using a code in which only one bit of a code word can be 1 at any time. (Friedman and Menon, 1968). The following example illustrates the multiple-rank realization of a given flow table.

**Example 6.13**

|   | $I_1$ | $I_2$ | $I_3$ | $I_4$ | $y_1$ | $y_2$ | $y_3$ | $y_4$ | $y_5$ |
|---|---|---|---|---|---|---|---|---|---|
|   |   |   |   |   | 1 | 2 | 3 | 3 | 4 |
| A | Ⓐ | D | Ⓐ | B | 0 | 0 | 0 | 0 | 0 |
| B | A | Ⓑ | A | Ⓑ | 0 | 1 | 0 | 0 | 0 |
| C | Ⓒ | D | E | B | 1 | 0 | 1 | 0 | 0 |
| D | C | Ⓓ | A | F | 1 | 0 | 0 | 0 | 1 |
| E | C | B | Ⓔ | F | 1 | 1 | 1 | 0 | 1 |
| F | C | B | Ⓕ | Ⓕ | 1 | 1 | 0 | 1 | 1 |

$$S_{y_1} = I_2\bar{y}_2 + I_3(y_3 + y_4) + I_4 y_5; \quad R_{y_1} = I_2 y_2 + I_3 \bar{y}_3 \bar{y}_4 + I_4 \bar{y}_5$$

$$S_{y_2} = I_3(y_3 + y_4) + I_4 y_5 \quad ; \quad R_{y_2} = I_3 \bar{y}_3 \bar{y}_4 + I_4 \bar{y}_5 + I_1$$

$$S_{y_3} = I_1 y_1 \quad ; \quad R_{y_3} = I_1 \bar{y}_1 + I_2 + I_4$$

$$S_{y_4} = I_4 y_5 \quad ; \quad R_{y_4} = I_4 \bar{y}_5 + I_1 + I_2$$

$$S_{y_5} = I_2 y_2 + I_3(y_3 + y_4) \quad ; \quad R_{y_5} = I_2 \bar{y}_2 + I_3 \bar{y}_3 \bar{y}_4 + I_1 \, .$$

One desirable feature of fault analysis in combinational circuits is that it is possible to determine what set of faults are detected by a given test without simulating every faulty circuit for these tests. This can be done by determining what paths and partial paths in the circuit are sensitized by the given test input. This cannot be done so easily for an asynchronous sequential circuit, because the propagation of a fault to a state variable is not sufficient to detect the fault, even if the state variable is observable, since the failure condition may be unstable and thus may eventually be masked out by some other signal or by the failure feeding back on itself. A multiple-rank circuit design of a sequential function eliminates the possibility of a failure condition at a state variable feeding around a loop and eventually destroying the failure condition. This enables us to determine the set of faults detected by a given test in much the same manner as for a combinational circuit if the state variables are observable, or as a synchronous sequential machine otherwise, and hence greatly simplifies the problem of generating tests using an analysis procedure. Similarly, if a simulation procedure is used, the necessity for extensive signal flow simulation is eliminated, thus again resulting in a great saving in simulation time. A multiple-rank circuit contains no feedback loops, as defined below, except within the SR flip-flops which are used as memory elements. A closed loop is a *feedback loop* if the system variables may *simultaneously* have such values that a signal may flow entirely around the loop. If the system variables never have values which permit the signal to flow entirely around the closed loop, then it is called a *pseudo-loop*. For example in Fig. 6.12, if $I_1$ and $I_2$ can never be one simultaneously, then the loop is a pseudo-loop.

Restricting the set of faults to be considered to a single gate input or output s-a-1 or s-a-0, we see that the only single faults that cause a signal to flow entirely around the loop in the circuit of Fig. 6.12 are wires *a* or *b* s-a-1 and $I_1 = 1$ or wires *c* or *d* s-a-1 and $I_2 = 1$. Without loss of generality, assume that *a* is s-a-1 and $I_1 = 1$ and the failure causes the flip-flop $y_1$

## DESIGN TO SIMPLIFY TESTING

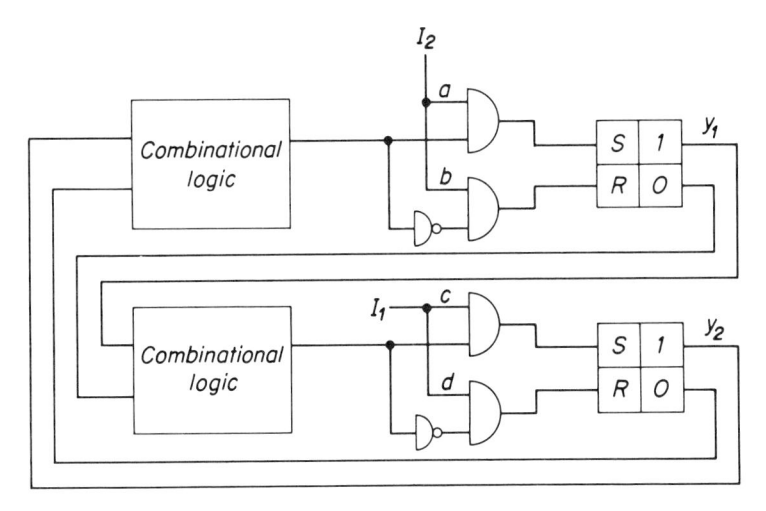

**Figure 6.12**

to be set. This failure can be erased only by resetting the flip-flop. When $I_1 = 1$, $I_2 = 0$ and $b = 0$, by our single-fault assumption, $y_1$ cannot be reset and the failure is "locked in". Thus we see that since every loop of our circuit is as shown in Fig. 6.12, no failure at a state variable caused by a single fault can feed back on itself and erase the failure condition. However, if $I_1$ or $I_2$ can become stuck at 1, it is possible for the failure condition to feed back around the closed loop and erase itself. This difficulty can be resolved by making $I_1$ and $I_2$ observable. In any case, a large majority of the faults do not result in closed loops, and hence analysis is greatly simplified.

Multiple-rank circuits also possess the property of "locking in" the failure as described above. Here again, it is necessary to ensure that no two inputs are 1 simultaneously by monitoring them.

If we consider the $p^{\text{th}}$ rank state variables as defining a submachine $M_p$, $p = 1, \ldots, k$, the following procedure determines the faults that are detected by a given test $(S, I_j)$, where $S$ is the state of the machine when input $I_j$ is applied assuming that the state variables are observable (If the state variables are not observable, the procedure is similar to that for synchronous sequential circuits.):

1. From the state assignment determine $N_{M_p}(S, I_j)$ (the next state of submachine $M_p$ for the correctly operating machine with present input $I_j$ and present state $S$ of the submachine $M_j$) for all $p \neq j$.

2. Use these next state values and state $S$ of submachine $M_j$ as pseudo

inputs and apply the path sensitizing technique to the combinational part of the circuit to determine what faults will propagate to flip-flops, and hence be detected, for this test.

The flip-flop or the set of flip-flops, at which a failure is observed gives a fairly accurate idea as to where the fault is located. If the present input is $I_j$ and the (previously undetected) failure is detected at a variable in submachine $M_j$ then the fault is in submachine $M_j$ and if the failure is detected at a variable in submachine $M_k$ but not at any variable in $M_j$ then the fault is in $M_k$. The following example illustrates the derivation of fault-detection tests for multiple-rank circuits.

**Example 6.14**

|   | $I_1$ | $I_2$ | $I_3$ | $y_1$ | $y_2$ | $y_3$ |
|---|---|---|---|---|---|---|
| A | Ⓐ | B | D | 0 | 0 | 0 |
| B | E | Ⓑ | Ⓑ | 1 | 0 | 1 |
| C | A | Ⓒ | — | 0 | 1 | — |
| D | E | C | Ⓓ | 1 | 1 | 0 |
| E | Ⓔ | C | B | 1 | 1 | 1 |

$$S_{y_1} = I_2\bar{y}_2 + I_3; \qquad R_{y_1} = I_2 y_2$$

$$S_{y_2} = I_1 y_1 + I_3 \bar{y}_3; \qquad R_{y_2} = I_1 \bar{y}_1 + I_3 y_3$$

$$S_{y_3} = I_1 y_1 + I_2; \qquad R_{y_3} = I_1 \bar{y}_1$$

The test $y_1 = 0$, $I_1 = 1$ takes the correctly functioning machine to state $y_1 = y_2 = y_3 = 0$. Thus by path sensitizing we can determine that the following faults are detected by this test.

In $M_1$, $a, b, c$ or $d$ s-a-1

In $M_2$, $e, f, g, h$ or $i$ s-a-1

$j, k, l, m, n$ s-a-0 if $y_2$ was previously reset

In $M_3$, $p, q, r, s$ s-a-1

$t, u, v$ s-a-0 if $y_3$ was previously reset.

The above set of faults detected by the given test is obtained under the assumptions that both outputs of each state variable flip-flop are observable and that both outputs of a flip-flop become zero when its

DESIGN TO SIMPLIFY TESTING 187

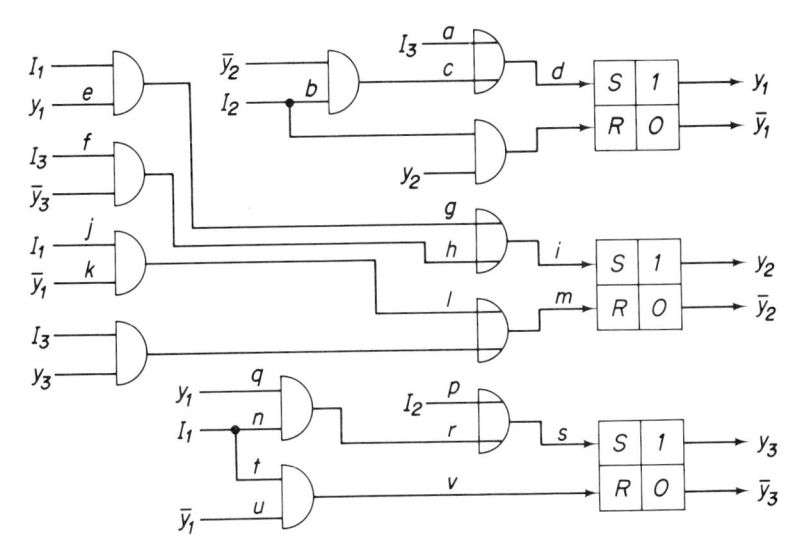

**Figure 6.13**

inputs are one simultaneously (as in the case of flip-flops formed by a pair of cross-connected NOR gates). Tests for specific faults are obtained as in the case of combinational logic by merely propagating the effect of the fault to the nearest flip-flop. For example, the set of tests for detecting the fault $b$ s-a-0 is $I_2 \bar{y}_2$ with $y_1$ initially reset.

*Circuits with Completion Signals*

Asynchronous circuits which generate completion signals (Muller, 1963; Miller, 1965; Armstrong et al., 1969) constitute another class of circuits that are relatively easy to maintain. Combinational and sequential circuits may both be designed in this manner. Though the primary purpose for the generation of completion signals is to ensure proper operation independent of the magnitudes of the delays associated with the gates in the circuits, these circuits also have the property that they stop operating for approximately one-half of all possible s-a-0 and s-a-1 faults. Thus a degree of self-checking is obtained.

In order to generate completion signals, the inputs and the outputs of the circuit are usually coded. One method (Armstrong, et al., 1969) codes the inputs and outputs as $p/q$ (each word has $q$ bits of which $p$ have the value one) and $m/n$ codes respectively. The transition from one code word (input or

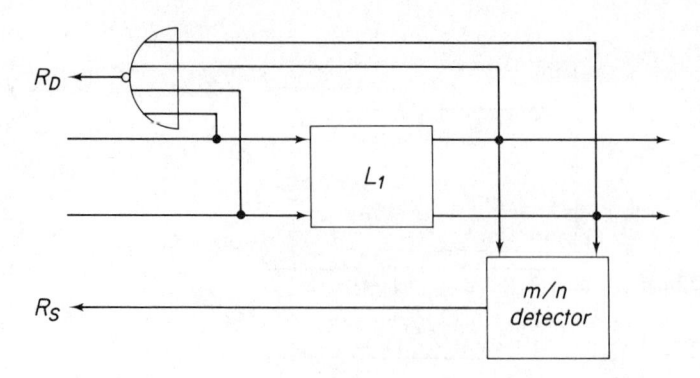

**Figure 6.14**

output) to another is always through the all-zero word called a *spacer*. The model is shown in Fig. 6.14. Here, the source supplies $p/q$ code to the circuit labeled $L_1$ when the data request signal $R_D = 1$ and the spacer request signal $R_S = 0$, and all zeros when $R_D = 0$, $R_S = 1$. Note that $R_D = 1$ when the inputs and outputs of $L_1$ are all zeros and $R_S = 1$ when the outputs of $L_1$ constitute an $m/n$ code word. The $m/n$ detector may be realized by a two-level AND-OR circuit.

Let $L_1$ be a combinational circuit realized as a two-level AND-OR circuit. If an input or the output of any gate in $L_1$ is s-a-0, this will cause some output of $L_1$ to be 0 when it should be 1 and prevent the generation of the completion signal $R_S$. Similarly, if any OR gate input or output is s-a-1, the completion signal $R_D$ will not be generated. However, a s-a-1 fault on an AND gate input may cause $m + 1$ outputs of $L_1$ to become 1 but may not stop the circuit because the $m/n$ detector produces a 1 output whenever $m$ or more of its inputs are 1. Similarly, s-a-1 on the NOR gate input will stop the circuit but s-a-0 will not. The class of faults in the $m/n$ detector that will halt the circuit is the same as that for $L_1$.

Flip-flops are used in realizations of sequential circuits and also asynchronously operating modules which generate completion signals (Armstrong, et al., 1969). In these circuits, all the flip-flops in a set are unexcited or all of them are excited. An additional degree of self-checking is obtained in these circuits because any error in a single flip-flop input will inhibit the generation of one of the completion signals.

Carter et al. (1970) have shown how other types of codes can be used for detecting single faults in combinational circuits. They have also shown that the detector itself can be made partially self-checking by suitably coding its outputs. Under the single-fault assumption, the detector will produce a correct coded output only if the outputs of the combinational circuit represent a valid code word. If the detector output is not a valid code word, this implies that either the combinational circuit or the detector is faulty. However, the detector can produce a valid code word at its output even when it contains a fault. This happens when the coded outputs of the combinational circuit do not constitute a test for the particular fault in the detector. Using the detector outputs as completion signals as discussed earlier, a system with a high degree of self-checking can be realized.

*System Organization*

In the preceding sections, we presented some techniques for designing individual circuits that are relatively easy to test. We shall now consider some aspects of system organization from the point of view of ease of testing.

A digital system is usually divided into a number of subsystems each of which consists of a number of functional modules. The size and complexity of the modules is dependent on the technology used. The module is usually the smallest replaceable unit and diagnostic tests are required to locate the faulty module (or determine a set containing only a few modules one of which may be faulty). Thus, the number of tests required will depend on how a circuit is divided into modules. An important problem in the design of easily diagnosable digital systems is that of dividing a given circuit into modules of a given size, so that the number of tests (or the length of the test sequence) required to locate the faulty modules is minimum. Unfortunately, very little is known about the solution to this problem.

Another desirable feature of an easily testable system is the ability to isolate subsystems logically during testing. The inputs and the outputs of each subsystem should be test insertion and observation points for ease of applying tests and observing outputs. Ramamoorthy (1967) has presented a graph-theoretic approach to the problem of dividing a given system into subsystems so as to minimize the interconnections between subsystems (and thereby the number of test insertion and observation points). It is also applicable to the problem at the circuit level, where a given circuit is to be divided into modules.

The system is represented by a directed graph whose nodes represent functional modules (or gates) and whose edges represent lines of signal propagation. Two types of subgraphs of the graph are used in the procedure. A *maximal strongly-connected* (*MSC*) *subgraph* is a subgraph containing all nodes that are strongly connected to one another. All MSC subgraphs of a graph are mutually disjoint; that is, no two MSC subgraphs of a graph will have any node in common. A *link subgraph* is a subgraph that contains no strongly-connected subgraphs or unconnected subgraphs in it.

Dividing a system into subsystems is accomplished by decomposing the graph of the system into MSC and link subgraphs. If the entrance and exit points of each subgraph are made test insertion and observation points respectively, the system can be effectively isolated into subsystems for testing. If any subsystem obtained by this procedure is still too large, it can be further decomposed by first removing a minimum number of edges in order to open all closed loops and then finding the MSC and link subgraphs in it. For every edge that is removed, the endpoints of the corresponding leads in the system are also made test points. This procedure can be repeated until subsystems of the desired size are obtained.

If every subsystem obtained by the above procedure is irredundant, the set of test points is sufficient for detecting all faults and also locating the faulty subsystem. However, all these test points may not be necessary for the purpose. A fault table similar to that discussed in Chapter 2 may be used to obtain a minimal or near minimal set of test points for the desired fault locatability.

Even if the system is divided into subsystems with test insertion and observation points for each subsystem, it is still necessary to have additional circuitry to generate and apply the necessary inputs or input sequences to these points and also monitor the outputs and print out appropriate error messages. If this subsystem, which is essentially *hard-core*\* is tested first and found to be fault-free, it can then be used to check the rest of the system. In order to reduce the amount of manual testing, this hard-core should be made as small as possible.

Another desirable feature in system organization is the ability for *boot-strapping*. Here a small hard-core is first tested manually. If it is normal, it is used to check another subsystem. At any time, all subsystems which have already been checked and found to be functioning correctly are used to test additional subsystems. With such an organization, a small hard-core is sufficient and the checking circuits "grow," as it were, as testing progresses. Although there are no systematic techniques for obtaining such a system organization, a functionally modularized design with a minimum amount of global feedback is likely to be useful.

The testing of some circuits is often simplified if certain input com-

---

\*The *hard-core* is that part of the system which must be fault-free in order to be able to test the rest of the system.

binations or input sequences that are not produced during the normal operation of the machine can be applied to them. Such inputs and sequences can be generated readily in machines with *micro-program control*. In such machines, the control sequences for executing different instructions are stored in *read-only-storage* (ROS). It is a relatively simple matter to store the various sequences required for testing also in a different part of the ROS, and apply them in the same manner as the execution of instructions.

An asynchronous control unit which stops automatically for a large fraction of the faults that may occur in it also simplifies the diagnosis of a digital system. The control unit could be made up of asynchronously operating modules, each of which generates appropriate completion signals when its outputs are valid. If a module fails to generate the appropriate completion signals, the system stops operating. The state of the control unit when the system stops is useful for locating the fault. This technique has been used in the *speed-independent* arithmetic control of Illiac II (Swartout, 1964) and also in the *cascade organized* control of the DSX-1 computer (Manning, 1966).

Several features for improved maintainability have been included in the design of the IBM System/360 (Carter et al., 1964; Hackl and Shirk, 1965). The tests can be read in from an external medium (such as magnetic tape) or a special read-only-store. All memory elements can be reset to values specified by the test. This procedure is called *scan-in*. The contents of all memory elements in the processor can be stored in a fixed part of the core memory by the *scan-out* procedure. During testing, it is possible to advance the clock in any desired manner, thereby making it possible to execute a small part of an instruction cycle.

In order to test the processor it is necessary that the special circuitry which performs the scan-in, scan-out and the clock advance be operating properly. These, together with the circuits which compare the actual response with the expected response constitute the hard-core of the processor and must be tested separately. If the hard-core is known to be functioning properly, the rest of the processor can be tested automatically by applying tests which have been stored and comparing the results with stored values.

## REDUNDANCY TECHNIQUES

The various techniques mentioned in the preceding section assume that a certain amount of down-time is tolerable and that repair is possible. In applications where continuous operation is required for a specified length of time, redundancy techniques become useful. The specific techniques to be used depend upon whether or not repair is possible and also on the required duration of reliable operation.

Redundancy techniques can be divided into two classes. In the first, called *fault-masking redundancy*, the effects of any fault (or up to a specified number of faults within any circuit) are masked by additional circuits. These additional circuits are part of the system and no switching is involved. Thus error-correction is instantaneous. In the second class are schemes which detect and locate any fault in the system and replace the faulty unit by switching in a spare unit. We shall refer to such systems as *self-checking systems*.

*Theoretical Estimates of Reliability*

If we assume that faults in a system occur independent of one another and with a constant mean failure rate which depends on the technology used, and if $\lambda$ is the mean failure rate, then the probability of survival of a component up to time $t$ is given by $R(t) = e^{-\lambda t}$. The mean time before failure or MTBF is

$$-\int_0^\infty t \, dR = \frac{1}{\lambda}$$

For a system composed of $m$ such components, if the system fails when any component fails, $R(t) = e^{-m\lambda t}$ and MTBF $= 1/m\lambda$.

Kneale (1961) has studied four different systems of redundancy and has determined the improvement in reliability for each. All of the systems consist of $n$ identical units and in each case the failure rate of a unit is assumed to be $\lambda_0$.

In the first model, all units operate in *parallel* and an ideal device determines the correct output using the outputs of all the units. The system fails when all units have failed. In the second model (referred to as *serial operation* in Table 6.2) only one unit is active at any time and the inactive units are assumed to have infinite life. When the active unit fails, the ideal device activates another unit. In the above two models there is no attempt to repair a failed unit. The third and fourth models are similar to the first two, except that a failed unit is repaired at an average rate of $\lambda_1$ (i.e., mean repair time $= 1/\lambda_1$). Table 6.2 shows the probability of survival and the mean time before failure for the four cases. (These formulas were derived under the

# FAULT-MASKING TECHNIQUES

assumption that the mean repair time of a unit is much smaller than the mean time before failure of a unit; i.e., $\lambda_1 \gg \lambda_0$.).

|  | Parallel Operation | Serial Operation |
|---|---|---|
| Without Repair | $R(t) = 1 - [1 - e^{-\lambda_0 t}]^n$ <br> $\text{MTBF} = \dfrac{1}{\lambda_0} \sum_{i=1}^{n} \dfrac{1}{i}$ | $R(t) = e^{-\lambda_0 t} \sum_{r=0}^{n-1} \dfrac{(\lambda_0 t)^r}{r!}$ <br> $\text{MTBF} = \dfrac{n}{\lambda_0}$ |
| With Repair | $R(t) = e^{-n\lambda_0 t / \lambda_1^{n-1}}$ <br> $\text{MTBF} = \dfrac{\lambda_1^{n-1}}{n \lambda_0^n}$ | $R(t) = e^{-(n-1)! \lambda_0^n t / \lambda_1^{n-1}}$ <br> $\text{MTBF} = \dfrac{\lambda_1^{n-1}(n-1)!}{\lambda_0^n}$ |

**Table 6.2**

The results shown in Table 6.2 indicate that switching in a good unit when the active unit has failed and repairing the failed unit both improve the reliability of the system. However, these results are based on the assumption of infinite life of a unit while inoperative and the use of a perfect error-detecting and switching device. In specific applications, it may be necessary to apply combinations of the different types of redundancy schemes.

## FAULT-MASKING TECHNIQUES

Fault-masking techniques are useful when the system is required to operate reliably over a relatively short period of time and repair is impossible. The fault-masking circuits are usually part of the system. The presence of this type of redundancy hinders testing as discussed in Chapter 2. Therefore additional test points should be provided to facilitate the initial check-out of the system.

We shall now examine some methods of fault masking. These include voting schemes, quadded logic, radial logic and the use of error-correcting codes.

*Voting Schemes*

A simple method for improving the reliability of a system without using switching or repair is triplication and voting. Consider the system shown in Fig. 6.15.

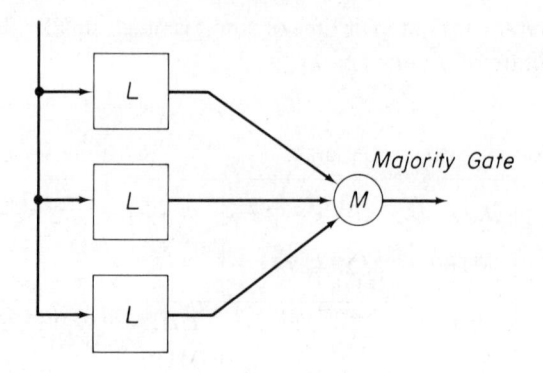

**Figure 6.15**

If we assume a perfect majority gate, the system will never fail unless two or more units fail. The probability of survival and the mean time before failure of the redundant system are:

$$R(t) = e^{-3\lambda t} + 3e^{-2\lambda t}(1 - e^{-\lambda t}) = 3e^{-2\lambda t} - 2e^{-3\lambda t}$$

$$\text{MTBF} = \frac{5}{6\lambda}$$

Thus the MTBF of the redundant system is less than that of the irredundant system. However, for small values of $t$ ($\lambda t << 1$), it can be shown that $R(t) > e^{-\lambda t}$. That is, the probability of survival of the redundant system is greater than that of the irredundant system for small values of $t$. Such systems are useful when a high reliability is required over a short period of time.

If the majority gate fails with probability $e^{-\lambda_1 t}$, the probability of survival of the redundant system is:

$$R'(t) = e^{-\lambda_1 t}[3e^{-2\lambda t} - 2e^{-3\lambda t}]$$

This assumes that the system will fail if the majority gate fails, regardless of whether or not the other units fail. This system is less reliable than the irredundant system for all values of $t$ if $\lambda_1 \geq \lambda$.

The method of multiplexing (von Neumann, 1956) is similar to the above method except that the original system is divided into subsystems and each subsystem is triplicated. A typical triplicated subsystem and the associated majority gates are shown in Fig. 6.16(a). An error in any element in a subsystem, including the majority gates will be masked by the system. Figure 6.16(c) shows how the system of Fig. 6.16(b) may be multiplexed. Here each

# FAULT-MASKING TECHNIQUES

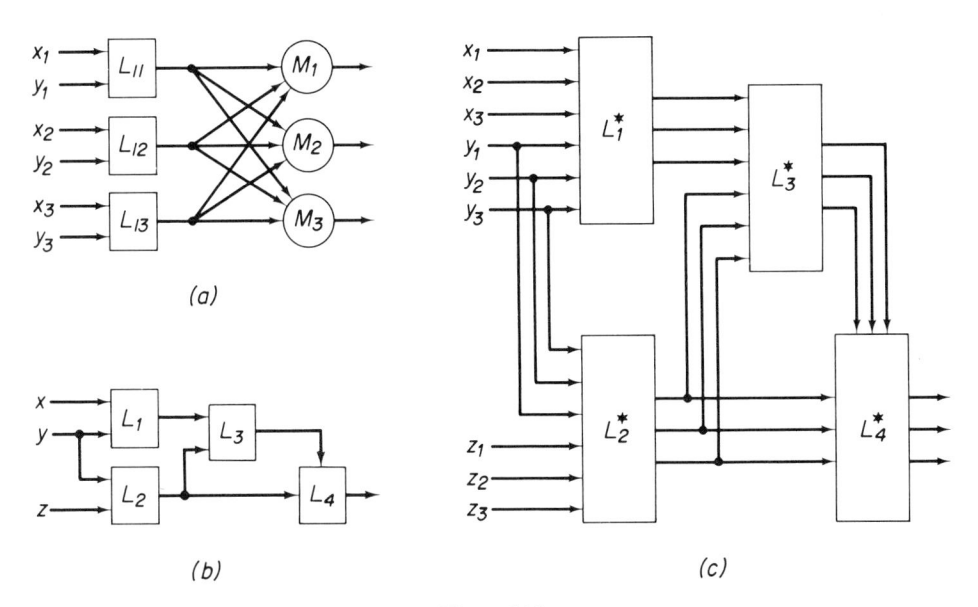

**Figure 6.16**

subsystem labeled $L_i^*$ is obtained by triplicating $L_i$ as shown in Fig. 6.16(a).

At the output of the system, it is necessary to select the proper output from among the three outputs either by a failure-free circuit or an observer. In the multiplexing technique, the majority gates serve as restoring organs. The redundant information available at their inputs is used to produce more reliable information at their outputs. Instead of using separate restoring organs, the elements that perform the logical operation can themselves be used to perform the restoring function also. We shall now examine some techniques which make use of this property.

*Quadded Logic*

Tryon (1962) has shown how reliable circuits can be constructed using *quadded logic*. As the name implies, logic elements appear in quadruplicate. Any error which appears is corrected at the next level. Thus all single faults except in the last two stages will be masked. Most multiple faults are also masked unless they appear in circuit elements which are close together.

The basic idea behind quadded logic can be demonstrated by the following example. Consider the AND gate shown in Fig. 6.17(a). This gate has two disjoint classes of single faults on its inputs—those which result

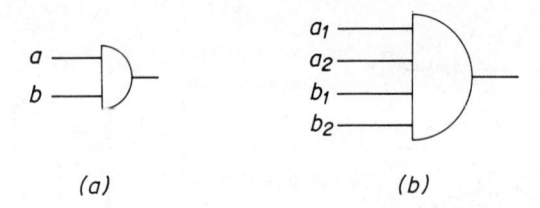

**Figure 6.17**

in an erroneous 1 output, and those which result in an erroneous 0 output. Now consider the AND gate shown in Fig. 6.17(b). Here $a_1$ and $a_2$ normally have the same value but are obtained from different sources and so are $b_1$ and $b_2$. Note that no single input fault can produce a faulty 1 output. Thus, the only faults that are critical on the inputs of the AND gate of Fig. 6.17(b) produce erroneous 0 outputs. The AND gate serves as a restoring organ for s-a-1 faults. An OR gate with similar redundant inputs can produce only erroneous 1 outputs. These facts can be utilized to mask errors in circuits containing alternating ANDs and ORs.

Consider the circuits of Fig. 6.18, where the circuit of (b) is obtained by replacing each of the AND gates of (a) by two gates with redundant inputs as discussed above. In the redundant circuit, erroneous 0 outputs of the AND gates are masked out on the OR gate. The only faults that can propagate to

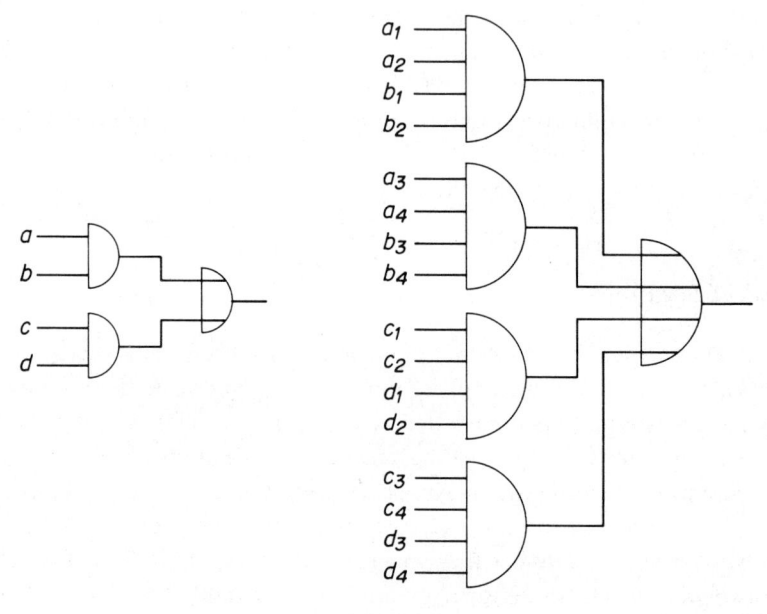

**Figure 6.18**

# FAULT-MASKING TECHNIQUES

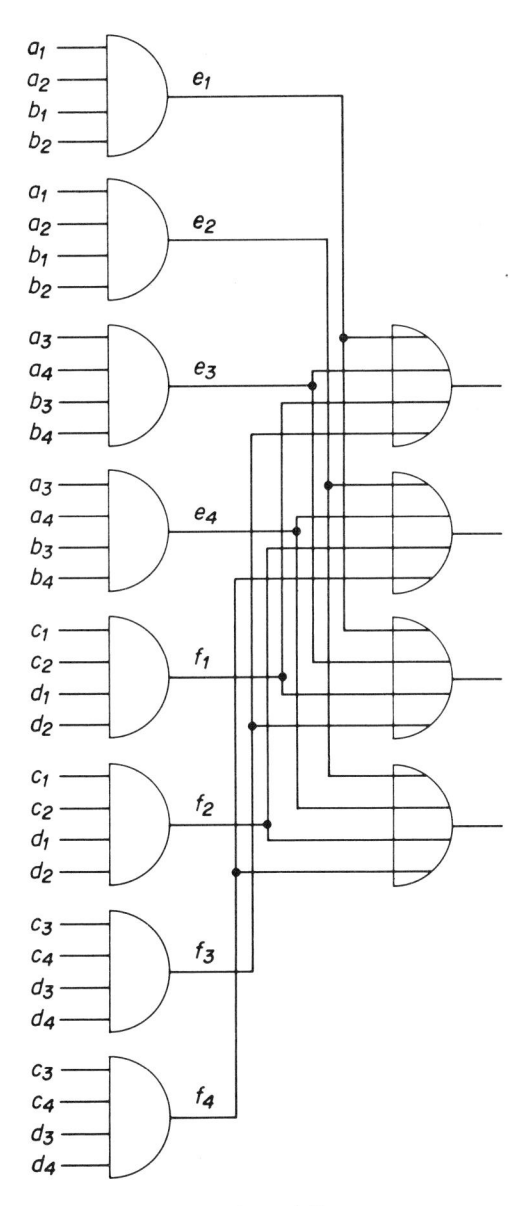

**Figure 6.19**

the output of the circuit are erroneous 1's on the OR-gate inputs (or equivalently, erroneous 1's on the AND-gate outputs). The OR gate serves as a restoring organ for faulty 0's but not faulty 1's.

Now suppose that each of the AND gates in the irredundant circuit is replaced by four AND gates which feed four OR gates as shown in Fig. 6.19.

With the interconnection scheme shown the OR gates correct the faulty 0 outputs from the AND gates. Furthermore, the outputs of the OR gates may be connected to another set of AND gates, which again will not produce faulty 1's.

Thus, if a combinational circuit of alternating AND and OR gates is realized in this manner, any single faulty 0 from an AND gate is masked at the next OR stage. A faulty 1 from an AND is masked at the next AND stage, provided the same interconnection pattern does not occur between successive logic levels. Note that two interconnection patterns are used in the circuit of Fig. 6.19. In the first level of AND gates, the two of the four gates replacing a single gate in the irredundant circuit have inputs labeled with subscripts 1 and 2, and the other two gates have inputs with subscripts 3 and 4. At the next level, the grouping of interconnections is 13, 24.

**Example 6.15:** Figure 6.20 shows an irredundant circuit and its quadded realization.

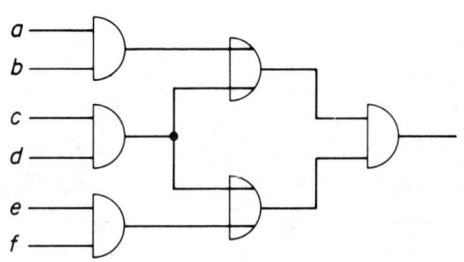

(a) Irredundant circuit

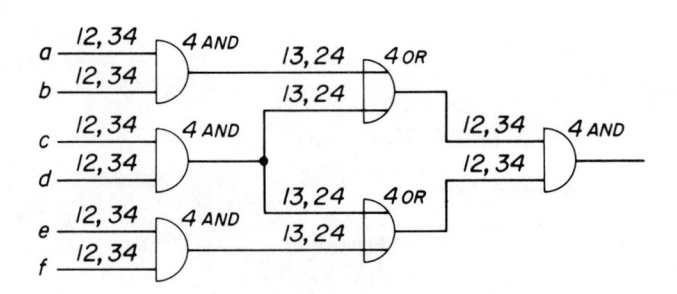

(b) Quadded circuit

**Figure 6.20**

# FAULT-MASKING TECHNIQUES

In the above figure the following compact notation is used: Quaduplicated ANDs and ORs will be denoted by 4AND and 4OR respectively. Quadded connections will be represented by single lines with a label indicating the pairing, e.g., 12, 34.

In order to obtain the correct interconnection pattern for circuits containing NOT elements, we construct an equivalent circuit with negations only at the inputs and determine the interconnection pattern for this circuit. In obtaining the equivalent circuit, it may be necessary to replace an AND gate by an OR gate or vice versa. However, we keep track of the gate in the original circuit that each gate in the equivalent circuit replaces. The original circuit is quadded with the interconnection pattern determined for the equivalent circuit. The NOT elements themselves have only one input each and therefore there is no cross-connection involved. This is denoted by $S$ on the input line to the quadded NOT. In connecting similar elements (i.e., AND feeding AND), the wiring patterns must be the same.

Any circuit containing ANDs, ORs and NOTs can be quadded using the method presented here. Similar quadded circuits can be designed using NAND or NOR gates (Jensen, 1963). Flip-flops can also be realized by treating them as circuits formed by interconnecting elements already considered, but containing feedback. For example, an SR flip-flop can be quadded by treating it as a pair of cross-connected NOR gates and quadding the circuit according to the usual rules.

The number of gates in a quadded circuit is four times that in the original circuit. Each gate in the quadded circuit (except NOT elements) has twice as many inputs as the original gate. Therefore, the redundancy ratio of quadded logic is approximately 8. (The redundancy ratio is the ratio of the amount of hardware in the redundant circuit to that in the irredundant circuit).

**Example 6.16:** Figure 6.21(b) shows the equivalent circuit and the interconnection pattern for the circuit of Fig. 6.21(a). The quadded circuit is shown in Fig. 6.21(c) using the compact notation of Example 6.15.

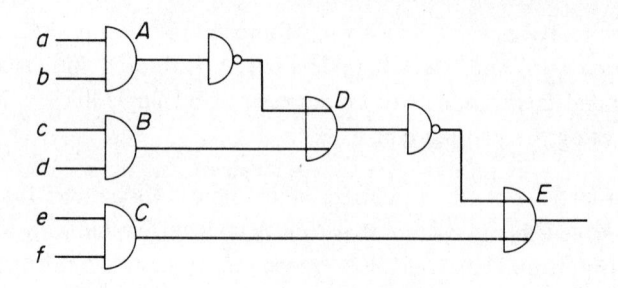

*(a) Irredundant circuit*

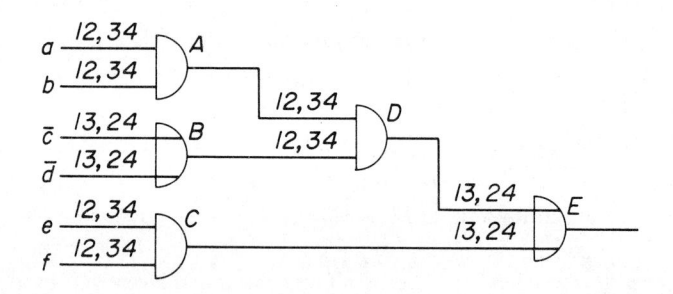

*(b) Equivalent circuit*

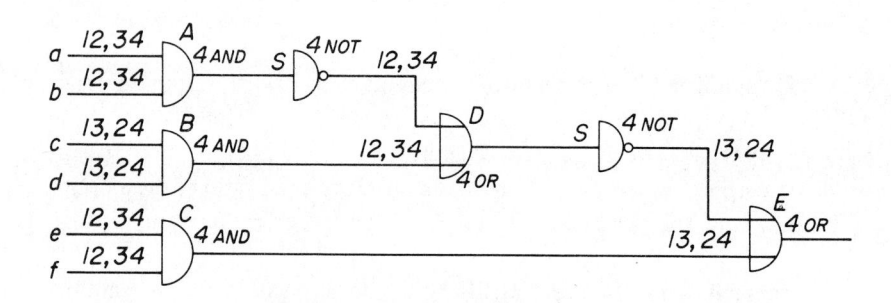

*(c) Quadded circuit*

**Figure 6.21**

Pierce (1965) has generalized quadded logic so as to correct multiple errors. Using *interwoven logic* where each gate in the irredundant circuit is replaced by $k^2$ gates each of which has $k$ repeated inputs, it is possible to correct $k - 1$ errors simultaneously.

## FAULT-MASKING TECHNIQUES

*Radial Logic*

Another redundancy technique which is capable of correcting most single errors is *radial logic* (Klaschka, 1967). It makes use of the fault-masking properties of the NOR gate (or NAND gate) with duplicated inputs. Consider the NOR gate of Fig. 6.22 with duplicated inputs from independent

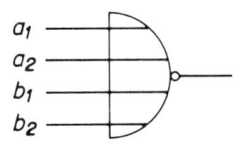

**Figure 6.22**

sources. The only single input fault that results in a faulty output is a s-a-1 fault on an input. The faulty 0 output produced in this case will be corrected at the next stage. Similar results hold for a NAND gate with duplicated inputs.

In radial logic of order 2, the irredundant circuit is first realized using only NOR gates. Each $k$-input NOR gate in this realization is then replaced by a pair of $2k$-input NOR gates with the duplicated inputs feeding both gates. As in the case of quadded logic, radial logic can be generalized to order $r$ which is capable of correcting $r - 1$ errors. Here each $k$-input NOR gate is replaced by $r$ NOR gates with $rk$ inputs. Fan-in and fan-out limitations may make radial logic of order greater than two impractical.

The only type of single fault that is not masked is a s-a-1 on the output of a gate. The faulty 1 can propagate to two gates in the next stage and cause two faulty 0 outputs to be produced even though these gates receive correct 0 inputs from another gate. This problem does not arise if the output of a gate is s-a-0 because the faulty 0 input will be masked by the correct 1 input received from another gate. The following example illustrates this point.

**Example 6.17:**

In Fig. 6.23(b), if the output of $A$ is s-a-1, the outputs of both $C$ and $D$ will be 0. This causes both signals which are normally the same to be incorrect at the same time, making fault masking impossible in successive levels. If the output of $A$ is s-a-0 but the output of $B$ has the correct value of 1, both $C$ and $D$ will produce the correct output.

(a) Irredundant circuit

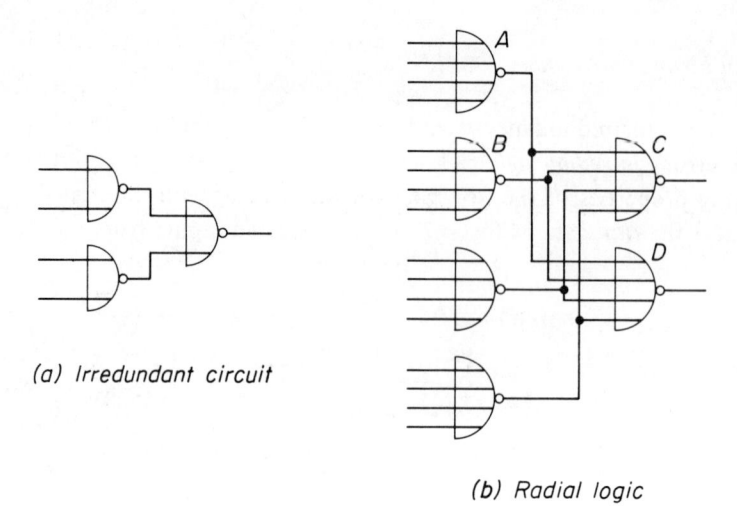

(b) Radial logic

**Figure 6.23**

Although radial logic requires only half the amount of logic required for quadded logic, the former does not correct one class of errors which the latter does. Radial logic may be desirable when the type of technology used makes this class of faults unlikely to occur. Radial logic using AND's and OR's can be obtained as a simple extension of the NOR realization, but certain classes of faults still cannot be masked.

*Use of Error-Correcting Codes*

Armstrong (1961) has proposed a method which makes use of error-correcting codes to obtain reliable systems. The method is actually a generalization of the triplication and voting procedure discussed earlier. The technique is applicable to combinational and sequential circuits. We shall consider the former case first.

Let us consider how an $m$-input, $n$-output combinational circuit can be designed so that it produces the correct outputs even in the presence of a single fault. If there is no shared logic between the different outputs, we could add $k$ check bits and use a single error-correcting code. Hamming (1950) has shown that the number of check bits required is the smallest integer $k$ such that $2^k \geq n + k + 1$.

If shared logic is allowed, a single fault may affect several outputs and the error-correcting code should be capable of correcting all errors that may

## FAULT-MASKING TECHNIQUES

result from a single fault. A more efficient technique, suggested by Armstrong (1961), is to break the given $m$-input, $n$-output circuit into $r$ subunits, each subunit realizing $p \leq n$ of the output functions. There may be shared logic between outputs within the same subunit, but no shared logic between subunits. This restricts the errors that can be produced by a single faulty subunit to the outputs of that subunit.

Errors produced by a single faulty subunit can be corrected by adding $q$ $p$-output subunits, as shown in Fig. 6.24. The outputs $z_{ij}$, $i = r + 1, \ldots,$

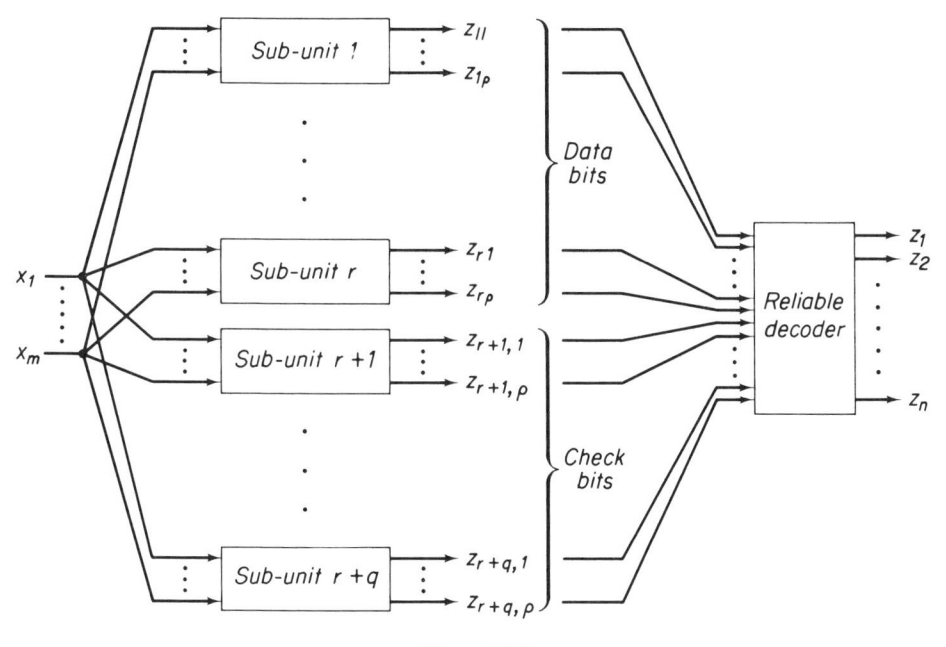

**Figure 6.24**

$r + q$ serve as check bits for $z_{kj}$, $k = 1, \ldots, r$, and $j = 1, \ldots, p$, in a Hamming single-error correcting code. The number of additional subunits $q$ is the smallest integer such that $2^q \geq r + q + 1$. Used in this manner, the Hamming code will not only correct errors in the outputs of a single subunit, but also correct errors in different subunits, provided that no two subunits have errors in the same bit position simultaneously; i.e., $z_{ij}$ and $z_{kj}$ cannot both be incorrect for all $i \neq k$. If errors are restricted to the outputs of one subunit at any time, more efficient codes can be obtained. Armstrong has computed bounds on the length of the code words needed and presented some codes. Ray-Chaudhuri (1961) has developed a general theory of minimally-redundant codes for this application. Note that in the case of a single subunit, both the Hamming code and Armstrong's code are the same as triplication.

**Example 6.18:** Consider a system which has 6 binary outputs. In order to correct single errors, 4 check bits are necessary if a Hamming code is used (Hamming, 1950). In the realization, the circuits generating the 10 bits of output (6 data bits + 4 check bits) should not have any shared logic in order to justify the assumption that at most one bit can be in error. Dividing the system into subunits with two outputs each, we see that single error correction is required over 3 data bits. Since 3 check bits are required for 3 data bits, the system must contain 6 subunits, each with two outputs. Though this system has 12 outputs it can correct double errors, provided that one of them is on the first output of any subunit and the other on the second output of any subunit. Using the code derived by Armstrong (1961), 5 subunits are sufficient, even if both outputs of any subunit may be in error at a time. Shared logic within a subunit is allowed and any incorrect output produced by any type of fault in one subunit will be corrected. This method seems to be preferable over the direct application of error correction to the outputs because of the greater error-correcting capability with about the same amount of redundancy.

In applying error-correcting techniques to sequential circuits, it is necessary to perform error correction on the outputs as well as the state variables. If no error correction is applied to the latter, a fault in a subunit whose outputs are state variables may be fed back, resulting in errors in more than one subunit at a later time. Since the system is capable of correcting errors in only one subunit, incorrect outputs may be produced.

As in the case of the triplication and voting scheme, the error-correcting circuitry has to be highly reliable in order for the redundant system to have a longer MTBF than the irredundant system. This can be accomplished by testing the correctors frequently and repairing faults rapidly. Alternatively, self-error-detecting circuits with replacement of faulty units by spares may be employed.

## SELF-CHECKING SYSTEMS

So far, we have discussed systems operating under two different sets of conditions. In the first, scheduled interruptions and repair were possible.

of the features of the *Self-Testing And Repair* (STAR) computer (Avizienis, 1968) developed at the Jet Propulsion Laboratory, Pasadena, California.

*Self-Testing and Repair (STAR) Computer*

This is an experimental computer which was designed and constructed primarily for research and evaluation of self-repair techniques. Its performance characteristics are meant to be suitable for the guidance and control of unmanned interplanetary spacecraft. The computer is required to operate reliably over a period of several years. Temporary malfunctions may be tolerated provided they are detected and the computations are repeated. Time is also available for switching out faulty units and switching in spares.

The STAR computer has a fixed configuration of subsystems, with spares provided for each subsystem. Spares are permanently connected to the system through information buses, but are left unpowered. Replacement of a faulty subsystem by a spare is effected by turning off the power to the former and powering the latter.

All machine words are encoded in error-detecting codes and fault detection is accomplished by error-detecting circuitry. If an error is detected a segment of the current program is repeated in order to determine whether it is a transient error. Switching of the faulty unit is done if the error is found to persist.

The testing and repair unit contains the error-detecting circuitry, and the hardware for retrial and switching. In order to be able to retry a segment of the current program, all machine words that will be needed are stored in redundant storage. Since the testing and repair unit is the hard core of the system, three copies of the unit are operated at all times. There are $n$ standby units ($n = 2$ in the present version) which are partially powered and also contain data for re-starts. All outputs of the testing and repair unit are determined by a two-out-of ($n + 3$) vote. When one powered unit disagrees with this output it is put in the standby condition and a standby unit is fully powered. Reuse of a standby unit is attempted when the other spares are exhausted. Reuse will be successful only if it was put in the standby condition as a result of a transient fault.

The techniques discussed above are capable of detecting and repairing most of the faults that occur in the system. However, they do not include faults in the buses or the switches themselves. Reliable operation of these parts is ensured by using component redundancy and designs whose likely failure modes are such that they do not lead to system failures.

*A Theoretical Model of Self-Checking*

Preparata et al. (1967) have studied a model of a self-checking system comprising a number of units, each of which is capable of performing computation as well as checking another unit. They have obtained sufficient conditions for identifying the faulty unit (units) in such a system.

The system is represented by a directed graph whose nodes correspond to the units in the system. A directed edge $b_{ij}$ is drawn from node $u_i$ to node $u_j$ if and only if the unit $u_i$ can test the unit $u_j$. We define a binary variable $a_{ij}$ associated with each edge $b_{ij}$ such that $a_{ij} = 1$ if the testing of $u_j$ by $u_i$ indicates that $u_j$ is faulty and $a_{ij} = 0$ otherwise. Since $u_i$ itself may be faulty $a_{ij} = 1$ by itself does not imply that $u_j$ is faulty.

A system of $n$ units is defined as *one-step* t-*fault diagnosable* if all faulty units in the system can be identified without replacement provided the number of faulty units does not exceed $t$.

The system defined above is *sequentially* t-*fault diagnosable* if at least one faulty unit can be identified without replacement provided the number of faults does not exceed $t$.

Preparata et al. (1967) have proved the following two theorems:

**Theorem 6.2:** *If a system with* n *units is one-step* t-*fault diagnosable, then* n ≥ 2t + 1. *Conversely, if* n ≥ 2t + 1, *it is possible to provide a connection pattern to make the system one-step* t-*fault diagnosable.*

**Theorem 6.3:** *In a one-step* t-*fault-diagnosable system, each unit is tested by* t *other units.*

**Example 6.19**

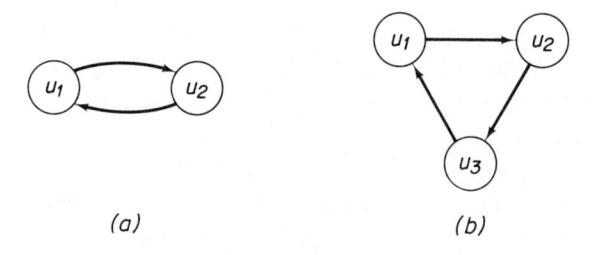

(a)          (b)

**Figure 6.25**

In this case, a system which is relatively easy to test was desirable so as to minimize the time required for maintenance. In the second case, repair was not possible but the system was required to operate with high reliability for a relatively short period of time. The fault-masking techniques discussed in the preceding section are ideally suited for this application.

A third type of environment is one in which interruptions in the operation are intolerable but repair is possible. Real-time systems such as the electronic switching systems used for telephone switching, belong to this category. In order to operate under these conditions, the system should be self-checking. It should be able to detect any fault within itself, identify the faulty subsystem and switch it out of the system. This should be done in a manner so that the system can continue to operate with the remaining units, but possibly with reduced capabilities.

*Electronic Switching System (ESS)*

The No. 1 *Electronic Switching System* (ESS) used in the Bell System for telephone switching is a highly reliable system, one of whose reliability objectives is that the system down time should not exceed 2 hours over its 40-year life (Keister et al., 1964; Downing et al., 1964). In addition to the use of long-life components and conservative circuit design, this high degree of reliability is attained by duplicating the vital parts of the system so as to retain an operational system in the presence of component failures. Circuits and programs are provided to determine the faulty unit and switch it out of operation. Diagnostic programs and maintenance dictionaries are provided to locate the faulty package in the failed unit, leading to rapid repair of the failed unit.

The first step in self-checking is to detect the presence of trouble. This is accomplished by the use of error-detecting codes or duplication, depending upon the unit. In units like buses and memory, error-detecting codes are used. In the central control unit where error detection by the use of codes is not possible, duplication and matching is employed. The system configuration is to be altered only if a permanent fault is found to be present or if the number of errors in a unit has exceeded a specified threshold. In certain units where single-error correcting and double-error detecting codes are used, a single error is corrected and the error count is updated, whereas a double error will require reconfiguration. When error correction is not possible, an automatic retrial of some of the instructions is made and a recurrence of the error is treated as caused by a permanent fault.

A different procedure is required to determine which of the two central control units is faulty. As mentioned earlier, the central control is duplicated and a match circuit compares certain internal signals of the two units. One central control is *active* and processes telephone calls, whereas the other unit serves as a *standby* and executes the same instructions. If a mismatch occurs and it persists on retrial, call processing is interrupted and both units test themselves by applying inputs which are stored in memory and comparing certain signals produced with values which are also stored. If one of them is found to be faulty, the active unit turns the normal unit into the active state and stops the faulty unit. Certain emergency action circuits have been provided to perform the reconfiguration when the active unit is unable to do it within a specified time. After each reconfiguration, certain "sanity tests" are performed before resuming call processing.

When only one central control is working, it applies diagnostic tests to the stopped unit, on a time-sharing basis with call processing. These tests and their results are stored in the memory. Special circuits are provided for applying these tests and transferring the outputs to be compared to the match circuits. When diagnosis is completed, the results are printed out and the circuit packs to be replaced are determined by looking up the printed results in a diagnostic dictionary.

The above procedure may be invalidated by a fault in the matching circuits. The likelihood of this happening can be minimized by checking the matching circuits periodically. In addition to this, certain exercise programs which exercise the seldom-used circuitry are executed periodically. Additional circuitry is provided for detecting clock failures, loss of power and locked-up sequences. Emergency action programs are provided for recovery after a total system failure.

The above is only an outline of some of the features of the No. 1 ESS, which improve its reliability and maintainability. The importance of an efficient and complete set of fault-detection and diagnostic tests to such a system is obvious. An efficient and complete set of detection tests is necessary to ensure that the faulty unit is identified rapidly and correctly. An efficient set of diagnostic tests enables the repair of the faulty unit by replacing only a few circuit packs. Rapid repair is necessary to minimize the likelihood of the active unit failing while the standby unit is under repair.

Self-checking is also useful where repair, in the usual sense is impossible. In such an environment, repair is effected by automatically switching in a good unit in place of a faulty one. As an example, we shall consider some

# SUMMARY

The system of Fig. 6.25(b) satisfies the conditions of Theorems 6.2 and 6.3, whereas Fig. 6.25(a) does not satisfy Theorem 6.2. Table 6.3 shows the error symptoms and the faults for the two systems. It is clear that the system of Fig. 6.25(b) is one-step one-fault diagnosable while the system of (a) is not. Note that No. 1 ESS may be represented by the latter model.

| $a_{12}$ | $a_{21}$ | Faulty unit |
|---|---|---|
| 0 | 0 | None |
| 0 | 1 | $u_1$ |
| 1 | 0 | $u_2$ |
| 1 | 1 | Unknown |

Table 6.3

(a) System of Fig. 6.25(a)

| $a_{12}$ | $a_{23}$ | $a_{31}$ | Faulty unit |
|---|---|---|---|
| 0 | 0 | 0 | None |
| 0 | 0 | 1 | $u_1$ |
| 0 | 1 | 0 | $u_3$ |
| 0 | 1 | 1 | $u_3$ |
| 1 | 0 | 0 | $u_2$ |
| 1 | 0 | 1 | $u_1$ |
| 1 | 1 | 0 | $u_2$ |
| 1 | 1 | 1 | Impossible with single fault |

(b) System of Fig. 6.25(b)

## SUMMARY

In this chapter, we have discussed several techniques for designing combinational and sequential circuits that are relatively easy to test and maintain. Some of the current techniques for designing reliable systems using redundancy were outlined. We also considered the concept of self-checking and presented some examples of partially self-checking systems. There are several important open problems in this area. Many more design techniques and guidelines are desirable for easily maintainable systems. The degree of self-checking and self-repair that is attainable is not known. An interesting open problem is: Is it theoretically possible to construct a completely self-repairing machine?

## REFERENCES

Armstrong, D. B., "A General Method of Applying Error Correction to Synchronous Digital Systems", *BSTJ* 40, 577–593, 1961.

Armstrong, D. B., Friedman, A. D. and Menon, P. R., "Design of Asynchronous Circuits Assuming Unbounded Gate Delays", *IEEE Trans. on Computers* C-18, 1110–1120, 1969.

Avizienis, A., "An Experimental Self-Repairing Computer", *Proc. IFIP Congress*, E29–33, 1968.

Carter, W. C., Montgomery, H. C., Preiss, R. J. and Reinheimer, H. J., "Design of Serviceability Features for the IBM System/360", *IBM Journal of Res. and Dev.* 8, 115–126, 1964.

Carter, W. C., Jessep, D. C., Bouricius, W. G., Wadia, A. B., McCarthy, C. E. and Milligan, F. G., "Design Techniques for Modular Architecture for Reliable Computer Systems", IBM Report No. 70-208-0002, 1970.

Downing, R. W., Nowak, J. S. and Tuomenoksa, L. S., "No. 1 ESS Maintenance Plan", *BSTJ* 43, 1961–2019, 1964.

Forbes, R. E., Rutherford, D. H., Stieglitz, C. B. and Tung, L. H., "A Self-Diagnosable Computer", *Proc. Fall Joint Computer Conference*, 1073–1086, 1965.

Friedman, A. D. and Menon, P. R., "Synthesis of Asynchronous Sequential Circuit with Mulitple-Input Changes", *IEEE Trans. on Computers* C-17, 559–566, 1968.

Friedman, A. D. and Menon, P. R., "Design of Generalized Double-Rank and Multiple-Rank Sequential Circuits", *Information and Control* vol. 15, 436–451, 1969.

Hackl, F. J. and Shirk, R. W., "An Integrated Approach to Automated Computer Maintenance", *Proc. Sixth Annual Symposium on Switching Circuit Theory and Logical Design*, 289–302, 1965.

# REFERENCES

Hall, A. D., "Synthesis of Double-Rank Sequential Circuits, *Princeton Univ. Tech. Report No.* 53, 1966.

Hamming, R. W., "Error-Detecting and Error-Correcting Codes", *BSTJ* 29, 147–160, 1950.

Hartmanis, J. and Stearns, R.E., *Algebraic Structure Theory of Sequential Machines*, Prentice-Hall, Englewood Cliffs, New Jersey, 1965.

Jensen, P. A., "Quadded NOR logic", *IEEE Trans. on Reliability* R-12, 22-31, 1963.

Keister, W., Ketchledge, R. W. and Vaughan, H. E., "No. 1 ESS: System Organization and Objectives", *BSTJ* 43, 1831–1844, 1964.

Klaschka, T. F., "Two Contributions to Redundancy Theory", *Proc. Eighth Annual Symposium on Switching and Automata Theory*, 175–183, 1967.

Kneale, S. G., "Reliability of Parallel Systems with Repair and Switching", *Proc. Seventh Symposium on Reliability and Quality Control*, 129–133, 1961.

Kohavi, Z. and Lavallee, P., "Design of Sequential Machines with Fault-Detection Capabilities", *IEEE Trans. on Electronic Computers* EC-16, 473–484, 1967.

Manning. E. G., "On Computer Self-Diagnosis, Part II—Generalizations and Design Principles", *IEEE Trans. on Electronic Computers* EC-15, 882–890, 1966.

Miller, R. E., *Switching Theory* Vol. 2, John Wiley & Sons, 1965.

Muller, D. E., "Asynchronous Logics and Application to Information Processing", *Proc. Symposium on Application of Switching Theory in Space Technology*, Aiken and Main, eds., Stanford Univ. Press, Stanford, California, 289–297, 1963.

Pierce, W. H., *Failure-Tolerant Computer Design*, Academic Press, New York, 1965.

Preparata, F. P., Metze, G. and Chien, R. T., "On the Connection Assignment Problem of Diagnosable Systems", *IEEE Trans. on Electronic Computers* EC-16, 848–854, 1967.

Ramamoorthy, C. V., "A Structural Theory of Machine Diagnosis", *Proc. Spring Joint Computer Conference*, 743–756, 1967.

Ray-Chaudhuri, D. K., "On the Construction of Minimally Redundant Reliable System Designs", *BSTJ* 40, 595–611, 1961.

Swartout, R. E., "New Techniques for Designing Speed Independent Control Logic", *Proc. Fifth Annual Symposium on Switching Circuit Theory and Logical Design*, 12–29, 1964.

Tryon, J. G., "Quadded Logic", *Redundancy Techniques for Computing Systems*, Wilcox and Mann, eds., Spartan Books, Washington, D. C. 205–228, 1962.

Von Neumann, J. "Probabilistic Logics and the Synthesis of Reliable Organisms from Unreliable Components", *Automata Studies*, Annals of Math. Studies No. 34, C. E. Shannon and J. McCarthy, eds., Princeton University Press, Princeton, New Jersey, 43–98, 1956.

## PROBLEMS

1. Let a combinational function $F$ be decomposed as shown below:

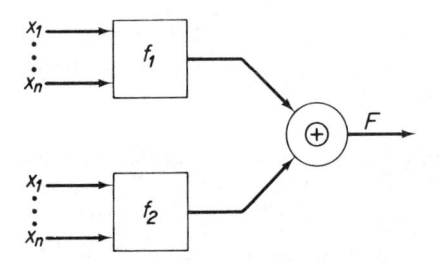

   **Figure 6.26**

   What are the conditions imposed on the functions $f_1$ and $f_2$ for all faults in such a realization to be detectable, assuming that the exclusive-OR is realized in the minimal two-level sum-of-products form?

2. Make the following flow table definitely diagnosable by adding the smallest number of outputs. Specify these outputs so that the order of diagnosability is minimum.

|   | 0    | 1    |
|---|------|------|
| A | A, 0 | B, 0 |
| B | A, 0 | C, 0 |
| C | C, 0 | A, 1 |
| D | D, 1 | D, 1 |

3. Assuming that the outputs of the flip-flops in Fig. 6.13 are observable, derive a test for the fault $u$ s-a-1.

4. A circuit is said to be zero fail-safe* (one fail-safe) if no single fault in it can produce an incorrect one (zero) output. Show that radial logic using NOR gates is zero fail-safe.

5. Consider the arrangement of 5 processors in a cycle each one testing its neighbor. Which double fault patterns can be distinguished from all other single and double fault patterns?

6. In the arrangement of 5 processors shown in Fig. 6.27, what double-fault patterns can be distinguished from all single faults and other double-fault patterns?

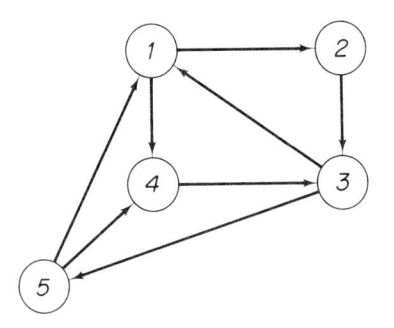

Figure 6.27

7. Consider an arrangement of $k$ processors in which each of the processors can test every other processor. What is the minimum value of $k$ to distinguish
   a) all single and double errors,
   b) all single, double ... and $p$-tuple errors for all $p$?

*Mine, H. and Koga, Y., "Basic Properties and a Construction Method for Fail-Safe Logical Systems," *IEEE Trans. on Electronic Computers* EC-16, 282–289, 1967.

8\*. Develop an algorithm for realizing any combinational function so that it can be tested for all single s-a-1 and s-a-0 faults by the smallest number of tests.

9\*. Characterize the class of functions which are essentially nfl.

10\*. Obtain a basic set of modules sufficient for realizing all combinational functions so that any single faulty module can be located.

11\*. Given a sequential circuit flow table, the actual realization of the circuit may determine the difficulty of testing. Investigate the relationship between the amount of feedback in the realization and the simplicity of testing, and also the effect of the relative amounts of global and local feedback.

# INDEX

## A

Adaptive schedule, 46
Armstrong's method (simulation), 158–164
  fault list, 159
  flip-flops, 162–163
Asynchronous sequential circuits:
  checking sequences, 97–100
  critical races, 6, 155
  definitions, 6
  double-rank, 182–183
  multiple-rank, 183–187

## B

Boolean difference:
  definition, 14
  test generation, 14–16
Boot-strapping, 190

## C

Cascade organized control, 191
Characterizing sequences, 80
Checking experiments, 71 (*see also* Checking sequences)
Checking sequences, 71
  *ad hoc* methods, 90–93
  asynchronous sequential circuits, 97–100
  Hennie's procedure, 73–85
  Hsieh's procedure, 85–90
  nesting technique, 79
  restricted fault assumption, 93–97
  synchronous machines, 70–97
Combinational circuits:
  definitions, 3–4
  fault-locatable, 171–178
  non-fault locatable (nfl), 171
  test derivation, 12–45
    Boolean difference method, 14–16

Combinational circuits (*Contd.*):
   D-algorithm, 19–34
      equivalent normal form, 41–45
      path sensitizing, 16–19
      Poage's method, 36–40
   totally fault-locatable, 174
   with small test sets, 169–171
Combinational schedule, 46
Completion signals, 187
Critical race, 6

**D**

D-algorithm, 19–34
   activity vector, 27
   consistency operation, 26
   D-cubes:
      intersection of, 26
      primitive, of a fault, 21–24
      propagation, 21, 24–26
   D-drive, 26–28
   formal, 20–32
   informal, 19–20
   multiple-fault, 32–34
   sequential circuits, 68–70
   test cube, 27
Deductive simulation (*see* Armstrong's method)
Definite event, 6
Definitely diagnosable machines, 179
Diagnosability, order of, 179
Diagnosing sequence (*see* Distinguishing sequence)
Diagnosing tree, 52, 53
Distinguishing sequence, 75
   sequential circuits with:
      design, 178–181
      testing, 75–76

Distinguishing tree, 78
Dominance, column and row, 47
Double-rank circuits, 182
DSX-1 computer, 191

**E**

Electronic Switching System (ESS), 205–207
Equivalent normal form, 41–45
   literal, 41
   near minimal test sets, 49–52
   scoring function, 49, 50
Error-correcting codes, 202–204

**F**

Failure-injection words, 154
Fault-collapsing, 48
Fault list, 159
Faults:
   multiple, 32–34, 37, 40
   s-a-1, 8
   s-a-0, 8
   short-circuit, 9
   shorted diode, 8–9
Fault-table methods, 46–48
Feedback loop, 184
   pseudo-loop, 184
Finite-state machines, 4 (*see also* Sequential machines)
Fixed schedule, 46
Flow table, 4
   normal mode, 6
   primitive, 99
Fundamental mode, 6

# INDEX

## H

Hard-core, 190, 191
Hennie's procedure, 73–85
Homing sequence, 77
Homing tree, 77
Hsieh's procedure, 85–90
Huffman analysis program, 155

## I

IBM System/360, 191
Illiac II, 191
Implicant, 3
Information, measure of, 157
Information gain, 157
Information-losslessness, 137
   of finite order, 144
   $x$-IL, 138
   $x$-ILF, 145
   $y$-IL, 138
   $x/z$-ILF, 145
Interwoven logic, 200
I/O canonical form, 85
I/O pair, 85
I/O sequence, 85
Iterative logic arrays, 106–150
   fault assumptions, 107
   one-dimensional, 108–125
      (*see also* One-dimensional arrays)
   sequential machines, 144–145
   testability, definition, 107
      (*see also* Testability)
   tree structures, 145–147
   two-dimensional, 125–144
      (*see also* Two-dimensional arrays)
Iterative system, 107

## K

Karnaugh map, 3

## L

Link subgraph, 190
Locating sequences, 80
Logic compiler, 154
Logic organizer, 154

## M

Machine identification, 70-100
   (*see also* Checking sequences)
   Moore's results, 71–73
Masking input, 120
   of degree $p$, 123
Maximal strongly-connected (MSC) subgraph, 189
Mealy machine, 4
Minimization of test sets, 46–53
   diagnosing tree, 52, 53
   enf method, 49–52
   fault-table methods, 46–48
Minterm, 13
m/n codes, 187
Moore machine, 4
Multiple faults, 32–34, 37, 40
Multiple-rank circuits, 183

## N

Nesting technique, 79
Non-fault locatable (nfl) circuits:
   essentially nfl, 174
   nfl pair, 173
Normal mode flow table, 6

## O

One-dimensional arrays:
  bounds on the number of tests, 119–120
  derivation of tests, 114–119
  location of faults, 120–125
  testability, 108–114

## P

Pair graph, 109
Partition, 71
  blocks, 71
  proper refinement, 71
Path-sensitizing, 16–19
  sequential circuits, 68–70
Poage's method, 36–40
  element propositions, 34
  literal proposition, 37, 38
    compressed notation, 38
  output propositions, 35
Prime implicant, 3
  covering problem, 4
Primitive flow table, 99
Product-of-sums, 3
Pseudo-loop, 184

## Q

Quadded logic, 195–200

## R

Radial logic, 201–202
Read-only-storage (ROS), 191
Reconvergent fan-out, 27

Reduced machine, 5
Redundancy:
  definition, 53
  effects on testing, 53–56
Redundancy techniques, 191–209
  fault-masking, 192–204
    error-correcting codes, 202–204
    quadded logic, 195–200
    radial logic, 201–202
    voting schemes, 193–195
  self checking, 192–209
    Electronic Switching System (ESS), 205–207
    Self-Testing And Repair (STAR) computer, 207–208
    theoretical model, 208–209
Reliability, theoretical estimates of, 192–193
Restricted-fault assumptions:
  iterative arrays, 107
  sequential machines, 93

## S

Scan-in, 191
Scan-out, 191
Schedules of testing:
  adaptive (sequential), 46
  fixed (combinational), 46
Selective trace, 152
Self-checking, 204–209
  Electronic Switching System (ESS), 205–207
  Self-Testing And Repair (STAR) computer, 207–208
  theoretical model, 208–209
Self-Testing And Repair (STAR) computer, 207–208

# INDEX

Sequential Analyzer, 70, 101, 153–158
  assumptions, 154
  failure-injection words, 154
  heuristics, 155
  Huffman analysis program, 155
  logic compiler, 154
  logic organizer, 154
  strategies, 155, 156
Sequential circuits: (*see also* Sequential machines)
  asynchronous, 6
  definitions, 4–6
  derivation of tests, 62–101
    circuit-testing approach, 62–70
    machine identification, 70–100
  double-rank, 182
  multiple-rank, 183
  synchronous, 6
  with distinguishing sequences, 178–181
Sequential function, 4
Sequential machines, 4 (*see also* Sequential circuits)
  arrays of, 144–145
  checking experiments, 70–100
  definitely diagnosable, 179
  reduced, 5
  strongly-connected, 5
  testing graph, 180
Sequential schedule, 46
Simple I/O sequence, 85
Simulation:
  functional, 153
  gate-level, 153
Simulation techniques, 151–165
  Armstrong's method, 158–169
  Sequential Analyzer, 153–158

Simulator:
  compiler-driven, 152
  table driven, 153
Singular cover, 20
Spacer, 188
Speed-independent circuits, 191
  (*see also* Completion signals)
State diagrams, 4
States, 4
  equivalence, 5
State table, 4 (*see also* Flow table)
Subgraph:
  link, 190
  maximal strongly-connected (MSC), 189
Successor graph, 127
Successor tree, 65–67
Sum-of-products, 3
Supersets, 126
Synchronizing sequence, 77
System organization, 189–191

# T

Tessellation, 126
  $+45°$, 127
  $-45°$, 130
  diagonal, 126
  of blocks, 127–129
Testability:
  definition, 107
  one-dimensional arrays, 108–114
  sequential machines, arrays of, 144–145
  two-dimensional arrays, 125–140

Testability (*Contd.*):
   application of cell inputs,
      126–133
   decidability, 126
   propagation of faults, 133–140
Testing graph:
  one-dimensional array, 114
  sequential machine, 180
Totally fault-locatable circuits, 174
Transfer sequence, 76
Tree structures, 145–147
Truth table, 3
Truth-table method, 12–13
Two-dimensional arrays, 125–144
   application of cell inputs,
      126–133
   bounds on the number of tests,
      141–142
   limitations of test-derivation
      procedures, 142–144

Two-dimensional arrays (*Contd.*):
   propagation of faults, 133–140
   tessellations, 126 (*see also*
      Tessellations)
   testability, 125–140 (*see also*
      Testability)

## U

Ultimately-distinguishable states,
   109
Unate function, 174
Usable tests, 109
   for fault location, 121

## V

Valid homing sequence, 86
Voting schemes, 193–194